ALSO BY MOSHE WALDOKS:

The Big Book of New American Humor:
The Best of the Past Twenty-five Years

The Big Book of Jewish Humor

The BEST AMERICAN HUMOR 1994

Edited by

Moshe Waldoks

TOUCHSTONE
Published by Simon & Schuster
New York London Toronto Sydney Tokyo Singapore

TOUCHSTONE
Rockefeller Center
1230 Avenue of the Americas
New York, New York 10020

TOUCHSTONE and colophon are registered trademarks
of Simon & Schuster Inc.

Designed by Irving Perkins Associates

Manufactured in the United States of America

10   9   8   7   6   5   4   3   2

ISBN: 0-671-89940-6

(continued at back of book)

Acknowledgments

I'd like to thank Mark Chimsky for initiating the idea of an annual collection of American humor. To my agent, Mildred Marmur, for making the match. To Carlo de Vito at Simon & Schuster, who made sure the project did not founder amidst the various corporate upheavals that marked the 1994 business season. To Bill Novak for his constant support. To Joan Leegant and Nancy Grodin for reading through much of the e.mail humor. To my brother, Phil, for keeping an eye out for possible candidates for the collection. To my life partner, Anne, and the girls, Shula, Brina, and Risa, hugs and kisses and thanks for the laughs.

Contents

MISCELLANEOUS

Contents 9

SHORT PIECES AND SHORT STORIES

EXCERPTS FROM NOVELS AND OTHER LONGER WORKS

Introduction

I am writing in a week when Olympic skater Tonya Harding was under suspicion for conspiring to break Nancy Kerrigan's knee; Lorena Bobbitt was found temporarily insane when she sliced off her husband's penis; the Menendez brothers, accused of killing their parents for an $11 million inheritance, had their jury deliberations end in deadlock; Los Angeles was cleaning up after a 6.6 Richter scale earthquake, not quite the Big One; *The New York Times* had a picture of Israeli Foreign Minister Shimon Peres holding hands with PLO Chairman Yasir Arafat; afternoon talk shows were devoted to body-piercing for teenagers and s/m marriage ceremonies; the Buffalo Bills lost yet again to the Dallas Cowboys in the twenty-eighth Superbowl; Dan Quayle appeared in a Lay's potato(e?) chip commercial; Michael Jackson agreed to pay off a thirteen year old who accused him of uninvited fellatio; ice storms covered the East Coast and parts of the Midwest; Bill Cosby returned to television as a lead in a murder mystery series on NBC; the Serbians were still bombing Sarajevo; Steven Spielberg's Holocaust blockbuster, *Schindler's List,* was making money at the box office; Staten Island was thinking of seceding from New York City; Bill Clinton made a Reaganesque State of the Union speech, leaving the Republicans not quite speechless; and did I mention that Tonya Harding was still under suspicion of conspiring to break Nancy Kerrigan's knee?

Now try to be funny after all that.

We live in an age that defies parody. The headlines seem like old contrivances on *The Show of Shows* or the late-lamented *National Lampoon.* The tabloids, in print and on television, offer up a panoply of the absurd, the ridiculous, the sleazy, and the weird that leaves comedy writers little more to do than let the headlines speak for themselves. Still, many of us still try to be funny.

For example, in order to dispel his wooden image, even Vice President Al Gore appeared on *The Late Show with David Letterman* with his own Top-Ten List:

Al Gore's List of Top-Ten Good Things About Being Vice President

10. Police escort gets you to movies faster.
9. You know the game tetherball? I played tetherball with the inventor of tetherball.
8. After they sign a bill, there's lots of free pens.
7. If you close your left eye, the seal on the podium reads "President of the United States."
6. I get intellectual property rights to my speeches.
5. Dan Quayle and Gerald Ford are pretty easy to beat during Vice Presidents' Week on *Jeopardy*.
4. You don't have to be funny to get invited on the Letterman show.
3. You get to eat all the french fries the president can't get to.
2. You don't have to be a good speller to get the job.
1. Secret Service code name "Buttafuoco."

By the way, in the late-night comedy wars, David has proven himself Johnny's true heir, albeit on another network, while Jay Leno hopes to wrest the NBC lifetime achievement mantle from Bob Hope. Chevy Chase's feeble attempt won't put any worse crinks into his already middling career, while Arsenio seems to have been eclipsed altogether. In our collection, Conan O'Brien, Dave's replacement on NBC, predicts his own demise in a *New York Times* Op-Ed piece.

The Op-Ed pages of the *Times* have also yielded other comic fruit, with Mark Leyner and Daniel Mendelsohn dissecting the body politic. Mendelsohn is sure that Republicans can be cured while Leyner looks for tattooed illustrations on American Senators. Ron Nyswaner, the screenwriter of *Philadelphia,* comments on Hollywood perks and Russell Baker reminisces about JFK on the thirtieth anniversary of the assassination. In *The New Yorker* Veronica Geng offers us political prognostications based on cheese trays and other hors d'oeuvres served at political gatherings.

Generation X, or The Boring Twenties, is represented by some pithy observations of Douglas Coupland that appeared in *The New Republic,* an odd showcase for the comic art (at least not intentionally). Another unexpected source of macabre humor is a wall poster announcing the end of the world. Don't miss it.

During the months I was putting this book together, I subscribed to two electronic bulletin boards. The first was called *humor,* the second, *giggles* (a third list started appearing at the end of the year called *Netwit.*) The humor, submitted from many parts of the globe, was often coarse, crude, and very often all too graphic. Bodily parts and bodily functions abounded and anecdotes laden with sexism, cannibalism, and nun-bashing often appeared on the screen.

The diverse humor transmitted was part sophomoric, part juvenile, sometimes cute, sometimes funny. Thanks to the discriminating use of my PC delete button it was possible to cull some delectable tidbits. I was particularly tickled by the list of slogans for National Condom Week, a compendium of computer viruses, a parable of organizational life ("How to Hunt Elephants"), and two parodies of the excesses of political correctness. The bursting global village and the imperialism of American popular culture is captured in "Euro English."

Populist humor can also be found on bumper stickers and tabloid headlines as well as in the occasional joke that actually sounded new to this editor. So few jokes really are that only a select few entered this collection.

These often anonymous contributions appear occasionally amidst the more stylized works of comic fiction. These sessions did lead to a discovery of excerpts from the Packwood diaries kindly furnished by Byron Lanning.

When you spend time each day looking at these lists you are struck by how hard it is to be funny and how difficult it is to find a new joke. You begin to appreciate even more those occasional humorous eruptions in 1993 that were chosen for this collection.

Of course many were already brewing beneath the surface as we stepped into the '90s. But the arbitrary nature of this annual dictates that to be included the material must have been published for the first time (or republished in a collection of stories) in 1993.

Thankfully there were also a few other restrictions. We could not include visual art (again with some exceptions), television or film scripts, or transcripts of stand-up routines. All of the authors in the collection are Americans and most of their protagonists are Americans. Some of the writers are well known while others made their debut in 1993.

This narrow confine proved a challenge; my last book was a selection from the last two and a half decades of American humor. While topicality was desirable I hoped that the pieces in the collection would retain a lasting measure of readability for quite some time after the actual events depicted. While humorous spontaneity is to be taken seriously, this is not a collection of *bon mots* or witty sayings, even though you'll find many examples of both. Whether or not you agree with all of my selections, you're in for quite a read comically and geographically.

On our excursion you'll join Transylvanian transplant Andrei Codrescu preparing to rediscover the margins of America on a documented road trip, if he learns to drive. Cathleen Schine takes us from the West Side of New York to Paris in search of the Enlightenment as the Mad Monks (Lane and Crotty) find their brand of '90s enlightenment in a madcap road trip from San Francisco's gay scene to New York's Soho sex scene, with Annie Sprinkle as their guide.

Crazy in Alabama takes us on a cross-country romp with a severed head to the set of *The Beverly Hillbillies.* Mark Childress's heroine, Lucille, is looking for herself. From the backwoods of Alabama to the bistros of Beverly Hills, she leads us on a wild chase accompanied by the disembodied head of her major impediment to upward mobility, her husband, Chester. Whether it's sentiment or folly, lugging your husband's head around in a Tupperware bowl can prove detrimental.

On our travels we go doppelgangering with Philip Roth and his double to the Demjanuk trial in Jerusalem and to a Palestinian town on the West Bank of the Jordan. This selection from Roth's *Operation Shylock* is a case in point. This ambitious mix of fact and fiction revolves around the unexpected foci for a comic novel, the issue of mistaken identities in the John Demjanuk trial in Israel and the appearance of a Roth-double preaching the case of the re-Dispersal of the Jews to their pre-War Eastern European haunts.

After the gradual depopulating of the State of Israel, Roth's diasporist double contends, Jewish security will be insured. Roth's novel is also a contemporary *midrash* (homiletical deconstruction) of the formative Biblical myth of Jacob and his struggle with the angel. The result of that struggle in Roth's novel provides the source of a new and renewed identity. The selection in this collection ("I Am Pipik") adds to the confusion when the "real" Roth pretends to be his own doppelganger in order to placate a former college schoolmate, now a West Bank Palestinian ideologist.

The humor of relationships is represented by Garrison Keillor in "Don Giovanni" as a cocktail bar piano player who glories in his past conquests and chronicles his resistance to marriage. In her first novel, *Nude Men,* Amanda Filipacchi records the travails of being involved intimately with a comic magician. Emily Prager offers the option of a blow-up beau while Cynthia Heimel and Linda Sunshine tackle the complexities of being female and forty in the '90s. Another baby-boomer, Wendy Wasserstein, ponders the power of celebrity while a prose-writing Garry Trudeau looks at the personal classifieds.

Georgia-based Frank Gannon is represented twice in our collection with an excerpt from his tongue-in-cheek anthropological essay, *All about MAN,* and his delightful confusion of poet Walt Whitman and bandleader Paul Whiteman.

There are also two short selections from Bruce McCall dealing with the various economic dimensions of our era: pre- or post-Christmas sales and the nature of our currency. John Updike is terrified by Christmas twelvefold while Robert Grossman hammers both Spiegelman and Spike in the pages of *The Nation.*

T. Coraghessan Boyle takes us time traveling to the birth of the Kellogg empire at the start of the twentieth century in Grand Rapids, Michigan. The selection from *The Road to Wellville* portrays self-introspection in a graphic way: as the search for the self via one's intestines and bowels. The victory of upper colonics in clearing the pathway to the pristine origins of the soul is spoofed in this account of the birth of bran and its ardent advocate John Kellogg.

These examples of American humor don't coddle or cajole. Michael Guinzburg's crack-heads at their twelve-step meeting and Harold Jaffe's playlet, "Drug Addict," on self-help twelve-step groups cast a withering glance at group therapy me-tooism.

In a year of global disillusionment and growing American isolationism, it is remarkable that these selections take you all around our planet. There is, of course, a considerable amount of attention to the diversity of cultures found within our own borders. From crack-heads to health-nuts, pederasts and political pundits, this admittedly idiosyncratic and subjective collection is dedicated to one central goal: a good read and good laughs along the way.

—Moshe Waldoks

ARTICLES
and
ESSAYS

THE MODEL COMPANION
Emily Prager

I had all but decided between the courting candlestick and the microwavable slippers when I saw him. He was in the Safety Zone catalogue, an anti-hazard shopping guide, nestled among radon gas detectors, hotel room locks and thief-proof wallets. "You're Never Alone With Safe-T-Man," the headline read. I abandoned all other decisions; here was something I really needed.

Safe-T-Man, the copy said, "is a life-size, simulated male that looks like a 175-pound man, yet weighs only four pounds." Perfect! I thought.

"Designed for use as a visual deterrent, Safe-T-Man tricks people into thinking you have the protection of a male guardian." Great!

The copy went on: "He is 5-10, yet is designed with a long torso, so he appears to be six feet tall when seated. In the car, Safe-T-Man's upright posture makes others believe there are two people, rather than just you alone. If you go out, sit Safe-T-Man near a window, it'll look like somebody's home." Miraculous!

And then, the best of all: "Clothing for Safe-T-Man is not included. Dress him according to your own preference." I could hardly wait. I ordered two, one white, one black, at only $99.95 a guy.

They arrived two days later. When I opened the boxes, it really was scary. They looked like dead men; staring victims of a gang-land hit. But as I lifted them out and sat them in a chair, I was thrilled. They were huge, really tall, not inflatables but, uh, stuffed, with big manly shoulders, Dynel hair and amazingly realistic faces. "Each face," it said on the tags, "has been handpainted to give your Safe-T-Man his own expression." My Safe-T-Man; I liked that.

The black one was otherwise a dead ringer for Burt Reynolds, complete with a moustache. The white one, painted to seem as if he had two days' stubble, looked like Don Johnson without the cuteness. Both were designed to sit in extraordinarily lifelike ways, even though their arms, legs and hands were rag-dolly. On the black one, someone had sewn toes.

They were both wearing Safe-T-Man T-shirts and nothing else. They were not anatomically correct. They were Safe-T-Men in every way.

As we sat at the table getting to know each other, I couldn't help noticing that their hair was flat and mussed from their journey. You know how it drives a girl mad when a man's hair looks scruffy and he won't let her fix it? I got out my brush and they let me. And I did it again and again. They didn't peep.

"Name them," their tags encouraged, and I chose Burt for the black one, Don for the white one.

I took Don shopping in cabs. Cabdrivers loved him. They were nicer to the stuffed man than any driver has been to me—a live woman—in years, but never mind. Don deserved it. Any guy who was in that good a mood on the way to shop for clothes had my vote. Of course they idolized him.

Brooks Brothers is so lovely at Christmas. How often I have wished to meander around the store looking at all the tasteful things with an acquiescent man at my side. Don was that man. As I carried Don to the elevator, a woman shopper was heard to say, "That's one way to get him to shop with you," and I knew he had struck a chord.

I asked Don what sort of Brooks Brothers man he'd like to be, but he didn't seem to care, so I chose for him. A buttoned-down white shirt ($48), gray flannels ($125), a striped tie ($48), wing tips ($32), a blue blazer ($350) and, of course, a camel-hair coat ($895). Don is a big man—16 neck, 42-long jacket, 32 inseam— and he was positively sweet about letting me dress him. He never pulled away, never snarled, and the minute I had buttoned up his shirt, I knew I had chosen correctly. Don went from undercover cop to Harvard man in an instant. It's amazing what clothes can do.

It was at Brooks Brothers that I learned that Safe-T-Man might be useful to men. "I could put him in the car and use the express lane, minimum two passengers," one salesman said, but not wishing to be a party to crime, we left the store.

On the street, everyone loved Don. Once they had done their double takes, they rushed right over and wanted to meet him. He made everyone smile, and I believe that if I carried him with me at all times I would never be mugged.

At the Barneys downtown, they were selling artist-designed limited-edition items, proceeds from which go to the American Foundation for AIDS Research. Don was a darling. Whereas other men might have balked at wearing both the Robert Rauschenberg tie ($125) and the Ross Bleckner vest ($39), feeling two abstract patterns were too much, Don adored it.

Some men simply refuse to wear clothes they look good in. I don't know why—they associate it with being feminine or something. All I know is, not my Don. When I stood him up and showed him how fabulous he looked in a Barneys New York three-piece gray wool suit ($595), he was struck speechless and just stared in awe.

Even after a whole day of shopping and changing clothes, Don let me carry him all around the women's store at Barneys. He never complained when I had to try on a few dresses. He didn't want to wait outside because it was getting to him. He didn't insist on meeting me back home later. He stayed right with me, arm around my neck, until I was ready to go.

We exited the store past the Fornasetti cravats, which at $85 are quite beautiful. I especially like the one with the big giraffe on it. But it was not right for Don. It really needs a man with a bit more sense of humor.

That evening, I went to the movies with friends. When I got back and entered my apartment, I saw Don out of the corner of my eye and nearly died. This is why it says on his tag, "not to be used in the presence of anyone suffering from trauma, strain, shock, discomfort, cardiac or nervous symptoms" or as a "practical joke." Absolutely right.

Still, life with Burt and Don was a delight. They liked my taste in music. They didn't grab for the remote. If only I had met them in my 20s.

I sat them by the fire-escape windows as I slept, and for the first time in years, alone in the house, I slumbered like a baby. The only drawback, I thought, was that if there were someone hiding in my apartment, I'd never notice because I would think it was Burt or Don, but I put that out of my mind pronto.

On the second leg of my shopping trip, I took Burt to the Emporio Armani. Since he was the more glamorous of the two, I thought Armani would be right, and he did not demur. The salesman helped me dress him in a shawl-collared tuxedo ($875), a blue velvet vest with mother-of-pearl buttons ($220) and a collarless denim shirt ($135). I added some mirrored sunglasses ($110) and Burt looked gorgeous, like Hollywood royalty, as if he had the Oscar speech right in his pocket.

As I gathered Burt up and carried him out of Emporio, I realized that what they say is true: high-quality men's wear all over this town is at least one-third cheaper than the equivalent women's wear. For $1,200, Burt and Don could get the best off-the-rack tailoring money can buy; the top. It really irked me. But it is gratifying that I could dress them so well without going bankrupt.

Since then I've taken them to parties and they fit in well with everyone. They don't mind if I repeat myself or if someone flirts with me. I don't care if someone flirts with them, and they never have to leave early to do some work.

The only problem is that my boyfriend hates them. He says I have a burglar alarm and don't need them. He says if I stopped watching "Cops" I'd feel better. He says they make him feel nervous and like we're never alone. I told him I'd send them back to the company on only two conditions: that he lets me dress him how I like and brush his hair. He hasn't gotten back to me, but he is considering it.

THE (ILLUSTRATED) BODY POLITIC

Mark Leyner

~

There are fascinating and eerie parallels between Arkady G. Bronnikov's study of convicts' tattoos in Russian gulags, which appeared in words and photographs on this page on Nov. 6, and my investigation into the shrouded world of tattooing in the U.S. Senate. Like the prisons that Mr. Bronnikov visited, the Senate is an insular, predominantly male culture with a rigid hierarchy that is articulated through an almost impenetrably encoded lexicon and iconography.

Although the gulag tattoo is typically rendered in a lurid pictorial style and the senatorial tattoo tends to be minimalist—designed for optimal legibility, like an Olympic mascot—both function as résumés of past deeds and indications of the bearer's place in the institutional pecking order.

Obviously, senators shun commercial tattoo parlors—they tattoo each other. As in the gulag, the methods are primitive and painful. But unlike their Russian counterparts, senators do not consider withstanding pain to be a sign of bravery—sour mash is the traditional anodyne.

Careful viewing of C-Span will occasionally yield a glimpse of a senator feigning sleep as, beneath the overcoat draped across his trunk, an esteemed colleague applies the ink with a sharp instrument—a honed paper clip, a tiepin, the nub of a pen. (Special status is accorded tattoos created with pens used to sign legislation that brought some windfall to the senator's state.)

Whereas Russian convicts are tattooed all over their bodies, senators adorn only their torsos, buttocks and limbs. The lower portion of the arm is never tattooed, enabling the senator to pose with rolled-up shirtsleeves for photo ops of him flipping burgers at a union barbecue or sparring in a senior-citizen tae kwon do class.

Committee chairmen are usually adorned with gavels or ball peen hammers across their chests. If a chairman has an egg tattooed on each knee, it means that he kneels before no man, not even a President of his own party. This can translate more specifically to "no gays in the military" or "no to Nafta."

The most common tattoo in the Senate is a red M & M candy on the thigh. This signifies "miscellaneous malfeasance." A Möbius strip indicates the senator has served consecutively for at least two decades, is a consummate Capitol Hill "old boy," and yet unabashedly campaigns for re-election as an outsider.

A tattoo can also signify that its wearer has extracted a lucrative quid pro quo from the President during a closely contested legislative battle. For instance, a mermaid wearing a Washington Redskins helmet means "I've kept an obsolete naval base in my state from being closed."

Often a tattoo indicates the senator's debts to campaign contributors. A cow with hypertrophic udders translates as "I'm pals with the biotech industry." A water skier skimming across the ocean on two pieces of yellowtail sushi means, "I'm free trade and anti-tariff." A golfer hitting a ball out of a steaming pot of polenta advertises that the senator is open to the blandishments of foreign lobbyists. A lawn jockey whose mouth is stuffed with cigars unmistakably announces: "I'm a pro-censorship racist in the pocket of the tobacco industry."

Frequently, a tattoo is a sign of past misdeeds and contretemps. The image of a student craning his neck to glimpse another student's quiz says, "I've plagiarized." The semiotics of the florid signature of the California savings and loan mogul Charles Keating, enclasped in a valentine heart, are self-evident.

The paw is the traditional symbol of the sexual harasser. Within this category is a special hierarchy. A skirt-chasing senator will adorn himself with a dog paw, a fox paw, a lion paw or a bear paw depending on the longevity and frequency of his practice.

The lowest of the low is the diary keeper. There is more invective argot for this creature in the Senate than there are words for snow in the Eskimo vocabulary. He is usually forcibly tattooed by other senators with the image of a simpering weasel poaching itself in a boiling caldron.

Like a Russian convict, the senator has almost nothing of his own. He is in the thrall of public opinion polls, buffeted by the vagaries of his constituency's moods and in political hock to his financial backers. The only thing that really belongs to him is his flesh—the canvas upon which he paints the icons of his prestige and infamy.

O'BRIEN FLOPS!

Conan O'Brien

~

There has been much speculation about the new "Late Night with Conan O'Brien." Little is known about the new host, and even less about the show's format. Last week, this writer had the opportunity to watch a test show in Rockefeller Center's legendary studio 6-A. Frankly, I was not impressed.

The crowd was visibly eager to like the young newcomer, but some seemed puzzled by the radical new set. The backdrop, consisting of 15-foot representations of Mr. O'Brien's laughing head, loomed over his desk and chair, both carved from illegally imported African ivory. While this was somewhat unsettling, an aura of eager anticipation still hung in the air.

Until, that is, the new Late Night band began to play. Composed of musicians cut by the Boston Pops, the band lurched into an interminable version of "Waltzing Matilda," apparently the show's theme song. The bandleader, a surly cellist, refused to make eye contact with anyone and hissed at a young girl who tried to clap along. As the music sputtered to a flaccid conclusion, thick jets of foam were dumped on the audience from hidden ceiling ducts. As people wiped the stinging lather from their eyes, Mr. O'Brien jumped out from behind a curtain and cheerfully quipped, "Ha, ha, you're all foamy!"

Unfazed by the lukewarm reaction to this ill-conceived prank, Mr. O'Brien launched into his monologue. Whipping out a large book, he read a string of childish "knock-knock" jokes. While the material was fair, Mr. O'Brien's delivery was halting, and he paused several times to adjust his reading glasses.

The worst was yet to come. Strutting arrogantly to his desk, Mr. O'Brien tried to converse briefly with his sidekick, an elderly Irish priest. But the old man seemed confused, and despite constant goading from Mr. O'Brien, sat in stony silence.

Sensing a loss of momentum, Mr. O'Brien quickly launched into a "Top Ten" list, something he'd repeatedly told the press he would never do. The list was rife with misspellings, and three of the 10 entries read "joke to come." Moments later, he tried playfully flipping a pencil at a camera, but missed and struck a woman in the eye. "At least it wasn't me," quipped the first guest, the former Mets outfielder Vince Coleman. O'Brien burst into laughter at this distasteful comment. "Now we're cooking with gas," said the cocky new voice of "Late Night."

Mr. O'Brien's guests that evening also included the deputy director of New York's wastewater collection bureau, the editor of the NBC interoffice newsletter and a man who could eat oranges without getting any juice on his shirt (although he failed to do so on camera). Inexplicably, all the guests were introduced at the same time. Mr. O'Brien then asked each, in turn, his favorite color. To every answer, he snorted that the chosen color was "for girls."

During a commercial break, several NBC executives entered the audience and asked for volunteers to hold up a gaudy "Nobody Beats Conan" banner, but the crowd jeered bitterly and one youth kicked the sign.

The last 20 minutes of the program consisted of Mr. O'Brien performing a strange, snake-like dance in front of his desk as audience members filed out in disgust. "You'll be back!" he shouted several times, until the entire studio was empty (except for the orange-eater and Mr. Coleman, who giggled frenetically under the closing credits).

As much as this writer would like to root for Mr. O'Brien, one can't help but have grave doubts about his prospects. Despite the considerable power of his raw sexuality and mesmerizing intellectual presence, this "Late Night" may very well end up the late "Late Night." Or not, I gotta go.

MAKING NICE: WHEN IS ENOUGH ENOUGH?

Wendy Wasserstein

Last month I was voted Miss Colitis. I was honored at the Waldorf-Astoria and presented with a Steuben glass bowl by Mary Ann Mobley Collins, a former Miss America. It's not that the treatment of colitis is an unworthy mission, but I have no personal connection to the cause except that I received a letter from the Colitis Committee asking me to show up. In other words, I became Miss Colitis because I am very nice.

Whatever *nice* means, I've been it all my life. In second grade when the *New York Post* announced that William Zeckendorf, the very successful real estate developer, had fallen on hard times, I became unduly concerned about Mr. Z. and his entire family. It wasn't as if I had ever met them—they certainly didn't run with my second-grade crowd. When I asked my father if the family

Zeckendorf would be moving from their Park Avenue penthouse to a fifth-floor walk-up, he told me I'd be much more successful in life if I learned to worry more about myself. It horrifies me to think that if I were a child now I'd be weeping over the misfortunes of Trump's Taj Mahal.

I'm not exactly sure where my overwhelming drive to be nice came from. Maybe it was from seeing *The Nun's Story* at an early age and being impressed with the sister's commitment to the Congo. I know I was never concerned about whether any male heroes of mine, like the Beatles, John F. Kennedy, or Hermann Hesse, were particularly nice. And I sort of always had a secret thing for the Duke of Wellington and Shakespeare because they probably weren't. But, for me, being nice—plain old accepting, decent nice—has always been the basic rule of any social interaction. In other words, I'm the last person who should be in charge of a totalitarian dictatorship.

Nice doesn't have to be drippy. It simply means no one's ever said they were sorry to meet you. When a nice person leaves the room, no one would ever mutter, "She's just horrible!" That's not drippy; that's a diplomatic and acrobatic feat of enormous proportions. Being nice seemed, at least when I was growing up, one of the good female qualities. It meant being truly considerate, caring, and even believing that people could connect for a purpose higher than self-aggrandizement. Being nice meant that kindness was a virtue as opposed to a naive miscalculation. The bad guys never worried about being nice—or finishing last.

Recently, I was on a panel discussing the future of the American theater—I should really join Good Causes Anonymous—and an argument about the state of criticism became quite heated. When the moderator said, "Let's ask Wendy what she thinks," one of my fellow panelists lovingly but dismissively remarked, "Oh, Wendy will never tell you. She's too nice." On cue I smiled, giggled, twirled my hair, did all the dumb nice things that I loathe that I do, as if to say, "Oh, yes, you're right, I'm nice, so I don't have any opinions that really matter, and you don't have to worry about me."

This is not to say that being nice isn't a virtue, which, like all virtues, has a definite kickback. Katie Couric seems nice in the best possible way: bright, hardworking, and personable. And frankly, my own niceness, a driving desire to be pleasant to every usher, concession-stand dealer, and ticket taker in the theater, has been very useful. Being nice, for me, has also allowed me to maintain a very pleasant distance. It's hard to get emotional or angry at someone who has just sent you a plant and, if she could, would throw in a co-op. I would just be being nice if I didn't say I've used my desire to please to the best possible advantage.

But the nice tables have turned. Nice is not very PC. Nice isn't an "in your face" kind of move. Nice doesn't stand up for what you believe in. Nice is wishy-washy, and it's almost appallingly nonassertive. Demand an answer from any assertion technocrat, and she'll agree. Nice is very noblesse oblige, very unicultural. Nice only happens when someone's in power and she can afford to be. Or even worse, nice underlines the unempowered; you're nice because you're not entitled not to be. Nice is very dated, very retro. It belongs on the shelf along with sugar and spice. And to top it all, nice isn't very sexy, it's certainly not dangerous, and it's too bland and forgiving for even a bimbo, which, by the way, isn't a very nice way to talk about a younger, attractive, differently talented blonde woman. Frankly, as personal qualities go, nice is currently rated below good dental hygiene. A bumper sticker was sighted last week outside Cleveland: I'D RATHER FLOSS THAN BE NICE.

Lately, whenever I'm complimented for being nice, I know the choice was hideously wrong. For instance, when a man says, "You're a very nice woman," the rest of the sentence is, "but you're not my type." The longtime lover of one of my best men friends received a message from him, extolling her for what a wonderful friend and nice person she had been recently. Two days later she learned that the same lover had left her—for another man. Of course, when my friend asked my advice about the incident, I suggested they all remain on good terms because life is short, and one doesn't make that many real connections. Sometimes I am ridiculously nice.

No one seems to care if Hillary Rodham Clinton, Janet Reno, Janet Jackson, or Barbra Streisand is nice. Difficult and demanding, even bitchy, seem to be far more desirable. Barbra may or may not be nice, but her heart's in the right place, she's for the right causes, and I've even read somewhere that she watches C-Span. You don't get to sleep in the Lincoln bedroom because you're nice. Nice will get you maybe to a bake-off, and that's valuable only if you can put a twist on a recipe for chocolate-chip cookies.

The only recent newsworthy woman who's come out of the spin cycle as "nice" is Tipper Gore, and she seems to be as evident in the public imagination as her husband. Mr. and Mrs. Nice are currently Mr. and Mrs. Nowhere.

Being nice seems to have been replaced with striving for an abrasive right and wrong. If you believe in the correct things, oddly enough from the point of view of the right or the left, then you are entitled to drive your vision home. In other words, dialogue, a differing of opinion, is now almost as wishy-washy as being nice. Nice means there's a possibility of communication. Of course, there's no reason to communicate when true power is manipulating the opposition to seeing things your way. Only gooey girls believe in conversation for conversation's sake. Real hard women, with bodies of steel, who lift railroads for breakfast, can squeeze any man, woman, or vegetable by the balls until they succumb and yell, "Auntie!"

I choose to believe that Audrey Hepburn and Eleanor Roosevelt were actually sort of nice. I choose to believe they had a generous spirit that motivated their concerns for others. I choose to believe they could use their charms for what they believed in. But what they believed in also made them charming. I know that sometimes I've played my "niceness" to my advantage. I know that certain powerful men are apt to be more helpful to earnest daughter figures than to scheming semiotics majors from Brown in Azzedine Alaïa tube dresses. I also know that women will often feel less competitive with a supposedly nice colleague than with a viper who eyes their office with a clear vision of redecorating. In other words, I'm not an innocent nice person. I've used it many times, as I'm sure others have for centuries.

At times of my greatest moral dilemmas, I often consult the teachings of my mother, Lola Wasserstein—housewife, mother, and aerobicist extraordinaire—for guidance. After all, she was the author of "Always look nice when you throw out the garbage—you never know who you might meet" and "Rich or poor, it's good to have money." On the subject of being nice, Lola Wasserstein makes two distinctions. According to her, "Sometimes it pays to be nice, and other times it's nice to be nice." What scares me is that right now it seems the only time it's all right to be nice is when it pays.

Next year when I get a call to be Miss Endometriosis, I'm going to try to just say no. And when a fellow panel member says I'm too nice to speak, I hope I wipe him right off the stage with my staggeringly acerbic brilliance. If my friend's ex-lover invites her out for too many weekends with his new lover, I'll tell her that at some point she becomes a doormat, and that's not nice. That's just stupid. She'd be better off getting down, getting mean, getting angry.

I wouldn't mind shedding the nice part of me that gets me taken for granted or is trying far too hard to be likable. But on the other hand, I would hate to not still care if Mr. Zeckendorf lost all his money (ridiculous though that may sound). Frankly, I never want to leave a room and be thought of as a horrible person. I prefer to be someone who always sends a thank-you card or a plant. Or maybe a co-op.

THE PACKWOOD DIARIES (AN EXCERPT)

Byron Lanning

~

Aug 13, 1989

I just got back from having dinner with Sen. Strom Thurmond at his house. He is the senior Senator from South Carolina. He must be over 150 years old, but he looks great for his age. He doesn't look a day over 110.

During my visit, I learned an amazing thing about Thurmond. He died five years ago. He died in a fire when his dyed black hair exploded. It seems he used a gasoline based dye and it ignited when Senator Pete Domenici mistook his head for an ashtray and put out his cigarette in it. However, the Republican Party and one of its affiliates, Extropians for Money, brought Thurmond back to life through Star Wars technology and RoboCop special effects.

In public in the Senate, Thurmond seems wide-awake for a Hollywood cyborg, at least as alert as Arnold Schwarzenegger. At home, it is another matter. I have met cordwood with more intelligence. For instance, Thurmond kept calling me Robert E. Lee and asked me several times, "General, may I date your horse Traveller? I assure you I have the most honorable intentions." I finally got him to stop asking me about this by telling him Traveller couldn't date him because he is engaged to Gen. Grant's mule.

During dinner, Thurmond picked up his meat loaf from his plate and held it to his ear and said, "Operator, I want to place a call to Jefferson Davis." He sat for a moment holding the meat loaf to his ear then slammed it back to his plate. "Damn," he cried, "an answering machine. I hate talking to answering machines." Later, he smeared his chocolate pudding all over his face and cried, "Look at me! I'm Al Jolson." After dinner, he got up and went into the bathroom where he sat in front of the toilet, flushing it constantly, complaining, "Look at this, 500 channels and nothing to watch." When I left, he walked me to his door. "Come on over again real soon General Lee," he said. "Next time, I'll let you floss my dentures."

Actually, it does not surprise me to know that Thurmond died. I suspected something strange about him a long time ago when he showed up for work one morning with bolts sticking out of his neck. What I find most startling about the man is that he dyes his hair black. Unbelievable! Who could have imagined such a thing. No wonder he looks good for his age.

Yet, this discovery has caused me great consternation. I now question my party and its policy towards dyed hair. One of the founding principles of the Republican Party, since its first convention, has been the belief in natural hair color. If a conservative Republican like Thurmond dyes his hair, what other Republicans have dyed their hair? Did Teddy Roosevelt dye his hair? My god, what if Lincoln did. I wonder now if Reagan dyed his hair. If so, what does this mean? Does it mean the Reagan legacy of low taxes, big defense spending, and US support of natural hair movements throughout Latin America to stop Castro is a fraud?

Questions, questions, too many questions. I have a headache. I must lie down. I must read my Penthouse, drink a twelve pack, and pass out.

THE CHEESE STANDS
ALONE

Veronica Geng

~

Will President Clinton bog down in political debts owed to Party bosses, heavy-hitter campaign contributors, labor leaders, early supporters, and prominent Democrats who didn't hold grudges against him when they could have—i.e., Governor Mario Cuomo? Not if Clinton makes good use of Michael Dukakis's most creative legacy to political discourse: the cheese tray.

Back in July, 1988, the *Daily News* reported, Dukakis met with Cuomo to

> begin planning for the fall campaign in New York. Cuomo [was] asked whether he felt snubbed because he [had] not been invited to appear on the [Convention] platform with Dukakis....
>
> "I was sitting there with him. He offered me cheese. He offered me food. I said hello to his mother. I didn't feel snubbed," Cuomo said.

Of course not! For no one feels snubbed when cheese is offered. In the Middle Ages, it was traditional for a man to indicate that a wheel of Cheddar was en route to the family of a woman he couldn't afford to rebuff; and today there is no more certain sign of eternally dangled promise than a nice hunk of fragrant Bel Paese presented on a Ritz cracker or, even better, held out on the palm of the hand. In politics, as in love—as in all human endeavors where we try to say more than we can say in words or deliver in costly and irrevocable actions—it is to cheese that we turn for the tendering of complex emotions, subtle hints, and just plain reassurance.

Dukakis has never been given full credit for the eloquence with which he spoke the language of cheese. Clinton is said privately to admire him for this skill, and during the 1992 New York Primary campaign, when a certain anti-Italian slur hung ominously in the air over the State Capitol, the timely offer of an herbed-chèvre gift pack, from Little Rock Fancy Fromages, allegedly turned the situation around. But now Cuomo is just one of a great many allies to whom favor is due, and it remains to be seen how well Clinton will use assorted cheeses to work the ambiguous area that lies between snub and ambassadorship.

The following document was leaked by a member of the Clinton transition team who has resigned his position on the Board of Directors of the National Council of Cheese Lobbyists:

THE HIDDEN LANGUAGE OF CHEESE

SWISS:	This is a nightmare.
STILTON:	There's a reporter right behind you. Don't make any kind of revealing gesture—just take the cheese.
PORT DU SALUT:	My wife will be doing that from now on.
CAMEMBERT ON WHEAT THIN:	Any government contract you want, if you can persuade me my conscience is clear about Jesse Jackson.
GOUDA:	A ceremonial spot on Robert Reich's necktie.
VELVEETA ON FLATBRØD:	More figures needed from O.M.B. on the worst-case scenario if we develop the courage to blow you off as a cynical parasite.
FETA ON PITA:	That was then, and this is now.
CUBE OF LAUGHING COW ON TOOTHPICK:	Sir (or Madam), does your hypocrisy know no bounds? The spectacle of you and your ilk turns even my stomach. Request denied.

PART-SKIM MOZZARELLA ON SALTINE: See that man? He's a U.S. marshal, here to arrest you for trying to bribe a federal official.

PROVOLONE: Get your snout out of the public trough!

TRIPLE-CRÈME ON CELERY STICK: Boy, if things were only different, we could be somewhere, just the two of us, the banks of a trout stream in the Dordogne, trailing our fingers in the water and talking about books and ideas till the sun goes down, then back to the inn for oysters and white wine and a serious discussion about philosophy and life—but instead you're laboring under the misapprehension that kissing my ass at a fundraiser bought you a free ride on the back of the American taxpayer, you toadying little weasel.

SCHMIERKASE ON TOAST WEDGE: Maybe by 1994 or 1995 something will shake loose, but I'd feel like a bum making promises I can't keep.

HERBED-CHÈVRE GIFT PACK: The Supreme Court.

AMERICAN: Would you like to say hello to my mother?

KNOW WHERE YOUR MONEY GOES

Bruce McCall

~

Efficiency consultants at the United States Treasury estimate that the U.S. economy loses $100 billion per year in productive time wasted by America's superrich and highly affluent looking for the right change. "This isn't rifling pockets and purses in search of a tip for the guy delivering Chinese," a senior consultant observes. "We're talking the kind of large-scale transactions that add up to big, big money when you multiply all such transactions by all of America's rich people on an annual basis." The solution: the Trans-action-Specific Banknote Program, now in pilot tests in affluent communities across America. Treasury consultants are set to soon add the Cristophe $200 hair-trim bill and the Benz $450 tune-up note, among others. And when Treasury officials and consultants return from their fact-finding junket to interview the sultan of Brunei, look for even more imaginative solutions!

Bruce McCall, courtesy *Esquire* magazine.

$39.95 BEFORE XMAS, $3.95 AFTER

Bruce McCall

~

You Can Go to Hell, That's What You Are, and I'm Just The One To Do It. Inspirational self-help, folk wit, and earthy wisdom from the author of "I Feel More Like I Do Now Than I Did When I First Came In."

Forbearance Notwithstanding: The Smelt Tariff Years. Until the official 1949–59 history of Canada's Department of fisheries—the "Cod Squad"—is written, this fair and evenhanded review (civil-service regulations prohibit ripping the lid off and telling all) should suffice.

Indy's 500 Greatest Crashes. Bucolic verse by the virtual assistant headmaster of Ruthenia's "Enchanted School" of poetry, reissued at last. Formerly titled "Song of the Mildew."

The Amelia Earhart Cookbook. Tasty fare any aviatrix downed on a remote Pacific atoll could—and who's to say didn't?—easily prepare, using only a Ronson lighter and a fishing line fashioned from a radio antenna!

A Glazier Reflects. What it's like to live in a brittle, shimmering mirror world—where one shattering moment can leave a career in shards.

The Enigma Conundrum. The boffins who built the "Crossword Puzzle Machine" were sworn to secrecy—so neither side knew what the other side knew: that the best-kept secret of the Second World War was that there was no secret. And that was the enduring, the ineffable, the maddening secret.

The Cellular Phone Murders. Something snapped—and now

someone's stalking everybody who blabs on the phone as they walk. Senseless vendetta, or justifiable cellucide? You be the judge!

Kids' Letters to RN. Stimulating parry and thrust between a well-meaning but misguided posse of inquisitor-antagonists and a man denied the advantages of a private-school education, who later uncomplainingly worked his way through college while the rich kids "partied it up."

Up from Narcolepsy. While other Hollywood stars were sleeping around, she was sleeping in. Then, with the aid of her astrologer, her dietitian, her personal trainer, and a mutt named F. W. Murnau, she overcame her shame and developed a hot new line of fashion bedclothes.

Golf Carts of the Third Reich. Fascinating historical document, golf nut's holiday, and art lover's delight, all in one lavishly illustrated volume. With many photographs never before taken.

The Buck Stops at Murder. A peppery president returns from the beyond to wreak mischief and mayhem on the campaign trail in Margaret Truman's taut, angry tale—climaxed by the comeuppance to end all comuppances!

The Coffee Table Book. From Pushkin's simple upturned keg to Imelda's three-million-dollar wonder, used as the ring for the 1972 Ali-Frazier "Thrilla in Manila," the history of the coffee table is almost as rich as this sixty-four-pound blend of literature and furniture—complete with four sturdy legs—that's not only about coffee tables, it is one.

Pâté Again! Accidentally locked into the commissary of Pillbox No. 32 on the Maginot Line in May of 1940 and discovered only in 1951, France's heroic "Lost Poilu" recounts his long, lonely ordeal without rancor or bitterness—or punctuation.

The Autobahn Society Bird Book. Banned at the Frankfurt Book Fair as "ornithological porno-violence"—but you'll see at a glance why it has brought bird-lovers and advocates of a speed limit on Germany's wide-open superhighways together in common cause as never before!

O. K. Fisbee: Giant Among Midgets, Midget Among Giants.
A balanced reappraisal. Fisbee invented the jump cut while editing
"Dreams of a Rarebit Fiend" during the 1910 Pasadena earthquake,
yet this visionary of a twentieth-century medium was at heart a
man of the previous century: his insistence on handcutting every
sprocket hole in his films, the author contends, tragically short-
ened his career, not to mention his films.

REPUBLICANS CAN BE CURED!

Daniel Mendelsohn

The startling discovery that affiliation with the Republican Party
is genetically determined, announced by scientists in the current
issue of the journal Nurture, threatens to overshadow the an-
nouncement by Government scientists that there might be a gene
for homosexuality in men.

Reports of the gene that codes for political conservatism, discovered after a long study of quintuplets in Orange County, Calif.,
has sent shock waves through the medical, political and golfing
communities.

Psychologists and psychoanalysts have long believed that Republicans' unnatural and frequently unconstitutional tendencies
result from unhealthy family life—a remarkably high percentage
of Republicans had authoritarian, domineering fathers and emotionally distant mothers who didn't teach them how to be kind
and gentle. But biologists have long suspected that conservatism
is inherited. "After all," said one author of the Nurture article,
"it's quite common for a Republican to have a brother or sister
who is a Republican."

The finding has been greeted with relief by parents and friends
of Republicans, who have tended to blame themselves for the

political views of otherwise lovable people—their children, friends and unindicted co-conspirators.

One mother, a longtime Democrat, clasped her hands in ecstasy on hearing of the findings. "I just knew it was genetic," she said, seated beside her two sons, both avowed Republicans. "I just knew nobody would actually *choose* that life style!" When asked what the Republican life style was, she said, "Well, you can just tell from watching TV, like at the convention in Houston: the loud outfits, the flaming xenophobia, the flamboyant demagogy—you know."

Both sons said they had suspected their Republicanism from an early age but did not confirm it until they were in college, when they became convinced it wasn't just a phase they were going through.

Despite the near-certainty of the medical community about Republicanism's genetic origins, troubling issues remain. The Nurture article offered no response to the suggestion that the startlingly high incidence of Republicanism among siblings could result from the fact that they share not only genes but also psychological and emotional attitudes, being the products of the same parents and family dynamics.

And it remains to be explained why so many avowed Democrats are known to vote Republican occasionally—or at least to fantasize about doing so. Polls show that three out of five adult Democrats admit to having had a Republican experience. In well-adjusted people, however, this experimentation rarely outlasts adolescence.

Surprisingly, some Republican activists hail the findings as a step forward rather than as an invitation to more conservophobia. They argue that since Republicans didn't "choose" their unwholesome life style any more than someone "chooses" to have a ski-jump nose, they shouldn't be denied civil rights to which normal people are entitled.

Other Republicans, recalling 19th century scientific studies that "proved" the mental inferiority of blacks, find the frenzied search for the biological cause of Republicanism pointless, if not downright sinister.

But for most real Americans, the discovery opens a window on a brighter tomorrow. In a few years, gene therapy could eradicate Republicanism altogether.

If conservatism is not the result of sheer orneriness (as many suspect) but is something Republicans can't help and probably even don't like, there's no reason why we shouldn't tolerate Republicans in the military or even high elected office—provided they don't flaunt their political beliefs.

TO GIVE IS SUBLIME
Ron Nyswaner

Paramount Pictures decided to do something quite nice for several people connected to its new film "The Firm." The studio bought new $100,000 Mercedes-Benz 500 SL convertible two-seaters for the film makers and star.

"The attempt is to make this a warmer and more human place, where people feel part of a family," [the Paramount chairwoman, Sherry] Lansing, said.

—The New York Times, July 12.

The other morning, I stopped into Bridget's Press and Go to pick up my dry cleaning. The air conditioner was down, the place smelled like formaldehyde. Sweat covered Bridget's forehead as she heaved my clothes off the motorized rack. I could see she was working hard, really hard.

I felt something. Gratitude, guilt. I decided then and there, I had to let Bridget know she was appreciated.

"That's $35," she said, holding out a hand muscled from years of tying hangers together with twisty-ties. It occurred to me Bridget was merely doing her job and being well paid for it. Wasn't that appreciation enough?

"We fixed the hem of your trousers," she said. "No charge."

There it was: She had gone the extra mile. Strangers do only what they have to do. But Bridget had done more, the way your family is supposed to do more than is required. I realized, Bridget *was* family.

"Take my Rolex," I said.

"What?" She was momentarily confused. But I wasn't. I was

opening my arms to a member of my extended family. It was a small gesture but one that would turn the sweltering shop into a warmer, more human place.

"I want you to know I appreciate what you've done," I said.

Bridget seemed moved, but she didn't take the watch. "Mr. Nyswaner . . ." she began.

"Please," I interrupted. "Call me Ron. No, call me Ronnie Lee." It's what my mother had called me until my 13th birthday. I'd always hated the name, but hatred is also a family feeling. "You're working so hard, Bridget. I insist."

"I'm not working *that* hard," she asked. "Not as hard as Tim."

She pointed to a young man on a ladder, his head swallowed up by the silent, 20,000 B.T.U. air-conditioner. His uniform was soaked through with sweat. He was working very hard.

"Usually, I've got air conditioning," Bridget continued, "even when it's 105. But think of Tim. He *never* gets to work in air conditioning, since it's his job to fix the air conditioner."

She had a point. "Tim?"

"Huh?" echoed from the unit.

"I want you to take this." I held out the watch. "Because you work so hard, and I want you to know I appreciate it."

"Wait a minute, damn it . . ." Tim's sleeve was caught on a freon tube. So I returned to Bridget, still concerned about showing my appreciation. I handed over the keys to my truck.

"It's red," I said, apologetically. "But if you don't like red, I'll pay to have it repainted. Your spouse can choose the color."

Bridget's spouse, Irving, backed away from a press. I could see that Irving was working hard.

"Does it have a driver's side airbag?" Irving asked. Finally, someone was getting into the family spirit!

Just then Armand, my plumber, stepped into the shop to pick up his head-to-toe protective jumper that filters out the asbestos fibers floating around my crawl space. Here I was drawing Bridget and Irving and Tim into my family, and I had completely forgotten Armand! It was one of those awkward moments.

I'll never forget the look on Armand's face when I handed over the deed to my house.

Later, standing on the highway holding my dry cleaning, homeless, without a vehicle, I reflected with satisfaction on my new, extended family. The sun was beating down as I stuck out my thumb to hitchhike to God knows where, but at least I was finally beginning to feel warm and human.

Really, really warm.

ADVT.

Garry Trudeau

~

Unlike those with more at stake, I fully accept that this space may not be the first thing you turned to this morning. Indeed, if you're like me, you've already visited the tiny classified ads at the bottom of page 1—an endless source of mystery and pleasure.

In this Lilliputian world of greetings, longings, seekings and salesmanship, it's always Harry's birthday and 1,000 singles are always converging on some hapless resort. But what makes these little postings unique is that they stud the front page of The New York Times, wisps of everyday life only picas away from the big, first drafts of history. Among my favorites:

THORNTON X. STANTON is cheating on his wife during business trips to New York, but she can't prove it. Can you? For confidential chat, call (710) 677-3333.—ADVT.

NEED TO CALL attention to me, Peter Gutnick, a young Harrison-Ford-meets-Woody-Allen. Willing to stretch. grow, as an actor. For glossy or to take meeting, call service at 870-1100.—ADVT.

SEEK TO ADOPT healthy, centered, inner child. Must have references. Call (212) 970-1202.—ADVT.

ATTRACTIVE, ECONOMICALLY VIABLE ethnic region seeks backers for full autonomy. Have access to seaport, intact colonial school system. For prospectus, contact: Deaver Associates, Washington, D.C. 20037.—ADVT.

ANGELA, DOES HE know you're 50? Happy birthday from your ex.—ADVT.

WSF AND BBIM desire to meet BMF or HGM with M.B.A. or Ph.D. to share TLC and quiet walks in the country. Reply PDQ or ASAP to Drawer A. N.Y., N.Y. 11045.—ADVT.

HAVE YOU EXPERIENCED a crime, fire or medical emergency within the last hour or so? If so, call 911.—ADVT.

GIRLS! BOYS! MAKE big bucks in your spare time. Apply NW corner of Amster. and 91st. Ask for Horse or Lucca.—ADVT.

FORE SAIL: SLIGHT lee used Newton Personal Digit Tall Assist pants. Call 212 78j-##8?—ADVZ.

DESPERATELY SEEKING VALIDATION, country house. Top drama critic will accept development deal from any discreet major. Fax elements to (212) 870-1202.—ADVT.

I LOVE YOU, Robert Kincaid. I love you for your muscles, your battered old pickup named Harry, your love of fresh vegetables, your muscles, your camera named Travis, your love of poetry, your light meter named Cody, your last-of-the-breed cowboy ways. I am not worthy. Go, go like the wind. You are the highway, the road, and I would not kill the wild, magnificent animal that is you. Francesca.—ADVT.

INVESTMENT-GRADE PEZ dispensers. Future superstars of the collectors market, destined to fetch prices far in excess of what conscience permits us to charge you. Our highly trained operator is standing by at (800) 201-5163.—ADVT.

HEALTH CLUB LYCRA singleswear, so light the U.S. Government says they're not technically clothes. Pop a pec and feel the fabric— and the room—respond. Order now to avoid delays at your end. (910) 787-8999.—ADVT.

IF YOU HAVE feelings of low self-esteem, worthlessness, call The Diva Institute of 970-1202. Qualified individuals only, please.— ADVT.

TOP PRIVATE SCHOOL, (two '91 grads to Harvard) losing lease, must offer two openings K, one opening Grade One to raise cash. Fax best offer to Ms. Kopelli at Admissions Office: 870-1100.— ADVT.

BOOTLEG LINDA McCARTNEY singing "Hey Jude" back-up vocal

on isolated track. Hilarious. CD or tape. $12 (800) 93-WINGS.—ADVT.

SUCCESSFUL, PROFESSIONAL, QUALITY-time couple seeks 24-hour, seven-day, live-in nanny to care for our two little miracles, 3 and 5, teach them manners, values, Spanish, etc. $110 wk. Call secretary at (315) 999-1515.—ADVT.

BILL, TAKE THE C train to 72D St. Station, catch crosstown bus to Riverside Dr., walk across park, West Side Highway to Hudson River. Jump in it. Meredith.—ADVT.

RUGGED, SPORTS-MINDED WBM, 40, in Federal Witness Protection Program seeks Kathleen Turner sound-alike for phone sex at an undisclosed number.—ADVT.

EXPERIENCED FORMER REPORTER will write professional obit for you or any member of your family. $79.95 includes quote from mayor or top show-business figure. Call (516) 510-2000, ext. 24.—ADVT.

BELINDA, I'VE FORGIVEN myself for my abusive behavior toward you. I still love myself very, very much. Do you? Call. Stanley.—ADVT.

SEEK FEMALE DEADHEAD companion to follow band on North American tour, share road expenses, cooking, light housekeeping. Send vibes to Star Keeper at P.O. Box 44, Astoria, N.Y. 20048—ADVT.

DISILLUSIONED POST-ROMANTIC, 40 long, 32 waist, seeks to divest entire Ralph Lauren wardrobe, accessories, bedclothes. Send best offer to Box 3356, Queens, N.Y. 17029.—ADVT.

WILL TRADE PORK bellies for Hamptons time share. Call beeper number (914) 777-1588.—ADVT.

NAFTA ENTHUSIAST SEEKS same to discuss implementation protocols. Photo a must. Write Box 4467, Washington, D.C. 24453.—ADVT.

AMAZING SEA MONKEYS, for less than you might expect. Also, air plants, jumping beans, other novelty life forms. For home delivery, call (800) 501-6339—ADVT.

---

415 EAST 37TH STREET has been liberated from the cable monopoly. Get quality, pirated cable at half the price. For confidential installation, call (212) OFF-BOOK.—ADVT.

HOW TO BE A CONSULTANT

Stanley Bing

~

It's a beautiful morning in American business. Not for *you,* but we're not talking about you. We're talking about me, because I'm a consultant! Guys like me, we run the planet. I'd say the future belongs to us, but that would be wrong, sort of. I mean, of course the future belongs to us. But the present belongs to us, too! Is it any wonder I'm so goddamned jolly? See my teeth? They're terrific! Know why? Because I keep them in extremely lean and productive shape, biting off heads of guys just like you! *Hahahahaha!*

Why aren't you laughing? You know what happened to the last guy who didn't laugh at my jokes? He's dead now! If you want to pick him up, you'll need a Dustbuster! Wow, just look at the time. I've got to run. I'm facilitating a meeting of senior people who are having trouble figuring out the company vision. At least I think that's what I'm doing here—maybe I'm just measuring your office for storage space! *Hahahahaha!*

What's that you say? You wanna be a consultant, too? Are you sure? It isn't easy. You have to work very, very hard. A lot of the time you might as well be in show business—you never know where your next gig is coming from. But it's a good life, too. You're not encumbered by boring ongoing loyalties or the need to retain consistent positions. That kind of flexibility is a wonderful asset. Just ask our boy David Gergen, now contributing valuable outside perspective to the highest CEO in the land, going from *GE Theater* to *Designing Women* without a blink or a burp. That's not good consulting. That's great consulting.

You really wanna learn the ropes? *Hmm* . . . time is money, son, especially my time. . . . But sure, why not? You could be a future client, couldn't you? I could write this whole thing off, couldn't I? Maybe even develop a book about it later. Make you one of the characters? Yeah! I like that! So take notes. I'll be testing you later to see if you were listening. Fail—and we'll have to kill ya! *Hahahahaha!*

First of all, unless you've never been employed in a real job at all (a serious possibility if you distinguished yourself at Harvard and went immediately into the pundit food chain), you're going to have to get yourself fired. This is not that difficult in this day and age, especially for people like you and me, who find it difficult to form lasting attachments. Start by suggesting quirky strategies that involve the wholesale destruction of the existing culture. This will get you noticed. Your superiors will see that you have trouble working with others, but of course so do they. They will also come to believe you are "brilliant," meaning that you say things that most people find difficult to understand, let alone refute. "We could outsource all centralized corporate planning," for instance. What does it mean? How would it work? *Nobody knows!* Eventually, you'll be found just too odd for organized life. But when you're gone, people will recall you as a weird guy, not uncreative, who was not a particularly good people-person.

You're on your way.

Now find a corporation you can really sink your teeth into. Once you get in the door, the tough part really starts. You can't just unload a ton of wet consulting all over the lobby. You're going to go through the whole listening thing, really tuning into the client, then *give back the exact thing you just heard.* If in your first meeting, for instance, Mr. Weevil says, "The industry is suffering a decline in sales of 20 percent this year, but we need to grow sales by 11 percent," you don't lean forward and yell, "Don't insult my intelligence! Get real!" On the contrary! After a good talk about, say, "reading both the short-term and out-year trend lines," feed back the original order in subtly changed form, like, "Any operating strategy we come up with has to be independent of assumed revenue growth and capable of building the bottom line into the low double digits." If you wait at least fifteen minutes between his statement and yours, there is a good shot the guy will think you came up with it on your own.

Then establish the big-time We. *We* includes everyone who is not *They*. *We* are willing to kick names and take ass. *They* are not. As H. Ross (the great consultant to the American people) Perot says, "It's that simple! Case closed!"

Next, get your Grand Concept together. You'll need it to find the Thing We Need to Do. Not two things. Not four. One. That's the kind of focus no intelligent business has by nature, so you'll be appreciated by people who hate complexity, i.e., senior management. Following are some Grand Concepts that are still available after the 1980s, when a lot of them got stuck to the bottom of the pan:

- Excellence (now being localized into Centers of Excellence).
- Chaos (as a good thing).
- Multi-tasking (getting one person to do six jobs).
- Outsourcing (good for consultants, as companies hire outsiders to perform crucial, formerly inner functions like benefits management and even sales).
- Decentralization (relinquishing all control of field operations and firing the entire headquarters management function; see *Soviet Union, former*).
- The Twenty-first Century (building for it, reaching to meet its challenge).

Any of these are good, until they're not. On the other hand, if you want to steer clear of buzz words, which have a half-life, it might be smarter to get to what the new breed of us guys are now doing: Introduce a massively gnomic, unknowable analysis engine that you have to keep running. Feel the pulse, take the temperature, take a survey that polls all 610 field managers on the way they account for inventory! It's detail so deep that nobody even thought it was achievable. And after six months, why, you've got that data, *which nobody even thought of asking for before!* Torment the business with this kind of inquisition continually and viciously, and nobody will ask what the fuck you're doing until you've run up a bill it would take a military contractor to justify.

What else? Let's see. Oh, yeah: Remain loyal to one guy and

one guy only. The guy who signs off on your bill. Beyond that, the entire system can sit on it, right? They're all potential enemies of change, anyhow.

And finally—and then I've really gotta run, my man—remember the basic equation of our business:

$$\sum = \sqrt{C}$$

That is, the cost of consulting (sigma) should be equal to (or even less than) the square root of the money you have saved (or made) the corporation. If there's a perception that every bit of money you save (or make) the company is going straight into your pocket, people will begin to resent you, no matter what kind of excellent work you are doing. Naturally, if you're helping the company actually *make more money,* you don't have to be killing people all the time, but that's *hard!*

Oh, and one very, very last thing: As insecure as the life sometimes gets, don't worry about tomorrow. For at the end of the day, after all the good ideas have been fielded, after all the meetings have been taken and the costs cut and new revenue streams activated (well, they *would* have been if people understood your ideas!), when the game gets old and you long for a regular paycheck with benefits you can count on—why not come inside?

That's right! There's plenty of room for you in the executive suite. You've helped to create the room, haven't you? And it would be cheaper, a lot cheaper, for everybody if you wanted to come home to stay, wouldn't it? You bet it would! Yeah! Come to think of it . . .

Mr. Bing, is it? Love your office! Love your job! In fact, from the look of the pictures on your desk, I think I could learn to love your wife and kids!

Ow! Ow! Leggo, will ya! I'll sue! I'll have your ass! No! Not out the window! I'm afraid of heights! Now, this isn't funny! Not one bit! You wouldn't let me go, wouldja? I'm a human being! You can't do this!

Aiiiieeeeee!

SPLAWPHGHT!

Perhaps that's not the right noise, I don't know. What *is* the sound of one trend hitting the pavement at about sixty miles an hour and exploding into a million mucilaginous pieces?

IT DOESN'T COUNT IF YOU DON'T KEEP SCORE

Jerry Adler

~

Today, ambitious, venal social climbers everywhere are fast discovering that the *Fortune* 500 has room for only five hundred CEOs at a time. More and more our thoughts turn toward someone like Roger D. Hansen—the subject of Calvin Trillin's best seller *Remembering Denny*—a man of such brilliance and charisma that his classmates sincerely believed he would be president someday but who became a professor of international relations at Johns

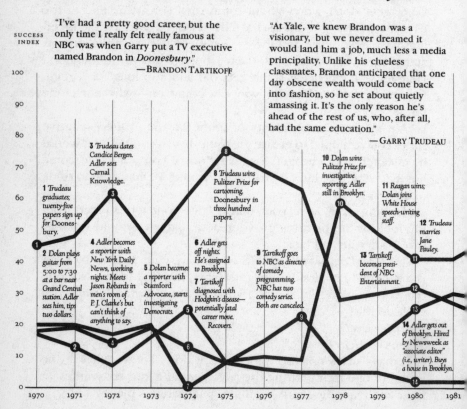

SUCCESS INDEX

"I've had a pretty good career, but the only time I really felt really famous at NBC was when Garry put a TV executive named Brandon in *Doonesbury*."
—BRANDON TARTIKOFF

"At Yale, we knew Brandon was a visionary, but we never dreamed it would land him a job, much less a media principality. Unlike his clueless classmates, Brandon anticipated that one day obscene wealth would come back into fashion, so he set about quietly amassing it. It's the only reason he's ahead of the rest of us, who, after all, had the same education."
— GARRY TRUDEAU

3 *Trudeau dates Candice Bergen. Adler sees Carnal Knowledge.*

1 *Trudeau graduates; twenty-five papers sign up for Doonesbury.*

2 *Dolan plays guitar from 5:00 to 7:30 at a bar near Grand Central station. Adler sees him, tips two dollars.*

4 *Adler becomes a reporter with New York Daily News, working nights. Meets Jason Robards in men's room of P. J. Clarke's but can't think of anything to say.*

5 *Dolan becomes a reporter with Stamford Advocate, starts investigating Democrats.*

6 *Adler gets off nights. He's assigned to Brooklyn.*

7 *Tartikoff diagnosed with Hodgkin's disease—potentially fatal career move. Recovers.*

8 *Trudeau wins Pulitzer Prize for cartooning. Doonesbury in three hundred papers.*

9 *Tartikoff goes to NBC as director of comedy programming. NBC has two comedy series. Both are canceled.*

10 *Dolan wins Pulitzer Prize for investigative reporting. Adler still in Brooklyn.*

11 *Reagan wins; Dolan joins White House speech-writing staff.*

12 *Trudeau marries Jane Pauley.*

13 *Tartikoff becomes president of NBC Entertainment.*

14 *Adler gets out of Brooklyn. Hired by Newsweek as "associate editor" (i.e., writer). Buys a house in Brooklyn.*

100   90   80   70   60   50   40   30   20   10   0

1970   1971   1972   1973   1974   1975   1976   1977   1978   1979   1980   1981

Hopkins instead. Rather than accept this as the mysterious workings of God's plan for his life or attempting to make the best of it in some other way, he killed himself—a reminder to all of us earnest middle-class strivers that *we are the pig in the python, and we're reaching the narrow end of the snake.*

Want to know just how bad you ought to feel about this? Try making a One-up Chart—a handy, at-a-glance guide to measure one's standing in the great game of envy that we call life. Select three to five people about your own age and of comparable endowments and ambitions whose achievements you can plausibly compare with your own. Plot their positions, year by year, on a success-index scale of zero to one hundred, showing how well any one individual is doing relative to the others. The rankings must at all times add up to exactly one hundred, so that nobody's success can be recorded except by diminishing everyone else's.

To illustrate, we can take my own chart, which I have compiled with reference to three randomly chosen members of my own

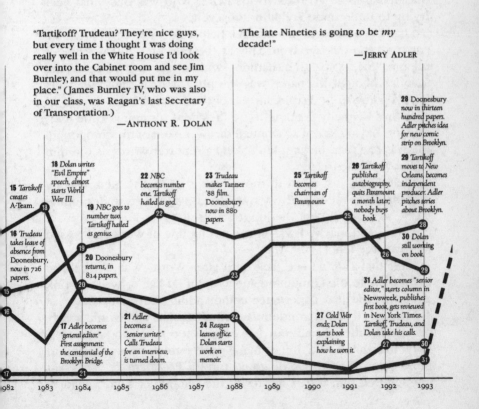

"Tartikoff? Trudeau? They're nice guys, but every time I thought I was doing really well in the White House I'd look over into the Cabinet room and see Jim Burnley, and that would put me in my place." (James Burnley IV, who was also in our class, was Reagan's last Secretary of Transportation.)

—ANTHONY R. DOLAN

"The late Nineties is going to be *my* decade!"

—JERRY ADLER

15 Tartikoff creates A-Team.

16 Trudeau takes leave of absence from Doonesbury, now in 726 papers.

17 Adler becomes "general editor." First assignment: the centennial of the Brooklyn Bridge.

18 Dolan writes "Evil Empire" speech, almost starts World War III.

19 NBC goes to number two, Tartikoff hailed as genius.

20 Doonesbury returns, in 814 papers.

21 Adler becomes a "senior writer." Calls Trudeau for an interview, is turned down.

22 NBC becomes number one. Tartikoff hailed as god.

23 Trudeau makes Tanner '88 film. Doonesbury now in 880 papers.

24 Reagan leaves office. Dolan starts work on memoir.

25 Tartikoff becomes chairman of Paramount.

26 Tartikoff publishes autobiography, quits Paramount a month later; nobody buys book.

27 Cold War ends; Dolan starts book explaining how he won it.

28 Doonesbury now in thirteen hundred papers. Adler pitches idea for new comic strip on Brooklyn.

29 Tartikoff moves to New Orleans, becomes independent producer. Adler pitches series about Brooklyn.

30 Dolan still working on book.

31 Adler becomes "senior editor," starts column in Newsweek, publishes first book, gets reviewed in New York Times. Tartikoff, Trudeau, and Dolan take his calls.

1982 1983 1984 1985 1986 1987 1988 1989 1990 1991 1992 1993

college class whose lives and careers I know a little bit about. They are Garry Trudeau, Pulitzer Prize–winning cartoonist; Brandon Tartikoff, former head of NBC and Paramount; Anthony R. Dolan, Pulitzer Prize–winning writer; and me, Jerry Adler.

ANOTHER INSIDE PEEK
Russell Baker

Memories of Jack Kennedy are once again filling the air, or at least the media. Mine go back to his father who was busy that year trying to undermine Franklin Roosevelt.

I had been watching young Jack help a slow-witted schoolmate parse a Latin passage from Livy at the rate of 1,200 words per minute. "Joe," said I to his father—which was what we called the founder, though his name was Joseph—"Joe," I said, "that boy Jack is going to be President one of these days."

"If any Kennedy is going to be President it's going to be me," said Joe, having Kenny O'Donnell throw me out of the compound. Joe was like that: Just couldn't stand a reporter who was too dim to know the score.

Well, I was just a kid in those days, so I said to Kenny as he was throwing me out, "How was I to guess Joe was undermining F.D.R. so he could get the job for himself?"

Kenny said maybe I was in the wrong line of work and tossed me over the fence.

After that I didn't see Jack until after World War II when he invited me to the compound and asked if I'd like to write a book about his wartime experience commanding a torpedo boat.

I said no. It was a wonderful story of heroism and would surely be a best seller, I said, but I liked him too much to write it. A book like that, I said, might make people think he was trying to build a heroic image so he could run for President.

I admired him too much to let the public get such a cynical

impression of him, I said: He thanked me profusely and had Arthur Schlesinger throw me out anyhow.

Arthur said maybe I was in the wrong line of work as he tossed me over the fence.

Jack was a Senator next time we met. I had been rowing in Nantucket Sound and lost both oars after accidentally bumping into his sailboat halfway between Martha's Vineyard and the compound at Hyannis Port. Jack had Pierre Salinger haul me out and revive me with a jolt of Chateau Latour '47.

To show my gratitude I gave Jack some political advice. "Jack," I said, "you've done good work in the Senate, but the Senate is a dead end. It's for gasbaggers, not can-do guys. It's time you moved up to where the action is."

Jack smiled in delight. "What you ought to do now," I said, "is quit the Senate, go back to Massachusetts and run for Mayor of Boston."

Jack had Pierre lower the dinghy, row me all the way back to the Kennedy compound and throw me over the fence. Not being in great condition, Pierre had some trouble making the heave, so out of gratitude for Jack's not having me thrown off the boat I helped out by climbing to the top of the fence myself and letting Pierre shove me over.

"You may be in the wrong line of work," I told Pierre.

When Jack ran for President he seemed to forget me. I figured, if that's how he's going to be, it's no skin off my nose. But when I heard he was going to debate Richard Nixon on TV humane instinct got the better of me.

"I like the guy," as I said to Jackie. "How can I let him walk unwarned into that meat grinder?"

Why was I talking to Jackie? To get into the compound I had disguised myself as a Baby-Tenda salesman, a Baby-Tenda being sort of a highchair on wheels that couldn't be tipped over to fracture baby's skull, the way old-fashioned highchairs could. Or so went the sales pitch.

After making the sale to Jackie, who naturally didn't want little Caroline's old-fashioned highchair tipping over, I told her the truth: I was there to save Jack from Nixon.

That dear girl, what else could she do? In an instant I was explaining to Jack why it would be a catastrophe if America saw a handsome young guy like him struggling helplessly on television in the coils of Nixon's smooth and deadly debating technique.

Previous experience had shown me that Jack's political wisdom was not very deep, so I patiently explained that since the whole country recognized Nixon while nobody recognized Jack it would be folly to give a mass audience its first glimpse of him in a debate he was sure to lose.

Ted Sorensen offered to throw me out, but Jack said he would do it himself, as it would make him look well exercised on television when he faced Nixon. What a terrific guy.

I HEAR AMERICA SWINGING

Frank Gannon

~

> Q. *During the swing era, there was a band leader named Whitman or Whiteman—I can't remember which. His first name was Walt, I think. Can you help me?*
>
> —*Parade* magazine

Our transportation was an old Greyhound bus. We took eight-week tours in that damn thing. There were 19 of us, and with our equipment and instruments we felt like sardines. Once, Al Platsky, a horn player, brought some sardines to eat on the bus. We laughed about it. Then we threw Platsky and his damn sardines off the bus. Then Walt revoked Platsky's union card. Then Walt wrote a poem about him.

That's the way it was on the road. We were always looking for the next gig. One time, Ralph Emerson, who handled our bookings, told Walt that we had a gig in Albany at 8 o'clock. We pull into Albany, nice and easy around 7:30. Next thing you know, it turns out Emerson meant Albany, Tex. After that everybody started calling him "Waldo."

One time, we showed up in Pennsauken, N.J., for a gig at an observatory. About six of us had started to play our opener, "I'll

String Along With Your Yawp," when the the guy who owned the observatory, unhappy with the ticket sales, put a "lugubrious topper" on the evening by shooting and killing himself. I remember I was looking over the song list right then; our next tune was "You're an Old Smoothie," followed immediately by "I Effuse My Flesh in Eddies but My Eddie's Not Like You." The observatory was dead silent. Walt stepped off the bandstand, walked over and looked at the dead guy. Then he looked out at the crowd, about 80 middle-aged people, and spoke:

"I pass death with the dying and birth with the new-sashed babe and am not contained between my hat and boots. And now, for your dancing and listening pleasure, a very wonderful old tune by Johnny Mercer and Harry Warren."

We went right into "Jeepers Creepers." A couple of attendants got the dead guy out of the way and the floor filled up. Let me tell you, those people *danced.*

Whitman didn't have many rules. With a group like ours, he couldn't. But you'd better be damn sure you didn't break the ones he did have.

1. I have no mockings or arguments. I witness and wait.
2. No smoking on stage.
3. If there's going to be any barbaric yawps, I'm going to be the one yawping.
4. For photographs, coat and tie. NO EXCEPTIONS!
5. We shall fetch as we go.
6. Do your own laundry.
7. Not I, nor anyone else, can travel that road for you. You must travel it by yourself.
8. No women on the bus.
9. Shoulder your duds, dear son, and I will mine, and let us hasten forth.
10. Remember, no women on the bus.

I roomed on the road with George (Lord) Byron, the slide man. As is well known, Byron was into the sauce pretty heavy. Before a show, he'd get himself a two-liter bottle of Mello Yellow, empty it out, then fill it almost to the top with Ten High bourbon. Then he'd pour a little Lysol in there and screw it shut. Right before

the show, he'd walk over in front of Whitman and make a big
show out of getting a cup of ice.

Byron thought he was fooling Whitman, but he wasn't. One day
Whitman walked up to him while Byron was doing his inane ice
thing.

"Hey, Lord," Whitman said, tossing him a little package. "Here's
your things."

"What's this," Byron asked, puzzled.

"A rainproof coat, good shoes, a staff cut from the woods and
a bottle of Lysol. You're finished with this organization, Byron."

Before Byron got to the door, we were already talking about
our next gig.

Once we played for a convention of catfish-farm owners. We
played "Something to Remember You By," "I've Got a Crush on
You" and "Anything Goes." One of the farm owners came up and
asked us why we didn't play anything that we brought the sheet
music for. I'll always remember what Walt told him, strictly sotto
voce. Walt looked the guy up and down. The guy had on some
kind of plaid polyester suit with a Ban-Lon shirt. Walt says: "The
spotted hawk swoops by and accuses me; he complains of my gab
and my loitering. Where's the turnip truck?"

The guy just froze. That's all, he just froze.

One night, unable to sleep after a gig in Terre Haute, Ind., I
went out for some coffee. I saw Blackie, our Moog synthesizer
gooser, sitting in back of the diner, and joined him. Just then, who
comes into the diner but Whitman. He slid into the booth next
to Blackie and a waitress came over with a cup of coffee.

"You boys played really well tonight," Walt said. He took a big
sip from his coffee. "I love to hear the boys when they play with
energy, I listen to them making their sounds and those sounds
are music and that music as fathomless as I am, and I am really
fathomless, as you know."

I looked at Blackie. Yes, I would get up first, and we would be
out of there in 90 seconds. We both liked Walt, but nobody wants
to sit around in a diner at 2 in the morning while Whitman
catalogues everything.

"I sit in this seat and see the diner around me and I say that it
is all good. I see that fat guy reading USA Today and I say that he
is good."

I got up. "Gotta get some sleep, Walt. I think I'm probably

getting the flu or something." Blackie was up, too. "I gotta go, too, Hoss."

Walt got up. We shook hands.

"Goodbye," Walt said. "We part again, but as we part we near each other and actually, at one point, change places. Am I right? And how about that waffle iron? That's good, I say, along with the bald guy eating that pecan waffle."

We left him and walked out into the clear cold night with silent stars. I never would have thought of that sentence if I hadn't spent those years on the road with Whitman. That's why the man is a legend among big band leaders.

A DECENT PROPOSAL

Libby Gelman-Waxner

~

Hey, I'm Josh Waxner, and I'm filling in for Lib this month because, as she said, Josh, this is your story, so you tell it, but keep it NC-17. It all started when we went to see this flick *Indecent Proposal.* Usually Lib goes to movies with her girlfriends—excuse me, woman friends—or with her cousin Andrew, the unemployed art director (don't get me started), but hey, it was her birthday, so I took off from work early and picked up a bottle of sangria, some yellow flowers at the Korean deli, a new lens for my Nikon, and this really pretty scarf with gold stuff on it from a sidewalk guy who didn't have a box, but he threw in this pink satin thing with an elastic band for a ponytail, so I figure I got Lib two presents. Even though I know that what she really wants are tickets to see *Sunset Boulevard,* this new Andrew Lloyd Webber musical that doesn't even open till, like, next year, the tickets are, like, 65 bucks each, and that Webber guy is English, so I said, Lib, we gotta support our own economy and make some sacrifices, and I really need the lens for my series documenting the effects of leather protectants on the padded dash of my Lexus, and that's why I got stuck going to the movies and wearing this turquoise cotton sweater she gave me that Andrew said will look great with my Dockers, the khaki pants that make me look like a laundry bag (every time Andrew says the word "Dockers," he starts giggling, then swears he's thinking of a joke he heard on the subway).

Anyway, so we go to this movie, which is about this architect, Woody Harrelson (yeah, right), and his wife, Demi Moore. They're broke, and they go to Vegas, and then Bob Redford shows up as some kind of billionaire and offers a million big ones for one night with Demi (yeah, right; it could happen). The couple talk it over and decide to go for it; Demi comes back in the morning, and you expect Woody to yell, Yippee, we're rich! and for Demi to go, What do you mean, *we?* But instead, she and the Woodster start getting all wussy about, like, relationship issues, and I'm thinking, Yeah, I really needed to pay $7.50 for couples counseling with the bartender from *Cheers,* even if Demi does sometimes discuss commitment with one of her nipples hanging out, kind of like Shari Lewis letting Lamb Chop in on things. So Demi goes off with Bob again, and Libby starts cheering; but when Demi and Woody get back together and their marriage is stronger, even if the Woodman donates the million bucks to save the hippos at some zoo—I'm not kidding. Woody also gives a speech about how architecture can uplift the human spirit, and he holds up a brick and shows a slide of the cathedral at Chartres and says that even a brick can aspire to be more than a brick—which, I guess, explains what Woody's doing in a feature film.

So we get out of the theater, and I'm feeling all cramped and gassy from waiting so long to see if Demi's gonna take a shower to cleanse her sins, and then it happens: Demi Moore is standing right outside Loews Tower East, staring at me. (I mean, I swear it was Demi, or at least an incredible body double.) She comes over to Lib and says, How much? and Lib assumes it's like a Richard Simmons Deal-A-Meal and says, Ten pounds and five inches from my hips and thighs, and Demi says, No, how much for a night with your husband?

And I go, like, Excuse me? and Demi says, My husband, Bruce Willis, only has a career in action films, and I didn't get a nomination for *A Few Good Men,* and I need some excitement in my life—how much? And Lib says, Wait, you want to have sex with my husband? as if she's on the cellular with *Ripley's Believe It or Not.* Demi explains that she's tired of actors and billionaires and that she wants a professional man, and I go, like, Whoa, how did you know I was an orthodontist? That's major psychic network! And Demi says, You have this air of healing authority and incredibly sensuous hands, and you're wearing a white nylon smock with a little mirror sticking out of the pocket. And then she says, I will give you $170 for one night, and I start to go, No way!—I mean, I've got the Fiedler twins coming in with killer occlusions at 8 A.M.—but I hear Lib say, Demi, do you by any chance know Andrew Lloyd Webber, like, personally?

So I pull Lib aside, and I say, What will this do to our relationship? How can you put a price on our love, and do you want me to be a cheap whore? And Lib says, Afterward, ask her what she uses on her hair for shine, and I say, Lib, I'm not some stud-for-hire, and Lib says, Ask her how tall Patrick Swayze is, and I say, Come on, this is pure human evil, and she says, Make sure the seats are orchestra or at least front mezzanine.

So Demi brings me back to this incredible suite at the St. Regis, and she says that I can have anything I want, and pretty soon we're knee-deep in Amstel Light, Doritos Tortilla Thins, and this great video game called Sonic the Hedgehog 2. I wanted to shove the furniture around and play Wiffle ball, but Demi says, Josh, it's time. She says, I stared at you in the movie theater and thought, I want what Libby has: I want one glorious night with a pudgy orthodontist with a bald spot from Lexington Avenue. And I go, Well, excuse me, Little Miss Flash-the-Works-on-the-Cover-of-*Vanity Fair*—I mean, I saw your mondo dud, *The Butcher's Wife*, on video, like everyone else. And we both laugh, and I say, Okay, babe, it's your dime, and I go to the bathroom to get ready. When I come out, she's in bed wearing only these white cotton G-string panties and French high heels, and I'm in my track shorts, my *ORTHODONTISTS DO IT IN YOUR MOUTH* T-shirt, and my flip-flops, and she says, Don't worry, you might like it, and I say, Don't bet on it, and she starts kissing my neck and moans and says, You're wearing Kouros, aren't you? and I say, You bet, babe—ever since Father's Day.

So when I get home the next morning, Lib asks, How was it? and I say, Let's never discuss it, and she says that she has to know for her own peace of mind, and I say, Here you go, row E, two on the aisle. And I ask, Was it worth it? but she's already on the phone with her mom, choosing a restaurant for after the show. So I head for the La-Z-Boy and put my feet up and think, Will I ever be truly clean again? Then I find this note in my pocket that says, Dear Josh, You will never look at me the way you looked at Sonic the Hedgehog. Libby is a saint. It was unsigned.

I told my partner, Marv Schlein, about my night with Demi, and he said, Right, like she really paid you for sex when she could get an oral surgeon. So I showed him one of the Polaroids I took that night, and he says, That's not Demi Moore. I say, It is too Demi, and he says, No way—that's Jaye Davidson. And suddenly, it dawns on me . . . Oh, my God! Oh, my God! But hey, at least I had sex with a movie star. And that's what counts, if you ask me.

—JOSH WAXNER

THE FRANKEST INTERVIEW YET

Ian Frazier

~

A: I was having sex. I had had sex previously, found that I enjoyed it, and so was having it again. With a sexual partner, I screwed all over the floor. Orgasms were multiple for the both of us. I took a lover, also. Plus I had a tryst with a fellow in the shower room of the old Grand Avenue Y. I turned an empty office at work into a snuggery, and made use of it. I became proficient not only in standard English, but also in tavern English. I cursed like a sailor or sometimes like a navvy. I mixed obscenities with profanities at will when the spirit moved me, using anatomical and physio-logical terms, inferences of parentage, and blasphemies. When called upon, I could turn the air blue.

Oral sex.

See what I mean? I did not (and do not) shrink from explicit language. If you are shocked, or perhaps are feeling ambivalent about what I am saying, good. Sexual practices should be more open, and no one knows this better than I. When the young shopgirls in their sheer blouses and blank faces come ankling into the elevator, my expression turns unmistakably sensual. I simply drip with sex. It oozes from my every pore, which I like, and they do, too. And when I see a strapping young hoss of a guy the experience is remarkably similar. I wiggle like a streetwalker and go right up to him and say, "Hello, my name is Mr. Bascom." I garden in the near-nude in the residential community where I live. I put on a pair of coveralls only when the weather is chilly or I'm doing landscaping. If my neighbors are offended, they shouldn't be. I have an excellent, heavyset body. We are all deeply sexual beings.

I met a young woman with a criterion figure and bedroom eyes at a sales event the other day. I mentally undressed her, then re-dressed her. She noticed the pertinacious quality of my stare, and asked, "What are you looking at, Mr. Johnsberry?" I mumbled a pleasantry and looked away. She knew as well as I did that if we wanted, we could screw. I could tell she was appraising me, wondering what I'd be like in the sack, and if I was a swordsman. I wouldn't have been at all surprised if she had a mental image of me bare-butt naked. So much the better. I informed her that my name was Mr. Bemis, and that I would very much enjoy her company in my hotel suite later in the evening. We began chatting. The sexual tension, undercurrents, and electricity in the air were so thick you could have seen them, while our colleagues leered at us with a casual knowingness.

Her name was Ms. Buxbaum, and Christ, what a great lay she turned out to be! After the obligatory postcoital cigarette, I immediately went to church and confessed my sins and was shriven for them, the peace of divine forgiveness filling me as I bent over the prayer rail in my fellow-congregants' holy, homely scent of soap and dry-cleaned wool and Sunday shoe polish. By the renewed light of the high chancel windows I signed my name, Mr. Randsworthy, in the registry. Then it was back to the hotel. My lover at the time was a male nurse, and you know how nurses are. He was lithe, sloe-eyed, and rather matter-of-fact about sex, as are many young men who work in hospitals. We discovered a mutual pursuit that gave us enormous pleasure: screwing our heads off.

Yes, I believe in lap dancing. Far from censuring it, I whole-heartedly encourage it as a healthy outlet. At the end of a long day, with my colleagues Mr. Pixley, Mr. Simpkins, et al., I often spend a few wickedly relaxing hours at a small club I know of where lap dancing is done. To have a well-built entertainer of either sex clad in little more than thong, pasties, and/or black bow tie sit in one's lap and gyrate has a marvellous effect. In this, of course, my views come into direct conflict with those of many. I believe that opposition to lap dancing is a destructive holdover from the Puritans, and have argued my point on a number of occasions, even with members of my own family—my children, and their spouses or companions. By now they know enough not to expect moralizing pabulum from me.

The children's mother, Ms. Frampton, and I had great sex throughout our long marriage and, quite candidly, before, when we were just a couple of randy college kids shacking up. In those days, Johnson (my pet name for my or any penis) could become an ivory wand virtually at command and achieve orgasm in just a few penile thrusts. Then, as now, I wore painted-on trousers with stirrups at the cuffs to pull them down even tighter, and my fiancée, Ms. Samples, did the same. We acquired a reputation on campus for unashamed and forthright behavior, which I have maintained ever since. All the kids except Gary know the time, place, and erotic circumstances of their conception, and are stronger for it. All the kids except Gary can tell you the particulars, thus freeing themselves and others from prudery and cant. When I heard that Gary was having problems at school, I flew up on the shuttle first thing the next morning, met with the Dean, Mr. Bentley, had sex, and thrashed out the whole situation. The following term, Gary's marks were back up where they belonged. Neither I, Gary's mother, nor his probable biological dad ever spared any effort with Gary, which is why I find some of his recent remarks unsubstantiated.

From the point of view of one who has spent the balance of his life pursuing vigorous sexual intercourse and sport-screwing, I can say that public attitudes have changed for the better. I give people like myself credit for this. How easy it would have been for me and my contemporaries to continue the backstairs bundling and fondling and frottage that characterized earlier times. But I am an avowed hedonist and sensualist, whose lasting legacy will be more of the same. I don't care how the future may judge me, Mr. Spradlin, as long as it acknowledges that I chased after anything in a skirt or trousers and mounted and was mounted freely. The sexual response is a pleasure given by God, in most cases. To deny this is to deny a natural desire to hear about my sex life and the sex lives of thousands of other businesspeople no different from ourselves.

THE TWELVE TERRORS OF CHRISTMAS

John Updike

~

1. SANTA: THE MAN. Loose-fitting nylon beard, fake optical twinkle, cheap red suit, funny rummy smell when you sit on his lap. If he's such a big shot, why is he drawing unemployment for eleven months of the year? Something scary and off key about him, like one of those Stephen King clowns.

2. SANTA: THE CONCEPT. Why would anybody halfway normal want to live at the North Pole on a bunch of shifting ice floes? Or stay up all night flying around the sky distributing presents to children of doubtful deservingness? There is a point where altruism becomes sick. Or else a sinister coverup for an international scam. A man of no plausible address, with no apparent source for his considerable wealth, comes down the chimney after midnight while decent, law-abiding citizens are snug in their beds—is this not, at the least, cause for alarm?

3. SANTA'S HELPERS. Again, what is really going on? Why do these purported elves submit to sweatshop conditions in what must be one of the gloomiest climates in the world, unless they are getting something out of it at our expense? Underclass masochism one day, bloody rebellion the next. The rat-a-tat-tat of tiny hammers may be just the beginning.

4. O TANNENBAUM. Suppose it topples over under its weight of explosive baubles? Suppose it harbors wood-borers that will migrate to the furniture? There is something ghastly about a tree—its look of many-limbed paralysis, its shaggy and conscienceless aplomb—encountered in the open, let alone in the living room. At night, you can hear it rustling and drinking water out of the bucket.

5. TINY REINDEER. Hooves that cut through roof shingles like linoleum knives. Antlers like a hundred dead branches. Unstable flight pattern suggesting "dry leaves that before the wild hurricane fly." Fur possibly laden with disease-bearing ticks.

6. ELECTROCUTION. It's not just the frayed strings of lights anymore, or the corroded transformer of the plucky little Lionel. It's all those battery packs, those electronic games, those built-in dictionaries, those robots asizzle with artificial intelligence. Even the tinsel tingles.

7. THE CAROLS. They boom and chime from the vaulted ceilings of supermarkets and discount stores, and yet the spirits keep sinking. Have our hearts grown so terribly heavy since childhood? What has happened to us? Why don't they ever play our favorites? What *were* our favorites? Tum-de-tum-tum, angels on high, something something, sky.

8. THE SPECIALS. Was Charlie Brown's voice always so plaintive and grating? Did Bing Crosby always have that little potbelly, and walk with his toes out? Wasn't that Danny Kaye / Fred Astaire / Jimmy Stewart / Grinch a card? Is Vera-Ellen still alive? Isn't there something else on, like wrestling or "Easter Parade"?

9. FEAR OF NOT GIVING ENOUGH. Leads to dizziness in shopping malls, foot fractures on speeded-up escalators, thumb and wrist sprain in the course of package manipulation, eye and facial injuries in carton-crowded buses, and fluttering sensations of disorientation and imminent impoverishment.

10. FEAR OF NOT RECEIVING ENOUGH. Leads to anxious scanning of U.P.S. deliveries and to identity crisis on Christmas morning, as the piles of rumpled wrapping paper and emptied boxes mount higher around every chair but your own. Three dull neckties and a pair of flannel-lined work gloves—is this really how they see you?

11. FEAR OF RETURNS. The embarrassments, the unseemly haggling. The lost receipts. The allegations of damaged goods. The humiliating descent into mercantilism's boiler room.

12. THE DARK. How early it comes now! How creepy and green in the gills everybody looks, scrabbling along in drab winter wraps by the phosphorous light of department-store windows full of Styrofoam snow, mockups of a factitious 1890, and beige mannequins posed with a false jauntiness in plaid bathrobes. Is this Hell or just an upturn in consumer confidence?

Kiss of the Spike

ROBERT GROSSMAN

Robert Grossman, courtesy of *The New Yorker.*

HOW DOOMED IS YOUR FAMILY?

Meredith Anthony, ET AL.

~

**MATCH YOUR FAMILY AGAINST THE GREAT DOOMED
FAMILIES OF HISTORY AND LITERATURE**

CATEGORY	Kennedys	Corleones
City	Boston	New York City
Family Empire	Politics	Rackets
Avaricious Patriarch	Joe Senior	The Don
Long-Suffering Powerful Matriarch	Rose	Mama Corleone
Reluctant but True Heir	John-John	Michael
Long-Suffering Anorexic Outsider	Jackie O	Kay Corleone
Long-Suffering Alienated Insider	Joan	Connie
Mistress of Choice	Marilyn Monroe	Any Bridesmaid
Family Sycophant	Peter Lawford	Johnny Fontaine
Family Shame	Mary-Jo Kopechne	Opera Singing
Family Stud	JFK	Sonny
Family Hothead	Bobby	Sonny
Family Glutton	Teddy	Clemenza
Family Nerd	Joe II	Fredo
Family Pit Bull	Willie Smith	Luca Brazzi
Family Rival	Rockefellers	Tattaglias
Family Joy	Football	Red Sauce
Identifying Traits	Good Teeth	Jacket Bulge
Preferred Method of Self-Destruction	Booze, Women	Gang Wars
Least Favorite Road Sign	Bridge Ahead	Stop and Pay Toll

House of Windsor	YOUR FAMILY
London	your home town
The Falklands	_____
The Queen Mum	_____
Queen Elizabeth	_____
Charles	_____
Diana	_____
Margaret	_____
Camilla Parker-Bowles	_____
David Frost	_____
Toe Sucking	_____
Randy Andy	_____
Anne	_____
Fergie	_____
Prince Philip	_____
Jack the Ripper	_____
France	_____
The Corgis	_____
Big Ears	_____
Lemon Peeler	_____
	_____

Men
Working

GUIDE TO THE FIVE DIMENSIONS

Douglas Coupland

~

	1st Dimension	2nd Dimension
Currently controversial population control technique	abstinence	condom
Dinosaur	trilobite	lizard
Cereal box cartoon character	Tony the Tiger	the Quaker Oats Quaker
Insidious labor practice	minimum wage	part-time workers
Object of middle-class desire	tennis ball	Picasso painting
Flight mode	Aeroflot	United (coach)
Elastic structure	rubber band	Silly Putty
Feistiness role model	the common cold virus	Lucky, the Lucky Charms leprechaun
Snack food	unpeeled carrot sticks	tub of chocolate frosting with wooden spoon

3rd Dimension	4th Dimension	5th Dimension
abortion	RU-486	lesbianism
Jurassic Park	Dino Flintstone	Eric Clapton
Count Chocula and Frankenberry	Jerry Seinfeld	Ross Perot
subcontracting	robots	slavery
ski chalet	three weeks in Provence	Charlie Rose
Concorde	the Star Trek beam thingy	astral projection
earthquake-proof Los Angeles skyscraper	theory of reincarnation	David Gergen
crash test dummy	Camille Paglia	Marxism
Norwegian lox with Maui onion and capers on pumpernickel	anabolic steroids	Clinton nominees

LOVE THY ENEMY

Paul Rudnick

~

*Place: **The Basement Meeting Hall of a Twelve-Step Program.***

DON: We all know why we're here, and remember, we're not into judgments. Who'd like to start? Yes?

TIM: Hi. My name is Tim, and I . . . I want to have sex with middle-aged straight guys.

EVERYONE: Hi, Tim!

TIM: That felt good! Lately, I've been having recurring fantasies about . . . Colin Powell.

There is general excited murmuring.

TIM: You know what I mean? I'm so sick of those male models in the magazines, with great bodies and abs and stuff. But I was watching Colin, during those hearings, and he was talking about how gays in the military would destroy cohesion, and—remember how his stomach sort of strained against his uniform? And remember those thick, rectangular eyeglass frames, kind of like the ones on Dennis the Menace's dad? And the chins? And all I could think was—foxhole. Just Colin and me. Only I guess it would have to be a kind of larger foxhole. Like a comfort-fit foxhole.

BARRY: Hi, my name is Barry, and I'm into chinos.

EVERYONE   [*with yearning*]: Chinos!

BARRY: What I mean is, I'm into guys who wear them. You know, like a paunchy yuppie with two kids and a pink polo shirt and Reeboks, and he thinks he looks like a preppy but he really looks more like a cleaning woman? I mean, sometimes I go to, like, malls, or Great Adventure, and when I see one of those guys pushing a double stroller and eating a DoveBar and using his camcorder—I have to find a men's room. I can't help myself.

ANDY: Hi, I'm Andy, and I have just two words—Sam Nunn.

TIM: Rudy Giuliani.

BARRY: Gene Hackman.

DON: Gentlemen, I think we're talking—comb-over.
Everyone screams in ecstasy.

ANDY: I'm only human!

TIM: I think about kissing the top of Sam Nunn's head, and I stay hard for *weeks.* I can't leave the *house.*

GARY: Hi, I'm Gary, and I have . . . a special problem. No, I'm sorry. I can't talk about it, it's too painful.

DON: Gary, you're among friends.

BARRY: I know what he's going to say.

TIM: We've all been there.

ANDY: Just say it. You'll feel better. It's the first step.

GARY: It's just . . . I love him. It's not about sex. Although, of course, I'd kill, I mean, just dinner, just . . . anything. He's like . . . okay, I'll just say it. My name is Gary and I want to make eternal, filthy, passionate, unending love to . . . Rush Limbaugh.

EVERYONE: *Rush!*

GARY: First it was just the audiocassettes of his book—I would listen to them in my car on the interstate, and suddenly one day . . . there was a pileup. This cop came over to me, I was wiping myself off with a Wash'n Dri, I was so embarrassed, but the cop takes one look and says, "Rush, huh? Not another one." For so long I thought there'd never be someone for me. I mean, Alan Burke, Tom Snyder, Morton Downey Jr.—all gone. Canceled. But . . . then came Rush. Making fun of abortion. Making up silly nicknames for Clinton. And the way he cracks himself up every time he says "feminazis" or "liberal wackos," and everything just . . . jiggles. I mean, forget Louie Anderson, forget Gleason, forget *Santa.*

DON: There was a man—maybe some of you are familiar with him. He came into my life and, well, nothing has ever been the same. And that man's name is Andy Rooney. *There is a pause and then a lingering sigh.*

DON: The uncombed eyebrows.

ANDY: No shoulders.

BARRY: *Jowls.*

DON: I know, what gay man hasn't at one time or another thought of chucking everything and just plain *stalking* the big A? Call it *Feeble Attraction.* Sometimes I'd fantasize an orgy, kind of *McLaughlin Group* sex. Me, Andy, maybe Mike Wallace, Morley. We'd start by passing around a bottle of Mylanta in a brown paper bag. Pretty soon we'd all be down to green-and-navy-plaid boxer shorts, Hanes V-neck T-shirts, garters, and Dr. Scholl's air-cushion insoles.

ANDY: Stop!

DON: But Andy—he was always the prize. The babe. I'm not saying he wears a truss, I have absolutely no evidence, but picture it. Picture it and try to keep your 501's buttoned. I would read his collected essays over and over again, especially the hot parts, the riffs on folding road maps and reading candy-bar labels. *The Story of A.* Remember when Andy was taken off the air for a couple of weeks because he called homosexuality life-threatening? Well, in my mind Andy spent those two weeks . . . in my arms. I imagined the two of us taking a honeymoon in Charles Kuralt's minivan. Discovering America and . . . each other.

TIM: But what did you do? How did you find help?

DON: Well, I tried the conventional forms of therapy. You know, placing electrodes on my penis during *60 Minutes,* picturing Andy having sex with other men, trying to transfer my obsession to someone more realistic, to a Perot or a Wilford Brimley. Nothing worked—I lost my job, my car, my condo—finally the police picked me up wearing just a raincoat, hovering in front of the remainders table at Barnes & Noble. I told the judge I would try to take control of my life. I told him that I knew Andy would never really love me. Let's face it, I'm attractive, I'm in decent shape, but I'm no Pat Robertson. And I decided to see if there were other gay men out there, the gay men whom Colin and Sam seem so preoccupied with. Gay men who want sex with middle-aged straight guys. The gays who are turned on by a Sansabelt label.

TIM: Power mowers.

BARRY: Golf cardigans.

ANDY: Monogrammed belt buckles from Swank.

DON: Calm down, fellas. . . .

GARY: The shins, where all the hair's been worn away by black nylon socks. . . .

TIM: *Brown* nylon socks.

BARRY: Father's Day neckties.

ANDY: Windbreakers.

TIM: Ear hairs.

GARY: Nose hairs.

ANDY: *Cholesterol.*

DON: One day at a time, guys—one day at a time.

THE IRONY BOARD II

Douglas Coupland

~

A Continuing Survey of Words That Have Become 100% Ironic

Some (but not all) criteria:

Might an in-flight magazine use this word to describe its merchandise?

Might this word be located on a Steak Hut menu?

Might a Boca Raton realtor entice me using this word?

Might this word inhabit a backlit plexiglass sign on Route 35?

Might this word describe Lou Grant or Mary Richards?

The List

appalled	baronial	bauble	beverage	bonanza	chick
ciao	collector's item	contemporary	crusty	curmudgeon	dig
exclusive	executive	gal	gruff	happening *(adj.)*	juicy
komedy	krazy	kustom	luxurious	majestic	melting pot
millionaire	mouthwatering	natural	-oid	-o-rama	outraged
perky	pert	plush	privilege	regal	sanitized
shocked	sizzling	sleek	smorgasbord	snazzy	square
stud	succulent	tantalizing	trinket	unique	verve

Bonus Party List:

Andy	Bianca	Calvin	Farrah	Halston	Jerry
Liza	Martha	Mick	Ryan	Truman	Warren

MISCELLANEOUS

DR. BENWAYS CENTER FOR SYMBOLIC MANIPULATION

In association with

THE INTERNATIONAL BROTHERHOOD OF PROPHETS OF THE APOCALYPSE

Present a Gala Fête to Celebrate

THE END OF THE WORLD

(as we know it)

To be Held at the Compound of the Greenlake Branch of the Old Davidians Home
5862 Mc Kinley Place North

Saturday 15 May, 1993

SPECIAL EVENTS TO INCLUDE:

ATF TARGET RANGE
LIVE AGENTS IN BOTH REGULAR AND OVER .50 CALIBER EVENTS

CHARLES MANSON LOOK-ALIKE CONTEST
Guest Judge Miss Squeaky Fromme

SEVEN SEALS BRAIN TEASER
Solve Them All And Win a Child Bride (Our choice)

INTER-SECT BINGO TOURNAMENT
Ammo to be Supplied by Contestants

For The Ladies: MISS HELLFIRE PAGEANT
MEN'S LONG DISTANCE CROSS BEARING
For the Kiddies: Pin The Tail on L. Ron Hubbard

JESUIT BAITING

DAVID KORESH MEMORIAL WEENIE ROAST

BUNKER CONSTRUCTION SYMPOSIUM
Exerpts from the Northern Idaho Chapter on hand to answer your questions

Fire Walking/Brimstone Toss

Casual Sex is Encouraged
Group Event Sign-Up (round robin) Begins at 8 pm

Free Kool-Aid Punch

Test your staying power on

DR. STRANGELOVE'S BUCKING BOMB RIDE

Media are respectfully requested to remain two statute miles from the event at all times

In the unlikely event of continuance of life on this planet as we know it this event will revert
to its default theme of birthday celebration for all those damn Taureans who seem to pop out
of the woodwork and expect a party around this time every year

—MICHAEL BINSKY

EURO ENGLISH

~

Having chosen English as the preferred language in the EEC, the European Parliament has commissioned a feasability study in ways of improving efficiency in communications betwen Government departments.

European officials have often pointed out that English spelling is unnecessary difficult; for example: cough, plough, rough, through and thorough. What is clearly needed is a phased programme of changes to iron out these anomalies. The programme would, of course, be administered by a committee staff at top level by participating nations.

In the first year, for example, the committee would suggest using 's' instead of the soft 'c'. Sertainly, sivil servants in all sities would resieve this news with joy. Then the hard 'c' could be replaced by 'k' sinse both letters are pronounsed alike. Not only would this klear up konfusion in the minds of klerikal workers, but typewriters kould be made with one less letter.

There would be growing enthusiasm when in the sekond year, it was anounsed that the troublesome 'ph' would henseforth be written 'f'.

This would make words like 'fotograf' twenty per sent shorter in print.

In the third year, publik akseptanse of the new spelling kan be expekted to reatsh the stage where more komplikated tshanges are possible. Governments would enkourage the removal of double letters which have always been a deterent to akurate speling.

We would al agre that the horible mes of silent 'e's in the languag is disgrasful. Therfor we kould drop thes and kontinu to read and writ as though nothing had hapend. By this tim it would be four years sins the skem began and peopl would be reseptive to steps sutsh as replasing 'th' by 'z'. Perhaps zen ze funktion of 'w' kould be taken on by 'v', vitsh is, after al, half a 'w'. Shortly after zis, ze unesesary 'o kould be dropd from words kontaining 'ou'. Similar arguments vud of kors be aplid to ozer kombinations of leters.

Kontinuing zis proses yer after yer, ve vud eventuli hav a reli sensibl riten styl. After tventi yers zer vud be no mor trublsm difikultis and evrivun vud fin it ezi tu understand ech ozer. Ze drems of Mr. Orvel vud finali hav kum tru.

COMPUTER VIRUSES

PAUL REVERE VIRUS: This revolutionary virus does not horse around. It warns you of impending hard disk attack—once if by LAN, twice if by C:.

POLITICALLY CORRECT VIRUS: Never calls herself a "virus," but instead refers to itself as an "electronic microorganism."

ROSS PEROT VIRUS: Activates every component in your system, just before the whole thing quits.

MARIO CUOMO VIRUS: It would be a great virus, but it refuses to run.

OPRAH WINFREY VIRUS: Your 200MB hard drive suddenly shrinks to 80MB, and then slowly expands back to 200MB.

AT&T VIRUS: Every three minutes it tells you what great service you are getting.

THE MCI VIRUS: Every three minutes it reminds you that you're paying too much for the AT&T virus.

TED TURNER VIRUS: Colorizes your monochrome monitor.

ARNOLD SCHWARZENEGGER VIRUS: Terminates and stays resident. It'll be back.

GOVERNMENT ECONOMIST VIRUS: Nothing works, but all your diagnostic software says everything is fine.

NEW WORLD ORDER VIRUS: Probably harmless, but it makes a lot of people really mad just thinking about it.

FEDERAL BUREAUCRAT VIRUS: Divides your hard disk into hundreds of little units, each of which does practically nothing, but all of which claim to be the most important part of the computer.

GALLUP VIRUS: Sixty percent of the PCs infected will lose 38 percent of their data 14 percent of the time (plus or minus a 3.5 percent margin of error).

TERRY RANDLE VIRUS: Prints "Oh no you don't" whenever you chose "Abort" from the "Abort, Retry, Fail" message.

TEXAS VIRUS: Makes sure that it's bigger than any other file.

ADAM AND EVE VIRUS: Takes a couple of bytes out of your Apple.

MICHAEL JACKSON VIRUS: Hard to identify because it is constantly altering its appearance. This virus won't harm your PC, but it will trash your car.

CONGRESSIONAL VIRUS: The computer locks up, screen splits erratically with a message appearing on each half blaming the other side for the problem.

AIRLINE VIRUS: You're in Dallas, but your data is in Singapore.

FREUDIAN VIRUS: Your computer becomes obsessed with its own motherboard.

PBS VIRUS: Your PC stops every few minutes to ask for money.

ELVIS VIRUS: Your computer gets fat, slow, and lazy and then self destructs, only to resurface at shopping malls and service stations across rural America.

OLLIE NORTH VIRUS: Turns your printer into a document shredder.

NIKE VIRUS: Just Does It!

SEARS VIRUS: Your data won't appear unless you buy new cables, power supply, and a set of shocks.

JIMMY HOFFA VIRUS: Nobody can find it.

CONGRESSIONAL VIRUS II: Runs every program on the hard drive simultaneously, but doesn't allow the user to accomplish anything.

KEVORKIAN VIRUS: Helps your computer shut down whenever it wants to.

IMELDA MARCOS VIRUS: Sings you a song (slightly off-key) on boot up then subtracts money from your Quicken account and spends it all on expensive shoes it purchases through Prodigy.

STAR TREK VIRUS: Invades your system in places where no virus has gone before.

HEALTH CARE VIRUS: Tests your system for a day, finds nothing wrong, and sends you a bill for $4,500.

GEORGE BUSH VIRUS: It starts by boldly stating, "Read my test . . . no new files!" on the screen, proceeds to fill up all the free space on your hard drive with new files, then blames it on the Congress Virus.

CLEVELAND INDIANS VIRUS: Makes your 486/50 machine perform like a 286/AT.

LAPD VIRUS: It claims it feels threatened by the other files on your PC and erases them in "self-defense."

CHICAGO CUBS VIRUS: Your PC makes frequent mistakes and comes in last in the reviews, but you still love it.

BUMPER STICKERS

IMPEACH CLINTON and her husband!
HELP!! I am having an out-of-money experience.
Nuke the unborn gay whales.
Auntie Em. Hate you, hate Kansas, taking the dog. Dorothy.
We're staying together for the sake of the cats.
It's been lovely, but I have to scream now.
My karma ran over your dogma.
Women who seek to be equal to men lack ambition.
This is not an abandoned vehicle.
I don't lie, cheat, or steal unnecessarily.
Beautify Texas. Put a Yankee on a bus.
Welcome to Texas, now go home.
It's as bad as you think and they are out to get you.
If you don't like the news, go out and make some of your own.
Life's too short to dance with ugly men.
Life's too short to dance with ugly women.
My wife says if I go fishing one more time, she's going to leave me. Gosh, I'm going to miss her.
When you do a good deed get a receipt (in case heaven is like the IRS).
I is a college student.
Sex on television can't hurt you unless you fall off.
Beer isn't just for breakfast any more.
Sorry, I don't date outside my species.
Eschew obfuscation.
Will Rogers never met a lawyer.
Happiness is seeing your mother-in-law's face on the back of a milk carton.

It's lonely at the top, but you eat better.

Don't steal. The government hates competition.

Is there life before coffee?

Never play leap frog with a unicorn.

Nobody's ugly after 2 a.m.

Cover me. I'm changing lanes.

The weather is here. Wish you were beautiful.

I Cayman went.

My other wife is beautiful.

I need someone really bad. Are you really bad?

Smile. It's the second best thing you can do with your lips.

Don't laugh. Your daughter could be in this vehicle.

Geez if you belive in honkus.

Friends don't let friends drive naked.

Save California; when you leave take someone with you.

I came, I saw, I did a little shopping.

There's one in every crowd and they always find me.

If money could talk, it would say goodbye.

When you're in love, you're at the mercy of a stranger.

Just when you think you've won the rat race along come faster
  rats.

If it's too loud, you're too old.

Wink. I'll do the rest.

The worst day fishing is better than the best day working.

An Irishman is not drunk so long as he can hold on to one blade
  of grass and not fall off the earth.

Cynics are people who know the price of everything and the
  value of nothing.

I may be fat but you're ugly, and I can lose weight.

Who cares who's on board?

No radio. Already stolen.

Crime wouldn't pay if the government ran it.

Want a taste of religion? Bite a minister.

Carlsbad Caverns: 22% more cavities.

Exxon Suxx.

Honk if you love cheeses.

Flying saucers are real, the Air Force doesn't exist.

I don't care who you are, what you are driving, or where you
  would rather be.

So many pedestrians, so little time.

THE PARACHUTE PARADIGM

~

You are one of two people on a malfunctioning airplane with only one parachute:

PESSIMIST: You refuse the parachute because you might die in the jump anyway.

OPTIMIST: You refuse the parachute because people have survived jumps just like this before.

PROCRASTINATOR: You play a game of Monopoly for the parachute.

BUREAUCRAT: You order them to conduct a feasibility study on parachute use in multi-engine aircraft under code-red conditions.

LAWYER: You charge one parachute for helping them sue the airline.

DOCTOR: You tell them you need to run more tests, then take the parachute in order to make your next appointment.

SALES EXECUTIVE: You sell them the parachute at top retail rates and get the names of their friends and relatives who might like one, too.

INTERNAL REVENUE SERVICE: You confiscate the parachute along with their luggage, wallet, and gold fillings.

ADVERTISER: You striptease while singing that what they need is a neon parachute with computer altimeter for only $39.99.

ENGINEER: You make them another parachute out of aisle curtains and dental floss.

SCIENTIST: You give them the parachute and ask them to send you a report on how well it worked.

MATHEMATICIAN: You refuse to accept the parachute without proof that it will work in all cases.

PHILOSOPHER: You ask how they know the parachute actually exists.

WRITER: You explicate simile and metaphor in the parachute instructions.

COMPARATIVE LITERATURE EXPERT: You read the parachute instructions in all four languages.

COMPUTER SCIENTIST: You design a machine capable of operating a parachute as well as a human being could.

ECONOMIST: You plot a demand curve by asking them, at regular intervals, how much they would pay for a parachute.

PSYCHOANALYST: You ask them what the shape of a parachute reminds them of.

ACTOR: You tie them down so they can watch you develop the character of a person stuck on a falling plane without a parachute.

ARTIST: You hang the parachute on the wall and sign it.

REPUBLICAN: As you jump out with the parachute, you tell them to work hard and not to expect handouts.

DEMOCRAT: You ask them for a dollar to buy scissors so you can cut the parachute into two equal pieces.

LIBERTARIAN: After reminding them of their constitutional right to have a parachute, you take it and jump out.

ROSS PEROT: You tell them not to worry, since it won't take you long to learn how to fix a plane.

SURGEON GENERAL: You issue a warning that sky diving can be hazardous to your health.

ASSOCIATION OF TOBACCO GROWERS: You explain very patiently that despite a number of remarkable coincidences, studies have shown no link whatsoever between airplane crashes and death.

NATIONAL RIFLE ASSOCIATION: You shoot them and take the parachute.

POLICE BIGOT: You beat them unconscious with the parachute.

ENVIRONMENTALIST: You refuse to use the parachute unless it is biodegradable.

OBJECTIVIST: Your only rational and moral choice is to take the parachute, as the free market will take care of the other person.

BRANCH DAVIDIAN (David Koresh): You get inside the parachute and refuse to come out.

SPORTS FAN: You start betting on how long it will take to crash.

AUTO MECHANIC: As long as you are looking at the plane engine, it works fine.

MIRROR, MIRROR ON THE WALL

A newly married couple did not have time to unwrap all their wedding presents before they went on their honeymoon. So after they returned from their honeymoon, they proceeded to open the remaining presents. They came upon one gift that did not have a card to indicate who gave it to them.

It was a very old but nice full-length mirror. The wife decided it would be a nice addition to their bedroom. Later that evening, the wife was getting ready for bed. She was standing in front of the mirror, looking at herself critically. She said, "I wish I had boobs out to here," indicating a 38C or better. Instantly, with no warning, her breasts grew out to her hands. She called excitedly for her new husband to come quickly. He said, "What happened to you!" She told him the story of her wish and the magical power of the mirror. He stood in front of the mirror. He said, "I wish I had a pecker that hung down to the floor." Again, the mirror reacted instantly and without any warning. His legs were cut off at the hips!

THE NEWLYWED GAME

~

A young girl is getting married and she's scared of what will happen on her wedding night so she asks her mother to get the hotel room next to her and her husband.

The big night arrives. The girl goes to the bathroom to get ready for bed.

When she comes out, her husband is taking off his shirt. She runs next door to her mother. "Momma, Momma, he's taking off his shirt!"

"That's perfectly normal, dear," the mother says. "Calm down." And the girl went back.

This time the husband was taking off his shoes. The girl ran back to her mother again, and again her mother told the girl it was all right. So the girl went back to her own room. What the husband hadn't told his wife was that he had been in a lawnmower accident when he was younger and lost part of his foot.

When the girl comes back to the room she sees his foot and runs back to her mother.

When she gets there she says, "Momma, Momma, he's got a foot and a half!"

The mother says, "Stay here, honey, I'll take care of this."

FOREPLAY

~

A man is marooned on an island for ten years and has given up all hope of ever being saved, when one day, suddenly, a woman washes ashore. Her clothes are all tattered, and she is clutching a waterproof bag. It seems that her ship also hit the coral reef off the island and has sunk. She, too, was the only survivor.

The man, overjoyed at seeing another person, blurts out his whole story, about how he learned to live on the island alone, how he learned to live off the land, surviving by his wits. When he has finished his story, the woman says to him, "You mean you've been on this island for *ten* years?"

"That's right," says the man.

"Tell me," she asks, "did you smoke cigarettes before you were marooned?"

"Why yes I did," he says. "Why do you ask?"

The woman says to him, "Well since you haven't had a cigarette in ten years, here!" And with that she pulls a cigarette out of her little bag and gives it to him.

"Oh, wow!" he says, "Thanks a lot!"

As she lights it for him she says, "Say, were you a drinking man before you got shipwrecked?"

"Well," says the man, puffing on the cigarette, "I would have an occasional whiskey or scotch now and then."

The woman reaches into her little bag and says, "You haven't had a drink in ten years? Here!" And from her bag she produces a small flask of the finest scotch and hands it to him.

He takes a full and deep pull from the flask and is thanking her when she suddenly says, "Gee . . . I just realized. You've been on this island for ten years. I guess you haven't uh, well, you know, played around in ten years, have you?"

"Good God!" says the man. "Do you have a set of golf clubs in that bag!"

NOT IN THE CATALOG

~

A young, newlywed couple moved to a small midwestern town.

Wanting to fit in right away, they applied for membership in the town's largest church. The minister of the church brought them into his office for an interview.

"We're pleased to have you apply to our church," said the minister, "but you must understand that we are a very strict congregation and in order to join you must prove your faith by abstaining from any kind of sex for a whole month. Do you think you can do that?" the minister asked, looking at both of them in turn.

The couple both nodded their agreement so the minister asked that they meet with him weekly to report on their progress.

"Well how are you two doing?" asked the minister the following week.

"Not too bad," said the man. "I was tempted a few times but I was able to call on my faith and resist."

"Very good," said the minister. "See you next week."

When next they met, the minister again asked about their status.

The young man, showing a slight twitch, confessed that the temptation was greater and he was having more difficulty controlling it but had thus far succeeded.

The next week the young man, now pale and tense, told the minister that the temptation was now mighty and almost beyond control. The minister tried to encourage him as best he could, urging him to abstain for just one more week.

The last meeting finally arrived. "Well," said the minister, "did you succeed?"

The young man squirmed in his seat and replied, "Last Thursday my wife had on her shortest skirt and she bent down in front of me to pick up something and I just couldn't control myself any longer. I tore off her clothes and we had wild sex right there on the floor!"

"Oh dear," said the minister, "I'm afraid we won't be able to let you back in our church."

"That's okay," said the young man, "they probably won't let us back in Sears either."

NATIONAL CONDOM WEEK SLOGANS

"Put a helmet on that soldier!"
—Sam Kinnisson

Cover your stump before you hump.
Before you attack her, wrap your whacker.
Don't be silly, protect your willy.
When in doubt, shroud your sprout.
Don't be a loner, cover your boner.
You can't go wrong if you shield your dong.
If you're not going to sack it, go home and whack it.
If you think you're spunky, cover your monkey.
If you slip between her thighs, be sure to condomize.
It will be sweeter if you wrap your peter.
She won't get sick if you wrap your dick.
If you go into heat, package your meat.
While you're undressing venus, dress up that penis.
When you take off her pants and blouse, be sure to suit your
    trouser mouse.
Gift wrap your member January through December.
Never, never deck her with an unwrapped pecker.
Don't be a fool, vulcanize your tool.
The right selection: protect your erection.
Wrap it in foil before checking her oil.
A crank in armor will never harm her.

If you really love her, wear a cover.
Don't make a mistake: muzzle your snake.
Sex is cleaner with a packaged weiner.
If you can't shield your rocket, leave it in your pocket.
No glove, no love.
Wear a stealth condom and she'll never see you coming.

YOUR HOROSCOPE

Aquarius: Jan. 20 to Feb. 18

You have an inventive mind and are inclined to be progressive. You lie a great deal. On the other hand, you are inclined to be careless and impractical, causing you to make the same mistakes over and over again. People think you are stupid.

Pisces: Feb. 19 to Mar. 20

You have a vivid imagination and often think you are being followed by the CIA or FBI. You have a minor influence over your associates and people resent you for your flaunting of your power. You lack confidence and are generally a coward. Pisces people do terrible things to small animals.

Aries: Mar. 21 to April 19

You are the pioneer type and hold most people in contempt. You are quick-tempered, impatient, and scornful of advice. You are not very nice.

Taurus: April 20 to May 20

You are practical and persistent. You have a dogged determination and work like hell. Most people think you are stubborn and bull-headed. You are a communist.

Gemini: May 21 to June 20

You are quick and an intelligent thinker. People like you because you are bisexual. However, you are inclined to expect too much for too little. This means you are cheap. Geminis are known for committing incest.

Cancer: June 21 to July 22

You are sympathetic and understanding about other people's problems. They think you are a sucker. You are always putting things off. That's why you'll never make anything of yourself. Most welfare recipients are Cancer people.

Leo: July 23 to Aug. 22

You consider yourself a born leader. Others think you are pushy. Most Leo people are bullies. You are vain and dislike honest criticism. Your arrogance is disgusting. Leo people are known thieves.

Virgo: Aug. 23 to Sept. 22

You are the logical type and hate disorder. This nit-picking is sickening to your friends. You are cold and unemotional and sometimes fall asleep while making love. Virgos make good bus drivers.

Libra: Sept. 23 to Oct. 22

You are the artistic type and have a difficult time with reality. If you are a man, you more than likely are queer. Chances for employment and monetary gains are excellent. Most Libra women are good prostitutes. All Libras die of venereal disease.

Scorpio: Oct. 23 to Nov. 21

You're shrewd in business and cannot be trusted. You shall reach the pinnacle of success because of your total lack of ethics. Most Scorpio people are murdered.

Sagittarius: Nov. 22 to Dec. 21

You are optimistic and enthusiastic. You have a reckless tendency to rely on luck since you lack talent. The majority of Sagittarians are drunks or dope fiends. People laugh at you a great deal.

Capricorn: Dec. 22 to Jan. 19

You are conservative and afraid of taking risks. You don't do much of anything and are lazy. There has never been a Capricorn of any importance. Capricorns should avoid standing still for too long as they are apt to be mistaken for inanimate objects.

OLD BLUE

A Southern boy graduates from high school and is going north to college.

Just as he is about to leave, his parents say to him, "We know you're going to be mighty lonely up there with all them Northerners, so we decided to let you take Old Blue with you. He has been our family dog for so many years, we know that Old Blue will be good company for you."

So the boy goes north with Old Blue and is only there a few weeks when he gets a call from Mary Lou, his girlfriend from back home. It seems that in about eight more months they will be having a problem unless he can take care of it now, and it will cost five hundred dollars.

The boy tells Mary Lou that he will get back to her. Then he calls his folks.

"How are you?" they ask.

"Oh, I'm just fine," he says.

"And how," they ask, "is Old Blue?"

"Well, he's kind of depressed. You see, there's this woman up here who's been teaching dogs to read, and Old Blue is feeling kind of left out 'cause all the dogs can read, exceptin' him. The woman charges five hundred dollars."

"Well," say the parents, "we won't let Old Blue down. We'll send you the money."

When the boy receives the five hundred dollars a few days later, he sends it off to Mary Lou and everything is taken care of.

The boy goes home for a quick visit, and a little over a month after he gets back to school, he receives another call from Mary Lou. It seems they have the same problem again and she needs another five hundred dollars.

So the boy calls his parents and tells them that while he, himself, is fine, Old Blue is depressed again. "Old Blue's been reading up a storm," he tells them. "He's been through all the books in the library and is now reading all the newspapers and magazines. But now the lady is teaching dogs to talk, and Old Blue is feeling left out again. She charges five hundred dollars for talking lessons."

"We can't let Old Blue down," say the parents. "We'll send you the money."

Once again the boy gets the money and sends it off to Mary Lou.

Then the boy is driving home in his pickup for the holidays with Old Blue sitting on the seat next to him, and he just can't figure out what he is going to tell his parents. When he is in front of the Buford's farm, the farm next to his parents', he takes his shotgun and Old Blue out of the truck and shoots the dog, killing him.

When the boy reaches his parents' farm, he sees his father standing out in the driveway.

"Hello, son!" says the father. He then looks at the pickup and says, "But where's Old Blue?"

"Well, Pa," says the boy, "I was driving down the road and Old Blue, he was a reading Shakespeare and Plato and pontificating on Newton and Socrates and Einstein when we passed the Buford's farm. Old Blue, he said to me, 'Say, what do you think your mother would do if I told her that your father has been running over to the Buford's farm and having his way with Mrs. Buford when old man Buford was away from the farm over all these past years?'"

The father looks at his son—quite solemnly—and says, "You shot that dog, didn't you boy!"

DESCARTES

~

Everyone knows that Descartes is famous for his axiom:

> Cogito ergo sum.

It took a lot of work to develop this little homily. Among his earliest efforts was:

> Cogito ergo spud.
> (*I think therefore I yam.*)

Descartes goes into a bar one day, and the bartender says to him: "Bonjour, M. Descartes, would you care for something to drink?" Decartes looks up and replies, "I think not," and promptly disappears!

One of Descartes' unsuccessful experiments was with animal intelligence. He tried to see if horses thought. However, face to face confrontation proved to be impossible. You can't put Descartes before the horse.

CITY OF LOS ANGELES HIGH SCHOOL MATH PROFICIENCY EXAM

~

NAME: _____GANG: _____

1. Johnny has an AK47 with a 30 round clip. If he misses 6 out of 10 shots and shoots 13 times at each drive-by shooting, how many drive-by shootings can he attempt before he has to reload?

2. Jose has 2 ounces of cocaine and he sells an 8 ball to Jackson for $320 and 2 grams to Billy for $85 per gram. What is the street value of the balance of cocaine if he doesn't cut it?

3. Rufus is pimping for three girls. If the price is $65 for each trick, how many tricks will each girl have to turn so Rufus can pay for his $800 per day crack habit?

4. Jarome wants to cut his half pound of heroin to make 20% more profit. How many ounces of cut will he need?

5. Willie gets $200 for stealing a BMW, $50 for a Chevy, and $100 for a 4×4. If he has stolen 2 BMWs and 3 4×4s, how many Chevys will he have to steal to make $800?

6. Raul is in prison for 6 years for murder. He got $10,000 for the hit. If his common-law wife is spending $100 per month, how much money will be left when he gets out of prison and how many years will he get for killing the bitch that spent his money?

7. If the average spray can covers 22 square feet and the average letter is 3 square feet, how many letters can a tagger spray with three cans of paint?

8. Hector knocked up 6 girls in his gang. There are 27 girls in the gang. What percentage of the girls in the gang has Hector knocked up?

HOW TO HUNT ELEPHANTS?

ENGINEERS hunt elephants by going to Africa, catching gray animals at random, and stopping when any one of them weighs within plus or minus 15 percent of any previously observed elephant.

ECONOMISTS don't hunt elephants, but they believe that if elephants are paid enough, they will hunt themselves.

STATISTICIANS hunt the 1st animal they see N times and call it an elephant.

CONSULTANTS don't hunt elephants, and many have never hunted anything at all, but they can be hired by the hour to advise those people who do. Operations research consultants can also measure the correlation of hat size and bullet color to the efficiency of elephant-hunting strategies, if someone else will only identify the elephants.

COMPUTER SCIENTISTS hunt elephants by exercising Algorithm A:

1. Go to Africa.
2. Start at the Cape of Good Hope.
3. Work northward in an orderly manner, traversing the continent alternately east and west.
4. During each traverse pass
   a. Catch each animal seen.
   b. Compare each animal caught to a known elephant.
   c. Stop when a match is detected.

Experienced **COMPUTER PROGRAMMERS** modify Algorithm A by placing a known elephant in Cairo to ensure that the algorithm will terminate. Assembly language programmers prefer to execute Algorithm A on their hands and knees.

LAWYERS don't hunt elephants, but they do follow the herds around, arguing about who owns the droppings. Software lawyers will claim that they own an entire herd based on the look and feel of one dropping.

VICE PRESIDENTS of engineering, research, and development try hard to hunt elephants, but their staffs are designed to prevent it. When the vice president does get to hunt elephants, the staff will try to ensure that all possible elephants are completely prehunted before the vice president sees them. If the vice president does see a nonprehunted elephant, the staff will:

(1) compliment the vice president's keen eyesight and
(2) enlarge itself to prevent any recurrence.

SENIOR MANAGERS set broad elephant-hunting policy based on the assumption that elephants are just like field mice, but with deeper voices.

QUALITY ASSURANCE INSPECTORS ignore the elephants and look for mistakes the other hunters made when they were packing the jeep.

SALESPEOPLE don't hunt elephants but spend their time selling elephants they haven't caught, for delivery two days before the season opens. Software salespeople ship the first thing they catch and write up an invoice for an elephant. Hardware salespeople catch rabbits, paint them gray, and sell them as **DESKTOP ELEPHANTS.**

SPELL CHECKER?

I have a spelling checker
It came with my PC;
It plainly marks four my revue
Mistakes I cannot sea.
I've run this poem threw it
I'm sure your pleased too no
It's letter perfect in it's weigh
My checker tolled me sew.

DOGS

Three dogs were in a cage at the city pound: a Pit Bull, a German Shepherd, and a Great Dane. The Pit Bull told the others, "I was eating dinner and my owner's two-year-old niece tried to grab my food, so I ripped out her throat. Now they are going to put me to sleep."

The German Shepherd said, "I chewed up all my master's shoes yesterday, now they are going to put me to sleep."

The Great Dane said, "My master is a beautiful twenty-two-year-old woman. The other day she came out of the shower and bent over in front of me, so I mounted her and did my thing!"

"So are you in here to be put to sleep, too?" asked the others.

"No, I'm here to have my nails clipped!"

WEEKLY WORLD NEWS

Front Page

Farmer raises four-foot-tall rabbits!

Family sues granny, 65, for snoring too loud!

1963 PLANE CRASH SURVIVORS FOUND: Castaways live in *"Gilligan's Island"* paradise for 30 Years!

Woman has taste buds on the bottoms of her feet!

KILLER LIGHTNING BUGS ARE HEADED OUR WAY... WARN SCIENTISTS!

Lady vampires demand their own blood bank!

On the Inside

Undertaker offers rent-a-corpse service to grieving families!

Hare-brained farmer breeds a rabbit with a cat! [Rabbit theme this week.]

Pet parrot eats $3,180!

Goats eat drug dealers' $600,000!

Two horsemen jailed for drunk riding!

Woman trains camels to wash office windows!

That's not ham hocks... it's HERMANN! RECIPE FOR MURDER: Wife chops up hubby—and serves him for dinner!

Photo of Jackie Gleason is ALIVE!

Was my husband reincarnated as a tarantula? (Letter to Serena Sabak, "America's Sexiest Psychic")

Black-belt karate champ KO's himself!

Survey Shocker: "According to a new study from Nice, France, people are more afraid of sending their food back to the kitchen at a restaurant than they are of dying."

Pope John Paul II: Enough is Enough! 300 priests to exorcise the Devil's Triangle!

Live longer—sleep on a brick bed!

Woman, 74, married 1,083 men in 57 years . . . and she's still looking for Mr. Right!

Snake spits up 2-year-old boy!

You get shorter when you're on vacation!

New study! Men marry women for their hips!

Most men would rather be a woman for a week than President of the United States!

Cavemen loved to gamble!

Glass-eating family shattered when bizarre diet kills daughter, 8!

HUMOROUS HEADLINES

Survivor of Siamese twins joins parents

Blind woman gets new kidney from dad she hasn't seen in years

Never withhold herpes infection from loved one

Smokers are productive. But death cuts efficiency.

Death causes loneliness, feelings of isolation

Stolen painting found by tree

Dealers will hear car talk Friday at noon

Victim tied, nude policeman testifies

Judge to rule on nude beach

Complaints about NHL referees growing ugly

Police discover crack in Australia

Caribbean islands drift to left

Women's movement called more broad-based

Men recommend more clubs for wives

Dr. Ruth to talk about sex with newspaper editors

Grandmother of eight makes hole in one

Two convicts evade noose; jury hung
Drunk gets nine months in violin case
Farmer bill dies in house
Iraqi head seeks arms
Prostitutes appeal to pope
Enraged cow injures farmer with ax
Hitler, Nazi papers found in attic
2 sisters reunited after 18 years in checkout counter
British left waffles on Falkland Islands
Students hear reptile lecture

ONE-LINERS

Jay Leno: "In Connecticut, a prisoner on death row has gone on a hunger strike . . . here's a problem that pretty much takes care of itself."

A hypocrite is someone who complains about the sex and violence on his VCR.

Why did the man cross the Moebius strip?
To get to the same side.

POLITICALLY CORRECT NFL

Washington Native Americans
New York Very Tall People
Dallas Western-Style Laborers
Los Angeles Uninvited Guests

Minnesota Plundering Norsemen
Green Bay Meat Industry Workers
San Francisco Precious Metal Enthusiasts
New Orleans Pretty Good People
Phoenix Male Finches
Miami Pelagic Percoid Food Fishes
Denver Untamed Beasts of Burden
Cincinnati Large Bangladeshi Carnivorous Mammals
Tampa Bay West Indies Freebooters
Detroit Large Carnivorous Cats
Chicago Securities Traders in a Declining Market
Indianapolis Young Male Horses
New England Zealous Lovers of Country
Atlanta Hovering Birds of Prey
Philadelphia Largely Non-Hovering Birds of Prey
Seattle Oceanic Birds of Prey
Tampa Bay Ocean-Going Unlawful Salvage Personnel
Houston Liquid Fossil Fuel Devotees (or taking a different inter-
    pretation of oilers) Wheel Rotation Perpetuators
Los Angeles Male Horned Largely Mountain-Faring Ruminants
New York Air-Fed Inertial Reaction Propulsion Systems
Kansas City Native American Leaders
Pittsburgh Ferrous Heavy-Industry Personnel
Cleveland Subtle Mixtures of 66% Red and 33% Green
San Diego High-Voltage Capacitor Technicians
Buffalo Men Named William, on Familiar Terms with Associates

SHORT PIECES
and
SHORT STORIES

from RAMEAU'S NIECE

Cathleen Schine

~

THERE IS A KIND OF EGOTISM THAT SHRINKS THE UNIVERSE; and there was Edward's kind. It dominated the world not by limiting it, but by generous, almost profligate recognition of everything, like sunlight, illuminating whatever it touched, and touching whatever it could.

Margaret's husband was a wonder to her, a loud, handsome Englishman, a Jew from Oxford with gray hair that stuck up in tufts, like an East European poet's, an egotist whose egotism was of such astonishing proportions that he thought the rest of the world quite marvelous simply because it was there with him.

Margaret Nathan was herself a person of no mean ego, although she knew her own egotism shone less like the sun than like a battery-operated flashlight, swinging this way and that way, lighting short narrow paths through the oppressive darkness of other people. Margaret was a demanding person, hard on herself, certainly; harder by far on everyone else.

But turning her restless beam toward Edward, she could find nothing there to be hard about. As to Margaret's demanding nature, she felt immediately that here was a safe haven for it. Edward seemed to demand demands, so that he might have the joy of satisfying them.

Margaret marveled at her husband, awed that he had come to be hers at all. They met in New York when he was visiting an old friend of his and her boyfriend at the time, Al Birnbaum, a Marxist graduate student who spoke, in so far as he was able, like William F. Buckley. It occurred to Margaret that at some secret, buried level Al aspired not to change the world, not really, but to present the opposing view on "Firing Line"—to costar. She could envision him quite clearly: slumped, languorous and slack, in one of those low-backed chairs, right beside Bill, his own head rolling back on its own pale neck, the evil twin of the evil twin.

She took one look at his friend Edward, who was looking rather closely at her, and she saw that he was looking at her in that way that suggested that his old friend was not, after all, *such* an old friend. And she looked back at him in a way that she hoped said, Nor of mine.

"Why, you must come with me, of course," he said when he heard she was writing her thesis about an eighteenth-century female philosophe. He took her hand in both of his. "What a wonderful idea. We'll visit her château. Did she have a château? Surely the woman had a château! I was planning to go in the autumn, through France to the Alps, into Italy. A long and leisurely trip across Europe by car. We'll stop at Venice. Then we'll turn around and come back. Will you come with me? Of course you will. Oh God, what luck."

They were joking, playing around in front of the Boyfriend. But the Boyfriend wasn't paying much attention (he was sick of Margaret, who had become increasingly unpleasant, subscribing to *Dissent* and reading long, liberal anticommunist articles aloud to him); and Margaret and Edward, fooling and flirting in that self-conscious and ostentatious way one employs when one is indeed joking or when one is wholly in earnest, made a mock promise to meet the next night (ha ha ha, went the chorus), which they both breathlessly kept.

Madame de Montigny's château had long ago turned to dust, but Edward Ehrenwerth did take Margaret on a trip across Europe that fall just the same. They drove in a gentle, gray mist from London to the ferry, where Edward then had a long and apparently satisfying chat with one of the crewmen about model trains, then on to their first stop, a renovated farmhouse in a village just north of Paris, belonging to some friends of Edward's. Jean-Claude and Juliette, two exquisitely thin persons in identical, droopy black cashmere sweaters, were French academics who studied and taught American literature: he specialized in neo-Gothic romances written by former housewives, she in slim, laconic novels of a style she referred to as *minimalisme*. They pored over paperbacks and called them texts.

"You don't mind that these books are, you know, shitty?" Margaret asked after several glasses of the wine that had been brought ceremoniously from a cool cellar.

"But on the contrary, American culture, this is its vitality, life's blood, this"—*thees* is what he actually said—"aah, how shall I say it, this, this—"

Sheet, Margaret thought. Thees sheet.

"And you know, such judgment," Juliette interrupted, "such criticism is so patriarchal, so very, very logocentric."

"Margaret, Margaret, literature is, is what?" cried Jean-Claude. "The acquisition and distribution of cultural capital!" Jean-Claude, having warmed noticeably to both the wine and to his subject, slapped Margaret heartily on the back. "Good? Bad? Pooh! The project of the Enlightenment is dead! Invert the hierarchy of judgment!" He raised his glass and laughed. "Long live the liberation of the signifier!"

"Well," said Edward, after joining the toast, "the wine is awfully good. Thank God, my dears, you haven't inverted that particular hierarchy."

"Ah, well, the wine," said both the host and hostess, grinning with pride, shrugging in their lovely, loose sweaters. "The wine—of course."

In honor of the visiting American, Juliette had adapted her cuisine, making hamburgers. Then Edward and Margaret retired to the guest room, which was the entire top floor of the house, a beautiful room, and when she saw it, Margaret thought, with some envy, Ah, the French, so much taste, so little brain, for the room was decorated in the most luxurious velvets and brocades and tasseled cabbage-rose drapes and a Herman Miller sofa and butterfly chairs and original Eames and Knoll pieces, a marvelous, elegant, witty combination, a happy marriage of *minimalisme* and Gothic romance.

Outside, the wind howled, rattling the shutters. Margaret sank her head into the square feather pillows and listened. Creak creak. Clunk clunk. "Is this the attic?" she said. "Are we in the attic?"

"I suppose it is. The attic. That sounds a bit portentous. What will happen here? What will happen here tonight? This very drear and drafty night? Perhaps the enraged Enlightenment will haunt us, armed with sharpened quill. 'I have been wronged!' Ah, Juliette and Jean-Claude—they open cultural doors. They *are* cultural doors."

"Did you see the door of their refrigerator?" Margaret said. Juliette and Jean-Claude had proudly shown them the refrigerator, a high-tech, extremely wide, remarkably shallow apparatus behind a door of elaborately carved wood.

"Yes," Edward said. "Theirs is a very pure and cerebral socialism."

Creak creak, said the shutters.

Margaret picked up a paperback from the bedside table. The cover showed a dark-haired (raven-haired, she corrected herself) woman, her head thrown back, and beside her a beautiful black woman, head thrown back too, both of whom seemed to be bound, in an indistinct way (perhaps they were just sort of tangled) on a dock. The book was called *Desire's Dominion.*

"Well, they're very considerate, your friends, aren't they?" She lay back, closed her eyes, and listened to the wind outside. "Do you like France, Edward?"

Edward leaned down and whispered, " 'Thanks to the human heart by which we live, thanks to its tenderness, its joys, and fears, to me the meanest flower that blows can give thoughts that do often lie too deep for tears.' "

"To whom is that addressed?" she asked. "Who is the meanest flower that blows? Me or France?"

"Neither. It's my manifesto. Neither of you is in any way mean. I just like Wordsworth. And you. And France."

"How very un-British of you."

But Edward had spent most of his childhood summers in France. It was where he'd met Jean-Claude, on one of those summer holidays. Margaret thought of Jean-Claude and Edward, skinny boys in skimpy but still baggy bathing trunks, digging among the rocks on the Normandy shore. She thought of the "Immortality" ode. Now, whenever she thought of Jean-Claude, she would think of Wordsworth's lines, she would remember a boy she never met, until he'd become a considerate, fatuous postmodern man, on a beach she'd never seen, and tears would come to her eyes. How annoying, to be so vulnerable to poetry, to Edward.

"Did you ever see *Splendor in the Grass?*" she said, as some kind of revenge. "*That* was a post-Gothic romance."

Before that trip, Margaret never drank, not even wine; and she rarely drank after it. But during those weeks, she was quite thoroughly drunk every day.

The sun came up each morning to find her snoring in the starched white sheets of some plump little pension bed. No, she thought, when Edward tried to wake her. No, you see, I've moved in, I'm quite settled here and cannot be shifted, not ever, certainly not by you, Edward, whoever you are. And through half-open eyes she watched him get dressed, marveling at how the British could have conquered the world with such skinny, sunken chests.

"Maybe you should wear tight pants tucked into boots, you know?" she said. "Like Mick Jagger."

"Undoubtedly."

Sometimes she could pull him back to bed, sometimes not. She didn't care. She didn't care about anything except scenery and wine and food and pictures in echoing galleries and churches in echoing squares and Edward in the same ill-fitting brown suit.

Driving through the Rhone valley, passing a party-cake castle in the distance, rushing to make a reservation at a four-star restaurant, still hours away, Margaret leaned her forehead against the cool glass of the window and thought, This is the last phase of my long, long childhood. This is the last time I will sit in a car, still drunk from lunch, staring at fairy castles while someone else drives and worries and frets and checks the road map and the odometer. It's the first time, too, but I know what I mean.

Rows of poplars lined the road. The sun had come out from the clouds, which now glowed and reddened. This is bliss, Margaret thought. No wonder Edward likes Juliette and Jean-Claude. No wonder people drink wine, so red and velvety, rolling on your tongue. Margaret let her head fall back. She closed her eyes.

"*Tu baves, ma chérie,*" Edward said gently, patting her knee.

"I'm what?" Margaret said.

"Drooling, darling."

The restaurant was dark and quiet and seriously comfortable. Yum, yum, Margaret thought, gazing lazily at the menu. Yum, yum. Little lambs and little bunny rabbits and little fluttery quail—all manner of gentle, innocent beasts. I will have pork, the forbidden flesh scorned by centuries of my ancestors, but big and ugly. Yum, yum, yum. Medallions of pork with chestnuts.

"Too many pets on the menu," she said. "If I ran this joint, I would offer *boeuf sous rature.* Get it, Edward?" She heard herself laughing.

"Yes, Margaret, I get it," Edward said.

He was not laughing, but looking at her rather dryly. Still, she could not stop herself. What was the point of having read so much incomprehensible Derrida if one could not make philistine deconstruction puns? "*Sous rature,*" she continued. " 'Under erasure.' And then they'd serve you—nothing! They'd take the beef *off* the plate!"

"Is this what they teach you poor children in graduate school these days?"

"And then on the menu you could draw that line through the word *boeuf,* as the deconstructionists do in order to denote when a word is, well, when a word is whatever it is that makes them draw that line through it . . ."

As she rambled on, drunk and delighted with her erudition, Edward ignored her and ordered the wine, which was even better than what they'd drunk at lunch. She held the glass to her lips and drank slowly. If she was not mistaken, Edward was talking to the waiter about medieval husbandry. She could see the lights in the dim restaurant reflected in her wine glass, in the wine-dark wine. Wine-dark wine. She giggled. She could see the lights twinkling there, like stars, like stars on a dark night. Oh, how banal. Oh, how sublime.

She staggered to bed that night and lay staring at the ceiling as Edward untied her shoes and recited in Latin a Catullus poem about a stolen napkin, and she thought she would marry him, would have to marry him, that it was a necessity, a rule of nature, like gravity. If, of course, he would have her.

" 'Give back my napkin!' " he shouted, straddling her, pinning her arms to the bed. " 'Or await three hundred hendeca-syllables!' "

The next day they drove to Les Baux, the cliff-top ruins of a castle where some medieval nobleman had grilled the heart of a poet and served it to his wife for dinner. When that lady had finished her meal and was told the ingredients, she said the dish had been so sweet that she never wanted anything else to pass her lips, and jumped off the cliff.

"Ah, the goyim," Edward said.

They drove to Vaucluse, where Petrarch had written his love poems to Laura, and to Avignon, where Margaret came down with a fever and stayed sweating and shivering in the little low-ceilinged hotel room within the city's high walls; and from her damp, febrile pillow she wondered if she would die right now, right here, dissipated with drink and lovemaking and museum-visiting.

When she recovered, they drove to the Italian Alps and spent

the night in an almost empty ski resort where she read while
Edward held a long, quiet, serious discussion that Margaret could
not understand with the Austrian chef's eight-year-old son. Edward knew seven languages, and accepted only with the poorest
grace that he could speak just one of them at a time. The others
were always waiting, eager and impatient, shifting from foot to
foot like children, until, at last, one of them would be allowed to
thunder out, full speed ahead. Edward spoke with resonant, distinct enjoyment, loud and clear, savoring each word, as if the
different languages tasted good. He was a show-off, talking, laughing, sometimes singing loudly, without fear, sharing his own wonder of himself. Margaret was so fully in love with him now that
she never knew if the flushed confusion she was experiencing
was from the wine or her boisterous companion.

"For our honeymoon," he said the next morning as Margaret
drove the left-handed English car on the right-handed Italian road,
"I propose—"

"But you never have proposed, you know."

"I propose Sri Lanka—Ceylon, as we old stick-in-the-mud im-
perialists prefer to call it. We shall discover the meaning of life
on the scented isle. When bored with copulation, we can go up
to Kandy and regard the Buddha's tooth."

When Margaret woke up in the Alps, the air was so clear she
blinked. Driving on the winding road, toward Italy, toward a whole
new land of new wines and new paintings and new beds to share
with her new fiancé, she stared ahead at the narrow, climbing
vine of a road, and her heart pounded with disbelieving pleasure.
Edward, in the mountains, was required by nature to recite Romantic poetry. He recited poetry as habitually as other people
cleared their throats. Verse was preverbal: a preparation for
speech, an ordering of one's thoughts and feelings, an exquisite
sketch, a graceful, generous, gratefully borrowed vision. Margaret
understood this and listened to his voice, as clear as the air, as
self-consciously grand as the surrounding peaks, as happy as a
child's, and then she drove off the mountain. Not all the way
off the mountain, she noticed. Just *aiming* off the mountain,
really.

"Shortcut, darling?"

Margaret never forgot driving off the mountain, and she never
forgot how Edward pretended she wasn't shaking, how he made

quiet jokes that guided her back to the road and back to the world where cars were aimed at Turin rather than at a heavily wooded abyss.

She drove slowly, with determination, ecstatic that she had not rolled hideously to a foreign death, and for a moment she felt about the world the way she thought Edward always felt about it, for thirty honking cars trailed irritably behind her, and, glancing in the rearview mirror, all she noticed about them was how brightly they sparkled in the mountain sunlight.

BEHIND THEIR LIVES STOOD EDWARD'S SCHEDULE, A FIRM yet supple structure that gave to each day a thousand opportunities. If there were only twenty-four hours, then let them begin! Edward rose not only with the sun, but as if he were the sun. I am here, he seemed to be saying. The day may, indeed must, begin. He ate the same breakfast each morning, but what a breakfast—kippered herring and pumpernickel bread, bacon and eggs, fried tomatoes and mushrooms, Cheerios and sliced bananas, toast and jam and muffins, too. It was a labor-intensive meal, which was perhaps how he could stay so thin and eat so much. He presided over this ecumenical array of bowls, dishes, pots, and pans with smooth efficiency, then, finished, turned to his coffee and his newspapers, sometimes reading aloud to Margaret, unless she objected, which, foul-tempered and puffy-eyed, she often did.

"I don't care, Edward. I don't care about the Czech Philharmonic just yet."

"Margaret, one of the things I love about you, and there are so many it fills my soul with joy, but one of the most endearing qualities you have is how sincere you become in petulance." He smiled.

Margaret, her senses blunted by fatigue and the rich potpourri of breakfast odors, would nevertheless experience his presence then, acutely and pleasantly—the look of him and his touch, without looking or touching—and she would feel rising within her the familiar tide of gratitude and astonishment that she had come to recognize as love.

Margaret put her hand out and touched his across the table. Far away in Prague, the Czech Philharmonic was actively participating in a democratic revolution. In New York, she was happy and married to Edward. Both of these occurrences seemed equally improbable to Margaret and nearly miraculous. Edward was right: the world was a marvelous place.

"You really don't mind me," she said. "You like me."

"Our marriage is a putrid sink of festering lies; a vile, infested prison house into which we have been flung by a careless and callous fate."

Edward had married Margaret and moved to New York, to Columbia's Comp. Lit. Department, adapting as enthusiastically as the English sparrow, shifting effortlessly from an ancient, orderly university town to the great noise of urban decay. An American-ophile, Edward was a scholar of (of all people and against all academic fashion) Walt Whitman, and he adored the home of his poet.

Mannahatta! " 'A million people—manners free and superb'!" Edward was a man at peace with New York.

For the next six years, each morning at 7:00, Edward ventured forth into Mannahatta to run around the reservoir. He maintained that it cleared his head, but Margaret noted that running was practically the only exercise that would not affect pectoral muscles in a positive way, and so she was convinced that he underwent the ordeal merely to assure that his British chest would remain sufficiently concave. When he returned home, at exactly 8:40, sweating and loquacious after so much time deprived of both students and books, he would quickly shower and change, eat his extensive breakfast, then walk up to Columbia for his 11:00 class. Home for lunch and a twenty-minute nap. Back to school, for conferences or research or petty, backbiting department meetings, each of which he embraced warmly and without reservation, for they belonged to his life, and therefore to him, and so beamed with a pleasant and interesting reflected light. Home for dinner at 6:30 sharp, whether he had an 8:00 class or not. When he did, home at 10:15. If not, work at home until 11:00. Asleep at 11:30. Up at 6:30 for another round.

If there were exceptions to this routine—a dinner date, a lecture to give, a concert—the schedule rippled effortlessly and made room. Margaret had never met a more orderly, less rigid soul. Edward's mind, nearly promiscuous in its passionate interests, opened to every new possibility, with one exception: the possibility of failing to do what he had planned to do when he had planned to do it, and of failing to do anything else he wanted to or was required to, as well. And so, every day, like the spinning of the earth, like the silent journey of the stars from one curved horizon to another, Edward's day followed its course. If "willful" and "blessed" were synonyms, they would describe Edward and the gentle, unvarying rhythm of his days.

Vigorous and effortless, the weeks passed and his life was full. Margaret gazed admiringly, for she herself had no schedule to speak of. Her contributions to the family income, while considerable, came irregularly and from far away. Margaret was almost famous. She had written a biography—a plain, sturdy little biography, a biography as unfashionable, as modest and unassuming as an aproned housewife, which had nevertheless caught the public's fickle eye. The subject, Charlotte de Montigny, had been assigned to her when she was a graduate student in intellectual history looking for a dissertation topic. Wife of a dissolute and ill-tempered minor eighteenth-century aristocrat, Madame de Montigny had consoled herself by becoming an amateur astronomer, an occasional portrait artist, and an avid autodidact of anatomy. "Oh, *you* might as well take *her*," Margaret's adviser had said. An aging, eminent professor who drank too much and married too many of his students, he ordered up dissertation topics as if they were dishes at an unsatisfactory restaurant, the only restaurant in town. But this time, the meat loaf had won a prize, several prizes. Margaret was the recipient of grants and royalties, of a postdoctoral sinecure, of a little office at Princeton that was too far away to use.

But grants and royalties and an unused office across the river did not require a schedule or regular habits. Margaret eavesdropped on Edward as he argued amiably on the telephone with a magazine editor for whom he was reviewing a book.

"Do you like James Schuyler?" Edward finally asked into the phone. "I do. So American. 'The night is filled with indecisions, to take a downer or an upper, to take a walk, to lie down and relax. I order you: RELAX.'" And then, with great satisfaction, as if that certainly settled the matter, he hung up. Sometimes, when Margaret saw a poem on the printed page, with all its punctuation, its short and long lines, its verses, she would be startled. Living with Edward, she had come to regard poetry as conversation.

At her desk in the study they shared, Margaret turned back to Voltaire. Voltaire and his mistress had worked together for years, she thought. But they shared a château, not a spare bedroom. They worked in separate, elaborately appointed quarters, a prudent arrangement that made it quite impossible for Madame du Châtelet to waste her working time by listening in on Voltaire's undoubtedly brilliant and entertaining telephone conversations— although she had regularly steamed open his mail. Still, she showed far greater independence than I do, sitting around gawking at my own husband as if he were my first beau, my secret lover, my only friend, and my lifelong mentor.

Sometimes the depth of her feelings for Edward annoyed her. Am I a domesticated household pet, to take such pleasure from the physical presence of a man reading the *Mississippi Review?* She got up and put her arms around his neck, burying her face in his silver unmowed lawn of hair. Who does he think he is, strutting around, being happy and punctual all the time?

"Let's go to Prague together," she said then. "Let's hear the Czech Philharmonic."

from POLITICALLY CORRECT BEDTIME STORIES

Jim Garner

~

LITTLE RED RIDING HOOD

There once was a young person named Red Riding Hood who lived with her mother on the edge of a large wood. One day her mother asked her to take a basket of fresh fruit and mineral water to her grandmother's house—not because this was womyn's work, mind you, but because the deed was generous and helped engender a feeling of community. Furthermore, her grandmother was not sick, but rather was in full physical and mental health and was fully capable of taking care of herself as a mature adult.

So Red Riding Hood set off with her basket of food through the woods. Many people she knew believed that the forest was a foreboding and dangerous place and never set foot in it. Red

Riding Hood, however, was confident enough in her own budding sexuality that such obvious Freudian imagery did not hinder her.

On her way to Grandma's house, Red Riding Hood was accosted by a Wolf, who asked her what was in her basket. She replied, "Some healthful snacks for my grandmother, who is certainly capable of taking care of herself as a mature adult."

The Wolf said, "You know, my dear, it isn't safe for a little girl to walk through these woods alone."

Red Riding Hood said, "I find your sexist remark offensive in the extreme, but I will ignore it because of your traditional status as an outcast from society, the stress of which has caused you to develop your own, entirely valid worldview. Now, if you'll excuse me, I must be on my way."

Red Riding Hood walked on along the main path. But, because his status outside society had freed him from slavish adherence to linear, Western-style thought, the Wolf knew of a quicker route to Grandma's house. He burst into the house and ate Grandma, an entirely valid course of action for a carnivore such as himself. Then, unhampered by rigid, traditionalist notions of what was masculine or feminine, he put on Grandma's nightclothes and crawled into bed.

Red Riding Hood entered the cottage and said, "Grandma, I have brought you some fat-free, sodium-free snacks to salute you in your role of a wise and nurturing matriarch."

From the bed, the Wolf said softly, "Come closer, child, so that I might see you."

Red Riding Hood said, "Oh, I forgot you are as optically challenged as a bat. Grandma, what big eyes you have!"

"They have seen much, and forgiven much, my dear."

"Grandma, what a big nose you have—only relatively, of course, and certainly attractive in its own way."

"It has smelled much, and forgiven much, my dear."

"Grandma, what big teeth you have!"

The Wolf said, "I am happy with who I am and what I am," and leaped out of bed. He grabbed Red Riding Hood in his claws, intent on devouring her. Red Riding Hood screamed, not out of alarm at the Wolf's apparent tendency toward cross-dressing, but because of his willful invasion of her personal space.

Her screams were heard by a passing woodchopper-person (or log-fuel technician, as he preferred to be called). When he burst into the cottage, he saw the melee and tried to intervene.

But as he raised his ax, Red Riding Hood and the Wolf both stopped.

"And what do you think you're doing?" asked Red Riding Hood.

The woodchopper-person blinked and tried to answer, but no words came to him.

"Bursting in here like a Neanderthal, trusting your weapon to do your thinking for you!" she said. "Sexist! Speciesist! How dare you assume that womyn and wolves can't solve their own problems without a man's help!"

When she heard Red Riding Hood's speech, Grandma jumped out of the Wolf's mouth, took the woodchopper-person's axe, and cut his head off. After this ordeal, Red Riding Hood, Grandma, and the Wolf felt a certain commonality of purpose. They decided to set up an alternative household based on mutual respect and cooperation, and they lived together in the woods happily ever after.

from ENOUGH IS ENOUGH
Karen Finley

~

Exaggerate

There is nothing worse than some bore who always has to tell a story exactly the way it happened. No one cares. People want to be amused by a good story. Exaggerate! Exaggerating makes all stories better. Exaggerators aren't liars, they're just entertaining personalities.

And always stay away from video cameras and people who film or tape every event and family gathering. Video cameras are the curse of the exaggerator. No one can embellish a story when confronted with the facts right in front of her on someone's TV. The best stories are always the ones that we exaggerate. A good exaggerator will never be considered a bore.

TIP:
Exaggerating makes our lives more creative and inventive without much money.

Keep It Simply Complicated

It's to your advantage to complicate your life. In this way you will appear to be doing so much in this world and it will seem that so much is happening to you. Make simple everyday events that happen to everyone into psychodrama. Take common fates that pass uneventfully through the lives of most people and turn them into grueling, heart-wrenching, soul-searching intrigues that last till the next trauma occurs.

Getting over the low hurdles in life is easy. It's getting over the high hurdles that attracts people's attention. A simple life is boring. Every complicated setback should be appreciated because overcoming it makes the triumph look that much greater.

HINT:
A complicated life has so many opportunities.

Being a Bitch

Being a bitch is when you can't be an asshole because you need to be mean to the people you *know*. You need to be mean because everything else is boring or bullshit and the people you are around are so stupid and proper that the only way to act is to be a bitch.

It's important to let people know that you are in pain but you control that pain. Perhaps they don't have the capacity for anything except the usual garbage normalcy and you are different because you are a bitch.

A bitch must dress well. You can't be a bitch and a lousy dresser. You must look good and prefer solids.

When bitching, don't look people in the eye. They don't deserve it. Say everything to the side with your head tilted up with authority, disdain and drama. A great bitch is someone who can say a cruel remark and everyone in the room is amused because for a few minutes their lives are not so awfully boring. The bitch is the performer.

It is very good to learn to be a bitch, because then we have personality, then we have fun, then we have friends who look up to us because we are a bitch.

TIP:
Be a bitch whenever possible. You always look better when acting like a bitch.

Being an Asshole

Being an asshole is a delightful way to behave with strangers. You don't say thank you. You are snide. You cut off slow drivers. You don't return phone calls. You always keep your answering machine on. You are a generally rude person. That means being rude to tourists, and when you are a tourist you are a total asshole too.

Being an asshole is beneficial because you can generally be rude to strangers and not take things out on your real friends. It is an etiquette that provides relief from always being courteous and thinking about others' feelings.

Taking a few minutes out of your day to be an asshole to strangers will provide the necessary relief. An asshole can make driving a good time by just honking for the hell of it. Everyone expects assholes in a city. The people who live in cities relish the asshole image, which keeps everyone at a distance, and small-town folk like seeing assholes in a city, for then they can convince themselves that it is better to live in their boring hometown.

It is difficult to be an asshole if you live in a small town because you are expected to be sweet and quaint, but you can get back at tourists who come to your town for events such as craft fairs. Craft fairs are a wonderful place to be an asshole by saying loud ugly remarks about the ugly goods people are trying to sell.

REMEMBER:
Being an asshole is quite a civilized tradition.

Talk Too Much

Stay away from those rigid, uncommunicative creatures who belch out, "You talk too much!" The best way to attack is to immediately make fun of them and then ignore them. That's right—don't talk to them at all. Let them be in their boring peace and quiet with no social life and no one to listen to.

Stop being embarrassed for talking on the phone all of the time or for having humongous phone bills. Phones were made to talk on. The only people who think that you are on the phone too much are people who don't have anyone to talk to.

When someone says, "You're still on the phone?" just reply, "Yes, I'm still on the phone, for I am lucky to have friends who enjoy speaking with me—not like you, who don't have any friends who call and want to talk to you. Your life must be pitiful if my friendships are of such great importance to you." Talking too much on the phone confirms to ourselves that we are popular and chatty.

REMEMBER:
When you aren't talking, you are working, and who the hell wants to work?

The Value of Unfulfilled Dreams

I say having dreams and staying in that dream state is euphoric. It's a lot of work to get off your butt and make something of yourself. It's a lot more fun to dream.

If someone cracks down on you for never realizing your dreams, just look at her and say pathetically, "Am I hurting anyone by dreaming?" Then try to attack her with her own accomplishments, like, "I wasn't built for bungee jumping, like you," or "I never had EST training, like you did."

If that doesn't work, ask her to lend you some money to pursue your dream. That'll shut her up.

TIP:
Wear a T-shirt that says, WHEN DREAMS COME TRUE, THEY STOP BEING DREAMS.

Rejecting Karma

Doesn't it make you gag when you do something minor in regard to the total cosmos such as call in sick to work or double-park your car and someone says to you, "You better watch out for your karma." Just look at him and say, "I hate karma. Karma was invented so that the poor and miserable would accept their condition without rebelling."

Karma only comes in handy when someone has fired you, takes your parking space or takes your clothes out of the dryer at the laundromat. In the world we live in, it is getting too risky to yell at someone. You may get shot. So then and only then can you call on karma.

TIP:
Never name a child Karma, not even as a middle name. Pets don't like it either.

WALKING TOUR: ROHNERT PARK
Molly Giles

The exercise bike might work for other people but after that policeman's wife on Debbie Street lost control of hers and rammed right into the television set face first I knew it wasn't for me. She broke her jaw which was a blessing compared to that poor woman on Brenda Way who was doing aerobics in her kitchen when she tripped and fell into her dishwasher and got stabbed to death by her steak knives; you should never load your knives tip up, I tell that to Bethany and Chelsea all the time. Eighty-two percent of all accidents happen at home and the other whatever percents happen within a ten-mile radius of your home so you're not really safe anywhere. I like to see what's coming at me so I walk. I leave every morning before Don or the girls are awake and the route I take is up Eva to Emily out to Ellen and back; it's not very scenic unless you like identical houses with identical front yards but at least I can't get lost and it does get my aerobics up.

The first house I see when I go out my front door is Barbara's and Barbara's is not identical any more because she just had the whole front redone for Krystal Lee's wedding. Even the grass is brand-new. She ordered one of those lawns they bring in a truck and unroll and we all went out and watched it like it was a movie and at the end we all clapped. Her rosebushes are new and so is that grapefruit tree, leave it to Barbara to plant something thin. The best part is that Barbara didn't have to pay for any of it; her ex-husband Lance paid for it all. He said that since Krystal Lee is his only daughter (and probably always will be, after his colostomy, poor guy) why not do things right, so he gave Krystal Lee a big check and she went and gave some of the left-over money to Barbara which has to be a secret from Lance because he thinks she spent it all on the wedding. She could have too the way things cost these days but I think she saved a little by having it at that Catholic church where the choirboy tried to crucify the homeless man and she got a deal on the country club too because one of her bridesmaids does hair for the pro there.

It was a beautiful wedding, I will give it that. The sermon was one of those long ones about joining of the flesh and how important it is to have babies but Krystal Lee's colors were pretty, peach and mint ice, and there was a real harpist and at the end they released a cage of white doves right out on the street. It turned out the priest knew the Pope, he met him in L.A. or someplace and he said the Pope said Hi and that made Barbara feel better about the whole thing because Barbara still isn't used to the fact that Krystal Lee wanted to marry an Italian. Don and I don't see what's the matter with Italians. But Barbara always has to have everything perfect.

Barbara's friend Greta Mooney who used to live next door to her liked things perfect too; you had to take your shoes off when you went over and she even had paper toilet seat liners in the downstairs bath for guests. One day her husband came home and she was in her rubber gloves scrubbing the walls and he said, "Clean this up why don't you," and he took a shotgun off the mantel and blew his brains out. And after Greta went back to Germany or wherever she'd come from, this other woman moved in and she was taking a shower one day and her uterus fell out.

So that house is bad luck and the one across from it will probably be vacant soon too. See that big sign on the lawn? "I Am Earl Miller's Neighbor"? Jim Parker puts it up every morning and every night Earl Miller kicks it down. Jim and Earl used to be best friends, they both like electric trains and they bought a pool table together. Now no one knows what happened. All of a sudden these signs are going up. "For A Good Time Call Earl Miller's Wife" and

then the number, the real phone number; she got the police out
for that. You'd think people would try to get along but Bethany's
new boyfriend Ar-Tee says that can't happen because human nature hasn't evolved since the cave age. Ar-Tee has a tattoo of Fred
Flintstone on his forearm so I guess he knows but Don and I have
our fingers crossed that Bethany will take a good hard look at
that beeper on his belt and break up with him soon anyway.

That lady over there says she wouldn't care who her daughters
go out with, she swears she gets along with everyone, oh yes,
she's so tolerant, she loves the world, she's always saying she
wants more of an "ethnic mix" and how we're so "limited" in
our "world vision" here. She used to be married to a Jewish man
and the story I heard was that he was molesting one of his own
children and the girl went along with it until she was fifteen and
found out how much prostitutes made. The minute she started
asking him for money he stopped. The girl who works at the new
nail place in the mall told me about that and she told me about
the man in the window over there too. He's newly paraplegic.
They think it's Lyme's disease but they don't know. They have to
do more tests. His wife got him a puppy to cheer him up but
when he was taking a nap one afternoon the puppy chewed one
of his toes off. He didn't feel a thing because no nerves, right, and
he didn't even know it was gone until his wife said, "Hey, what's
that dog got in its mouth?"They had to put the puppy to sleep
because once they taste blood they change. And if you think that's
sad, the girl who used to live next door, she was a year ahead of
Chelsea in high school and she was running out of Study Hall one
day and she didn't see where she was going and she bumped into
a boy running the other way and their heads hit and she died
instantly but he was fine. I always think of him, the guilt he must
feel, every time he washes his face, and I think of that girl's parents
too; they were best friends with that other couple whose baby
was stolen by a cult. They still don't know what cult. For a while
they thought it was that cult that pounds babies into hamburger
in the name of the Devil and then they cook the baby and eat
it—that's why the police can never find the evidence—but Don
says that cult is only in Berkeley, thank God. We are pretty sure
we had a cult living in that pink house for a while. It was a very
strange arrangement, six adults, and they were always dressed up,
even when they washed their cars the women wore high heels
and they didn't talk to anyone except Heather Lemon when she

went around with that petition to stop Dr. Wirtz from adding on to his garage.

Heather is still mad about Dr. Wirtz being the one to answer her Personal Ad but Don and I have talked about it and we think it makes sense: Heather and Dr. Wirtz are a lot alike. She's high-strung and he is too; Chelsea and Bethany told us he ripped a girl's braces off a whole year early because her father wouldn't pay the bill. Also frankly Heather should know better—she's been fooled by those Personals before: last year this guy said to meet him at Chevy's and he'd be the one in the cowboy hat and she turned up and he had a cowboy hat all right but he was a complete and utter midget, about three feet tall, and it was a cowboy hat from a toy store. Anyway Heather writes this new Ad saying she wants a kind, caring, professional man who is over six feet tall and this man writes back and says he's six feet one so they decide to meet and they take one look at each other and start screaming right there in the restaurant. The problem is: Heather and Dr. Wirtz hate each other. They've lived next door without speaking for four and a half years; she complains to the police about his leaf blower and he poured Clorox on her rock garden. The only thing they've ever agreed on is that new fence; Don says it's the strongest fence in the neighborhood but it's not the tallest, the tallest is that one over there where the Mormon lady found the ten cats hung from the trees. She had just climbed up a ladder to put seed in her bird feeder and there they were, every cat that had been missing from the neighborhood for the last six weeks tied up with fishing line and hanging from the branches and we had to chip in to hire a grief counselor for the kids they belonged to; it was even worse than the time someone went into the Fin-neys' back yard and shot their sheepdog with a bow and arrow to make it stop barking.

The sickest thing that's ever happened in those trees though is the rapist who tried to catch the seven-year-old girl by dropping dollar bills along the sidewalk. She followed the trail until she got into the trees and he grabbed her. Luckily she remembered to scream like they taught her in school and she ran into the street and this is the worst part because no one stopped to help her until her own father drove by on his way home from work, and the first thing he said was,"Where'd you get all that money?"

We're just too used to crazies, Don says. I remember that lady on Della Court who started out giving regular garage sales, once a month, like other people, and then something happened, she got addicted, and she had to have them all the time and pretty soon she was selling things like her kids' bunk beds when they were in school and their gerbil cage with the gerbils in it and all her husband's electric tools; I think she even tried to sell the car before they got her into treatment. I always think of her carrying all her living room furniture out to the street by herself every morning but of course she was harmless. Not all of them are. I know for my own peace of mind I won't take a shower when I'm alone in the house. When Don's at work and the girls are at school, I won't even go upstairs. I just put the folded laundry on the landing and when everyone's home I carry it up and make a lot of noise so if anyone is in the closet they have plenty of time to get out. They never did catch that rapist, after all, and there are plenty of others just like him out there. I always think of our Pastor, ex-Pastor that is, even Don won't go to his church any-more. Here he was, this perfect Pastor, always holding prayer circles to cure people of their homosexuality, and all the time he had AIDS and a whole double life like that young banker in Santa Rosa who drowned the call girl in his hot tub while his wife was on a Girl Scout overnight with their two little daughters. Don misses church, I know, and being an usher, and I hope he finds something soon because he's been in a terrible mood since Krystal Lee's wedding. At first he said it was a toothache but finally he told me the truth: Lance didn't recognize him in the reception line. Don *has* put on some weight lately but he hasn't changed that much. Lance is the one who's changed. I don't know what he's done but he's gotten so handsome; maybe it's the suffering he's been through but even Bethany and Chelsea noticed he looked better than he did when he lived across the street from us. He was wearing a royal blue tux at the wedding and if there was a bag inside I couldn't smell it and I'm usually sensitive to things like that. He danced with Krystal Lee and they looked so sweet together I wanted to cry.

The other one who danced was this girl, Shandora, who knows Krystal Lee from modeling school, and what she did was dirty dancing, I don't know what else you'd call it. I haven't seen it outside the movie but that's what it was. And there was this one man who started dancing with her. He was doing it too. I mean, he was ready to eat her up right there on the dance floor. And she was ready to let him. When the band took a break they went outside toward the cars and Don and I looked at each other and thought oh-oh and then she ran back in and the man was right behind her and he was even drunker than before and he was going to get her, I mean the Italians had to hold him back he was really going to get her, right in front of everyone. We all made a circle around her until they locked him in a car. Then Barbara took Shandora home with her and she slept on Barbara's bathroom floor, I know that doesn't sound so great but you should see Barbara's bathroom since she had it redone with Lance's money, and Shandora had a blanket between the toilet and the sink in case she needed it and I guess she did because the carpet was being steam cleaned when I went over to have coffee with Barbara last week.

And that was when Barbara told me this ... thing, this really strange thing. She said that after she got Shandora home she called Heather Lemon and Heather came over and the two of them examined Shandora to see if she'd had sex with the man. I mean, they *examined* her. They took off her clothes and pried her legs open and looked up inside her with a flashlight. Shandora was passed out the whole time. Heather's a paralegal and Barbara said if they found any sign of sexual activity, sperm or whathaveyou, they were going to sue that man for date rape. Lucky for him they didn't find anything. Shandora is still over there, in Krystal Lee's old room, and Barbara said she is thinking of moving in permanently. I wouldn't like someone like that living in my house. Also, I think: what is rape? Isn't what Barbara and Heather Lemon did to her rape?

I am puzzled by the whole situation. Yesterday I said to Don, if someone examined me they'd find out I haven't had sex since 1988 but I don't think Don took the hint. He was reading this diet book Bethany and Chelsea gave him for Father's Day, he wants to do this new one, it's all meat and potatoes, nothing else, which is basically all he eats anyway. I told him about this recipe for Top Ramen Salad I saw in the paper, you just add oil and vinegar to the Oriental Seasoning Packet and mix it all up with cole slaw and the dry noodles for crunch, but Don said he wouldn't touch that with a ten-foot stick. He's in a rut and I guess I'm in one too. Every morning I wake up early and lie in bed worrying that nothing will ever happen except I'll get older and the girls will grow up and go away and Barbara will always have better things than I do and Don will die from high cholesterol and I'll be all alone. And then—I can't help it—I imagine Don's funeral and what I'll wear and how Lance will stay after the service and say he's always been in love with me and I'll have to think: do I really want to get married again? To someone with those kinds of problems? But once the sun's up, and I'm on my walk, I forget my worries, and by the time I pass this house—this is where the girl lived whose silicon implants froze when she went on a ski trip— and that house—that's where they had to hire an exorcist because the television turned on to "Jeopardy" by itself every day—I feel better. There is nothing like fresh air to put things in perspective.

WOULDN'T A TITLE JUST MAKE IT WORSE?

Gordon Lish

I don't get it. I just don't get it. I mean, how come is it that I am always telling people stories of my life and people are always construing my stories to be stories as in *stories?* Why would I want to tell people made-up stories? I can't stand made-up stories. It makes me sick to hear a made-up story. Look, if your story is a made-up story, then do me a favor and keep it to yourself. Me, I would never tell a made-up story about anything, let alone about myself. I respect myself much too much for me ever to stoop to just making something up about myself. I don't get it why anybody would want to tell a made-up story about himself. But the even bigger mystery to me is why, when you tell them the truth, people go ahead and look at you and say, "Oh, come on, quit it— noooooooooooooo." Take this one, for instance. I mean, suppose we just get a squint at how this one works with someone like you instead of with anyone like them, okay? It was when I was lecturing in Austin once. I was there for the week, had to be there for the week, was signed up to teach fiction-writing there for the week—and was, for the week, being put up at the home of some very fancy folks, dignitaries in the English department or in the literature department or in one of those departments like that, both husband and wife. Anyhow, they were very grand and very nice and very kind, and I accordingly start to begin to feel so tremendously and irredeemably in debt to these folks even before I'd even slept under their roof for even one night. Well, I wasn't actually under their roof, as it were, but was in a sort of apartment affair attached to the main house by a sort of connective passageway, you might say, since passageways, I suppose, connect. I only mean to say that my place, my borrowed place, the place lent to me, that is, had its own window and its own door and when you went out of it, the door, you stepped into a little connective consideration that put you right up against the kitchen door of the grown-up house, as it also were—which is to say, the house of one's hosts. Anyhow, to get right to it if you don't mind all the hurry—you just have to appreciate the fact that I am the most fastidious little thing in all the wide and untidy world. In other words, let's say I happened to have been your house-guest for a period of ten years. Look, to give you an idea of how fastidious a little thing I am—at my usual base rate of one squillion tidinesses per year, it works out to the fact that you would find not just your house but your next-door neighbors' houses about ten squillion times tidier than they were when I had first put in an appearance in your neighborhood ten years ago. So I guess it goes without saying that this little tiny sort of garage apartment I was in was the last word in presentability the morning I was—the week's work now a job safely behind me—making ready to leave. Okay, I had to catch a plane, you see. So here's the deal—had positioned a box of candy on the table by the door, had leaned up against the box of candy a square of writing paper on which had been entered the written expression of my gratitude, had situated the key on the table so as for the key to act as a discouragement against the thank-you note's drifting to the floor, had taken one last look about to make certain nothing would offer the slightest invitation to reproach. Ahhhh. Good Gordon. I tell you, I felt as if, praise God, I was getting away with murder and was fooling them here and there and everywhere... *one ... more ... time.* And at this he shoulders his carry-all and goes for the knob with his other hand. But lets go of it, the doorknob, in the instant, it having just been disclosed to him that he is going to have to race to the latrine, and this with all possible speed. Now, then, we are hastening ahead in order that we might consider the forthcoming event from the dainty standpoint of hindsight, eh? Are you following me? Try to follow me. I have wiped. I have, as is my custom, wiped—wiping with soap, wiping with water—and wiped and wiped and wiped, flushing all the while. Good. I have not tarried for too long a time. I can make it to the airport in more than enough time. Wonderful, wonderful. I get to my feet, draw up my trousers, fasten them, yank a handful of toilet tissue free from the roll for to give a last finishing touch to the porcelain, to the seat, to the whole fucking glistening com-mode. When I see—in the bowl—*in the bowl*—a single, rock-hard, well-formed, fair-sized, freshly minted stool. So I activate the flushing mechanism. The water goes into its routine com-motion, the excretum gets itself sucked out of sight, but in due course—just as I had guessed, just as I had guessed—hell, *guessed*—KNEW, KNEW, KNEW—from the instant I was *born* I knew!—are you kidding, are you kidding?—it, this thing, this twist of Lishness lifts itself back into blatant view, grinning, I do be-lieve—even, it seemed to me, winking. Fine, fine—I hit the plunger again, already knowing what there is to be known, what there is *always* to be known—namely, that I and that all my descendants might stand here at our frantic labors flushing toilets until the cows came home, that when they did come home, this malicious, hainted, evil turd would still be here for them to see, and see it—it idly, gayly, gigantically turning in the otherwise perfect waters below—they, the bovine police, would. What to do, what to do, what to do? I mean, I could *see, foresee,* feel myself beaten by *forecast* galore. This blightedness, this fouledness, it would never be gone. If I snatched it up and hid it away in my carry-all, the contents thereof would smash into it and mash it into a paste that would then smear itself irremeably onto my favorite stuff, the best of which I had toted with me to Austin to show myself off in in front of whosoever might show up in my class. If instead I went to the window with it and dumped it overboard, would my hosts not come and discover it (it!) beneath the very porthole the very minute fate had seen me gone? What of taking it in hand, going to the door with it, and then going with it (oh, God, *it* again!) with me thither, thereafter to dispose of same in a suitable municipal receptacle as soon as I was well clear of the neighborhood? Yes, yes, yes, this seemed the plan! Until foresight (*stories, stories, stories*) made me to read in my mind—*in my mind*—the sentence predicating the presence of my hosts there in the passageway on the other side of the door, they foregathered in beaming bonhomie for the very purpose of embracing me the one last time, thereupon to send me all the more cheerily off. So are you seeing what I in my mind—*in my mind*—saw? I would fling open the door and *he* would be there to reach for my hand to clasp it quickly to his own. Whereas were I to have taken the precaution of having shifted the turd into my *other* hand, then would that not be the hand that *she* would then shoot out her hand to seize, *no es verdad?* I mean, I do not know what this means, *no es verdad?*—but can you think of what else there is for me to say? Except, to be sure, to report to you—yes, yes, yes—that, yes, yes, yes, I ate it. Well, of course, I ate it. After all, had it not been written that I would? Come on, quit it—has not every outcome by the teller—by me, by you, by Willie, by your aunt Tillie—already been foretold?

So now which is it, do you say—story or *story,* truth or *truth,* or words just working out as words?

from GET YOUR TONGUE OUT OF MY MOUTH, I'M KISSING YOU GOOD-BYE

Cynthia Heimel

~

"I WISH I WERE A LESBIAN"

A bunch of us went to the theater the other night. We saw a one-woman show starring a performance artist named Carrie, a woman who is funny, moving, attractive, and brilliant. During the show, she talked about being a lesbian, and every time she did, some women in crew cuts and work boots stood up and cheered.

"Those lesbians make me sick," said Carrie later. "I wish they would stop following me around."

"But why?" I asked nervously. With lesbians, I'm always afraid I'll say something politically incorrect.

"They're so damned politically correct," Carrie said. "They reduce me to a stereotype, they're not responding to me but just to my sexual preference, so fuck them." She took another swig of tequila. She was getting very drunk.

My friends were giving a party for her and she loved it. Her eyes were bright, she hugged anyone she could reach. I was fascinated. I'd never met anyone so honest, so warm, so sweet and smart.

Why can't I meet a man like this? I thought as she hugged me. She hugged me again. "You smell so good," she whispered. "Gee, thanks," I whispered back. She kissed me. On the lips. She tried to put her tongue into my mouth.

Oh my God! She tried to put her tongue into my mouth!

I know what guys think, they tell me often enough. They think that if they were women, they would definitely be lesbians. They also think of male homosexuality as a scary perversion, but of female homosexuality as, I don't know, kind of *wholesome*. Hardly anything excites them as much as the idea of two women doing it. (I would like to say for the record that the reverse is not true: The thought of two men doing it turns women off in a New York second.)

"So then what did you do?" asked my friend Brendan.

"I just kept my mouth closed and refused tongue penetration," I said. "I was flattered, but nervous."

"You gotta let her go down on you," he said. "It would be just too cool."

I wish I could.

It was at least a year ago when I had a small epiphany. I was working out at the gym and I saw two women spotting each other while doing bench presses. There was something about them. They seemed so confident, so strong, so self-sufficient. I couldn't understand it. Most women are tentative and conciliatory. They have an underlying urge to please. Most women seem like they're just about to apologize. Not these babes.

They're lesbians! I realized. They don't care if men like them!

I was jealous. I remember only once in my life feeling as content and confident as these women: It was 1979 and I was out of my mind on a combination of Quaaludes and cocaine. This method no longer strikes me as practical.

Oh, to be a lesbian! Never again to become tongue-tied and stupid and self-deprecating and laugh too much! To wear sweatpants my whole life long!

If I could be a lesbian, I could have chocolate cake for dinner every night and still get laid! Men, who have sex glands in their eyes and centerfolds in their hearts, are strange, deranged, picky and exacting about women's bodies! Other women are not! Other women would be empathetic about cellulite and bad-hair days! Plenty of lesbians are fat and loved!

Also, I'd probably drive better. I notice a lot of bad women drivers and I think, If she were a lesbian, she wouldn't be going twenty-five in the passing lane. Because women are taught that to please men, we should be incompetent and fluttery about certain things. We've learned to get hives at the sight of a lug wrench, to faint when a fuse blows. We've been taught that men like us to act as if we can't take care of ourselves. It supposedly makes them feel big and strong.

"I would adore being a lesbian," I told Brendan. "Mentally, I can picture it, but physically, get the fuck out of here."

"Come on, just be bisexual," he said. "Women have such beautiful bodies. Wouldn't you like to fondle a nice breast? Stroke a warm vulva?"

"Now I'm nauseous," I said. I wish I weren't.

What would I say to a lesbian? Men are amazed at how easily women fall into deep conversation the moment they meet. It's because we have a universal icebreaker: men. How annoying they are, how they never listen to us, how we can never figure out what they want, how cute that tall one in the corner is. The subject of men is the leitmotiv of heterosexual women's conversations. When I meet a lesbian, I find myself stopping my sentences in the middle.

But if I were a lesbian, I'd never have to wear one of those newfangled female condoms I've been reading about. Kind of like a diaphragm, only with a tail. A diaphragm with a tail! What fresh hell is this? I read in the paper that the device will "empower" women, that they'll no longer have to "negotiate with a man." Bullshit! The female condom means that women will again be entirely responsible for birth control.

There's that Texas saying, "The trouble with women is they have all the pussy." And the trouble with men is they have all the dicks. (And don't anyone write to tell me that lesbians strap on dildos, because that's the most disgusting thing I've ever heard, if it's even true, which I doubt.)

I am a slave to my hormones. I can put up with a lot of disrespect if a man has nice enough biceps. If he tells me that I should stop being so goddamned successful, that I should wear much shorter skirts and learn how to cook, I whine. I wheedle. I cajole. I try to argue him into having more respect, into being more sensitive—instead of simply telling him to go fuck himself.

If I were a lesbian, I would. Well, maybe. Maybe I'd be just as wimpy with women. Okay, never mind.

WOODY, WE HARDLY KNEW YE

The nation is reeling. We are sleepless and dazed, crashing into walls. The country's morale has never been lower. A pillar of our existence has collapsed. Our hero has destroyed himself in front of our horror-stricken eyes.

Woody, what could you have been thinking?

Maybe it was a setup. There are two kinds of people in the world: those who think Woody Allen is the genius spokesman of our collective angst, and those who think he's a filthy Jewish liberal gay-sympathizing cultural-elitist Communist madman. Another name for those two groups are Democrats and Republicans.

So I'm thinking the Republicans have something on Woody or maybe put a horse's head in his bed, because the timing is just too perfect. Right in the middle of the Republican convention, during a huge orgy of family-values hysteria, suddenly this. The Republicans figure that all Democrats will become so disheartened, so depressed, so disoriented by the fall of their hero that they'll just shoot themselves. And if they don't shoot themselves they'll be too demoralized to vote. This theory could be true. Woody himself said that politicians are "a notch beneath child molesters."

I personally have new lines on my face. I looked in the mirror just now and two furrows have appeared since yesterday.

Yesterday wasn't too bad. Yesterday was the day the news hit. Everybody's first impulse was to laugh it off.

"I just want to say," said this comedian I know, "that Woody Allen became my hero when I was in junior high, he's been my hero all through my life. So I'm not just latching on now."

Yesterday we had your traditional fight between men and women, with the men swallowing hard and then maintaining how cool it was, and the women sullen and snippy about yet another man turning out to be just a stupid git who cares more about youth and beauty than grace and spirit, another man who discards his mate for someone one-third his age.

"Come on, we'd all do it if we could," said a waiter.

"He's an asshole. I hate him," said a waitress.

But today the reality has sunk in. Plus there is the story of child abuse and criminal charges, not that anyone believes he abused those tiny children, but still, the ugliness! Then we saw Woody being ever so Woodyish during his news conference. (This has nothing to do with anything, but could men like George Bush, Paul Shaffer, Warren Beatty, and Woody please stop covering their gray hair with that cheap reddish brown hair-color stuff? It's ugly and an insult to our intelligence. Guys, go to a professional.)

Seeing Woody's face and hearing that familiar voice made us realize that this wasn't just a fun show-biz scandal about people we don't give a shit about like, oh, Rosanne's singing or Liz's drug abuse, this was about our beloved Woody. A man who shaped the way we think, a man we identify with, a man we believe we actually know. But humiliating your mate by falling in love with her daughter, a girl you've known since she was nine years old, is something we don't want to know.

I'm worried about my son. This is a kid who has seen *Annie Hall* fifty times and can quote anything in any Woody movie verbatim. A kid who after seeing *When Harry Met Sally* astonished me by listing the dozens of scenes that were Woody Allen rip-offs. A kid famous for not reading, who's never read a single book of mine (the little bastard) but who has read all of Woody's.

"It's his own tragic fate," says my kid.

"Total self-destruction that great artists are prone to," I said.

"I guess I could see the signs but didn't want to," he said.

We had lunch today with my friend Alan the director. "I feel betrayed," Alan said. "He's the father, the power in the relationship. He has a moral responsibility. I keep thinking of that scene in *Manhattan* where he's standing in a schoolroom with Michael Murphy and a hanging skeleton."

"Oh, yeah," says my kid, "where he points to the skeleton and says, 'It's very important to have some kind of personal integrity. I'll be hanging in a classroom one day and I want to make sure that when I thin out I'm well thought of.' "

A bearded man at the next table leaned toward us and spoke. "It's an issue of such complexity that a novelist should deal with it instead of a judge," he said. "This country has just gone into totally surreal black humor."

The woman sitting with him piped up. "Love is blind, but Woody, hon, get yourself a seeing-eye dog!"

"And anyway," said Alan, "he's got final cut, what more does he want?"

TIME: KILLER OR JOKER?

My childhood is like an acid flashback. Vague faces swim toward me when I try to remember grade school, junior high or high school. I had a best friend Amy but I only remember thick green leaves, her father's pipe in a white room, Amy on the swing with her braids flying backward. I had a friend named Polly Roach who drew horses incessantly. I was madly in love in the fifth and sixth grades with Jerry Bass, just like everyone else. I wrote his name over and over in my book. There was a boy named Ronnie Kessler, I think he was in love with me, I should have married him. There was Libby, who was boy-crazy . . .

But I am a grown-up now, I have reinvented myself. I live in New York, far from the Main Line. People who know me now don't know I was stupid and unpopular. I've escaped. So when my friend Sarah, who I met when we were four and still know and love, said she was going to the high school reunion, I said I'd go. It would be so funny.

We were early. Also early were two women named Karen and Cindy, whom I'd never seen before. Karen showed me her junior high yearbook. There was my picture, across which I had written, "Karen, It was a great time! Hope we see each other again! Love, Cyndy." Sarah found this hilarious.

Soon we were enmeshed in predinner cocktails and a blonde came up. "I thought of you yesterday," she said.

"Why, Gibble?" I asked. I hadn't thought of her yesterday. But now it was as if I'd seen her yesterday in study hall.

"Because I saw Reggie Jackson on TV," she said. She was obliquely alluding to the old scandal. I got very nervous and went and chomped on a carrot stick. Then I saw Polly Roach across the room and started choking.

"But you're blonde!" I said to Polly after she used the Heimlich maneuver. She had exactly the same face.

"I don't know what happened," Polly said. Then Debbie Lieberman wafted by and Polly went quiet. Only minutes ago I wouldn't have recognized the name. But now I pictured little Debbie Lieberman being mean to little Polly Roach because Polly didn't chase boys or try to be popular or anything, Polly just drew horses and sang in the choir and was nice to everyone.

"Hi, Cyndy," said a very pretty girl. I looked at her blankly. "Suzie Boyer," she said, "you don't remember me?"

"Oh of course I do," I said. I didn't really.

"Heartbreaker alert! Heartbreaker alert!" Sarah was running toward us and screaming. "Jerry Bass has arrived! He's still gorgeous!"

I felt a wave of fear. "I'm not talking to him," I said. "Fine," said Sarah, "I am." And she left.

"I remember you giving a book report in the eighth grade where you used the word 'Jew,'" said Suzie, "I'd never heard it before." She was beginning to look familiar.

"Oh my God, will you look at that, Nan is a redhead," I said to Polly.

Polly laughed. "Same old Cyndy," she said. Oh, no.

"Petey died of a heart attack three months ago," Nan whispered to me.

"Oh, Jesus," I said, "and Major has gone insane. This is terrible."

"And Harvey's in jail," said Libby, "for rape." Libby looked the same but was serene. "I didn't get married until I was twenty-nine," she said. "It was the right thing to do."

"I remember you," said a completely unfamiliar man. "My friend was so in love with you all through junior high and high school, until you left. He wanted to go out with you so much. You're all he ever talked about."

"Who? Who?" I asked frantically, wondering if it was too late.

"I can't remember his name, but all the boys were in love with you, you were a sexpot," he said.

I think he was talking about someone else and just got the names wrong.

Jerry Bass, looking so gorgeous, walked by, smiled, and waved. I looked around, realized I was alone at the table, and blushed.

"You didn't graduate with us," accused a very short girl.

"No I didn't," I snapped. "My parents pulled me out of school because I wouldn't stop going out with Major, okay?"

"And Libby was going out with Harvey, and Nan was going out with Petey, but it was just a fad with them, and you stayed with Major for years."

"Nobody would care if you went out with a black guy these days," said Gibble, "times have changed."

But the times hadn't helped Major, now insane, or Harvey, now in jail, or Petey, now dead. It had just been too hard.

Jerry Bass, who is now a psychotherapist, walked up to me and introduced himself! "I know," I said, "I was totally in love with you." And I still am. A deep and abject love was hurtling up from my unconscious, still insanely intact. "Everybody was."

"No, really? I had no idea. Really? I wish I had known," he said with that sweet stutter I'd forgotten. "Nobody ever knows. We're all prisoners of our own childhood fears."

I walked away from him with heart aching. Sarah and I hugged everyone and said good-bye. Suzie Boyer was now vivid in my memory, I pictured her in home ec, on overnights with the Brownies. It was as if I had known her all my life.

GAY BLADES

Nigel was rouging and powdering my cleavage, George was blow-drying my bangs, I was wriggling.

"Ow!"

"Stay still," said George. "Do you or do you not want to look like Christie Turlington?"

"Christ, now I've rouged your collarbone," said Nigel. "Stop fidgeting. There. You look fabulous."

"Fabulous," said George. "Stunning."

"So would either of you like to fuck me?"

"I would, but I must condition my chest hair," said George, sweeping from the room.

"Would you like to suck a large milky-white tit?" Nigel asked me.

"Please, Nige," I said.

"How about licking a pussy?"

"Please! Gross me out!"

"And that's how we feel," said Nigel.

Gender identification is a tricky thing. Should I resent Nigel and George for not paying me the ultimate compliment of their sexual desire? Should I consider them misogynists for their aversion? Or should I, as I do, love them because they're my dear friends and understand me better than a thousand straight men?

Not that there aren't gay misogynists:

What's the difference between a woman and a bowling ball?

If you had to, you could fuck a bowling ball.

Why are women like dog turds?

The older they are, the easier they are to pick up.

I heard both of these jokes from gay men about a decade ago, but I'll never forget them or stop despising the men who told them. But those are two instances in ten years, whereas every day of my life I am buffeted, no, fuck it, I am smashed in the face with heterosexual misogyny. Woman hatred explodes from my TV set, from the guys with jackhammers on my street, from waiters, from novelists. Straight men want to fuck women, and too often that makes them hate women.

So call me a fag hag if you want.

"You fag hag," says Nigel.

"There, you see!" I say, "gay men are always the ones to say it. They're always the first to put themselves down. Gay men are full of self-loathing!"

"So are women."

"That's true. Sometimes I think that self-loathing is the most humanizing of influences. We hate ourselves, therefore we have great compassion for others."

"Unless of course we hate ourselves and therefore go out and machine-gun an entire village."

"There is that. Maybe we feel bound to each other by our oppression. We are united in our helpless resentment of the opressor, the heterosexual white male. We identify with each other's plight."

"We identify with each other's tragically futile lust for Dennis Quaid, you silly cow."

"We have the same sexual impulses, yet we're not competitive, the way women can be. It's perfect."

"Has anybody seen my champagne-bucket earrings?" George called from the bathroom.

Gay men identify with women, in camp moments they yell at each other "girlfriend!" or even "girleen!," but they are not women. In their sexual behavior, they are alarmingly male.

Prowling, predatory, easily excited into lust, willing and able to have sex with those they regard with indifference or even hold in contempt. This explains the tragic promiscuity that went on before we knew about AIDS. Imagine what it would be like if you, a straight man, were met with a lusty, eager acceptance by every woman you ogled on the street or in a bar. That's what gay life was like in the seventies.

"Well, thank you very much," said George, "as if I would ever do it with anybody else but my Nige."

"You won't, George, but you might want to. Remember that guy who came to pick me up the other night?"

"Oh, he was so dishy. So gorgeous. Those eyes!"

"That's what I mean. Men, biologically, are helplessly promiscuous. The more evolved ones can rein in their animal impulses."

"Oh shut up and let's go to the party," said Nigel, making his James Dean face in the mirror.

At the party they got wild, Nigel danced with all the girls, holding them close, grinding into them.

"Nigel, be careful, she's a flower," George cautioned.

"You're just a closet heterosexual, Nigel," I accused.

Then the hostess brought out her wigs, and all the straight men in the room, heady with drink, tried them on and flounced around. They were adorable.

"That one doesn't know it yet," said Nigel, gesturing, "but he plays on our team."

"Yes," I said, "I thought he was awfully nice."

Yes, I mean it! Gay men are nicer! You can talk to them! And not because they're willing to chat about hairdos! You can say personal, complicated things to a gay man, and he won't look at you fishily, he won't make you feel like a fool.

There is a terrible pride about straight men. An implacable rigidity. They seem to forever be holding themselves in check, as if they're denying a convoluted maelstrom of feelings and fears churning within them. As if they're afraid that even one chink in their armor will make them fall apart.

So vehemently in control, and therefore so clearly vulnerable, straight men reduce women to uncertainty and delicacy. We're afraid we'll wound you and compromise your potency. We become your nursemaids.

The best, and perversely, the most masculine of straight men are the ones who have a strong dollop of femininity in their makeup. Give me a straight man who isn't afraid to gossip, whose mouth doesn't tighten when confronted by a woman being raunchy.

Femininity makes you strong.

from DATING IRON JOHN
Linda Sunshine

~

NICE GUYS vs. BAD BOYS

Keeping Score

There are only two kinds of men in this universe: Nice Guys and Bad Boys. Nice Guys are kind, attentive, and devoted. Bad Boys are aloof, selfish, and unreliable. As a general rule of thumb, we date Nice Guys but we fall for Bad Boys.

Why are we drawn to Bad Boys? The answer is revealed in the following chart, which analyzes and assigns points to the behavior patterns of both Nice Guys and Bad Boys.

It should be noted, by the way, that Bad Boys can be found in all age groups, from toddlers to old men, races, religions, colors, creeds, and neighborhoods.

NICE GUYS	BAD BOYS
Calls every day	Calls once every 2 weeks
Score:	
− 10 for being desperate	+ 10 for ever calling
Makes date 2 weeks in advance	Calls at last minute for date
− 10 for being too available	+ 10 for being popular
Has steady job (accountant, dentist, etc.)	Unemployed
− 10 for being ordinary	+ 10 for creativity, being artistic, anti-establishment
Wants to meet your best friend	Wants to date your best friend
− 10 for trying to toady his way into your life	+ 10 for making you jealous
Wants a serious relationship	Can't make a commitment
− 10 for not finding one	+ 10 for being a challenge
Works hard to please you	Only pleases you when he feels like it
− 10 for being dependent	+ 10 for independence
Takes you to expensive restaurants	Wants you to cook for him
− 10 for making you wear panty hose	+ 10 for eating your food
Extremely interested in your work	Extremely interested in his work
− 10 for asking too many questions	+ 10 for making you into a good listener
Talks about his feelings	Never discusses his feelings
− 10 because his feelings are never in sync with yours	+ 10 for allowing you to fantasize how he feels about you
Brings you roses	Never promised you a rose garden
− 10 for making you feel guilty for accepting gifts	+ 10 for honesty
Always dresses neat and clean	Doesn't care about clothes
− 10 for always wearing geeky jeans	+ 10 for looking great naked
Tells stupid jokes	Tells stupid jokes
− 10 for boredom	+ 10 for making you laugh

BONUS POINTS

+ 10 for always driving a nice car   + 250 for always being a great
                                               kisser

TOTAL SCORE

Nice Guys: − 110   Bad Boys: + 370

Any questions?

Ten Things You Should Never Tell . . .

Ten Things You Should Never Tell . . . Your Sister

1. When she was seven, you sold her to a neighbor kid for a quarter.
2. Mom always loved you best.
3. You hate the way she dresses.
4. Dad just lent you five thousand dollars for a new car.
5. You think her kids are spoiled.
6. People always ask, "Which one of you is the youngest?"
7. She was adopted.
8. You always wanted to be an only child.
9. Your boyfriend thinks she's far less attractive than you.
10. She's just like Mom.

Ten Things You Should Never Tell . . . Your Husband

1. His hairline is receding.
2. You sometimes think about having sex with someone else.
3. He always gives you a terrible birthday present.
4. His mother is on the phone.
5. Your mother is planning to spend her two-week vacation at your house.
6. He should stop at the gas station and ask for directions.
7. Your old college boyfriend asked you out to lunch.
8. You dented his car at the shopping mall.
9. You've been out pricing mink coats.
10. You didn't really have a headache last night.

Ten Things You Should Never Tell . . . Your Best Friend

1. Her diet isn't working.
2. Her boyfriend asked you out.
3. Her problems are stupid.
4. Her couch belongs on the far wall.
5. Your boyfriend thinks she's sexy.
6. Her apartment smells like a cat box.
7. She looks flat-chested in her new hundred-twenty-five-dollar swimsuit.
8. Your parents think she's a bad influence on you.
9. Her eye makeup is very dated.
10. Her dinner parties are boring.

Ten Things You Should Never Tell . . . Your Mother

1. You've had sex.
2. Your mother-in-law is a better cook.
3. You aren't wearing clean underwear.
4. You aren't wearing *any* underwear.
5. You're spending Thanksgiving with your in-laws.
6. You used to steal money from her purse.
7. You lied about the dog breaking her Waterford vase in 1968.
8. You don't believe in marriage.
9. Your new boyfriend is married.
10. You used to wish she was more like Donna Reed.

THE SUCCESSFULLY DYSFUNCTIONAL FAMILY

All happy families resemble one another, but each dysfunctional family is dysfunctional in its own way.

—LEO TOLSTOY,
Anna! (the made-for-television screenplay
adapted from his novel)

Dysfunctional families come in all shapes and sizes. Mine was a size 38 extra long, with a little extra room sewn into the seat.
My childhood was greatly affected by the fact that I was born

long before the invention of quality time. Back then, mothers and fathers spent huge quantities of time with their offspring. Call it ignorance. "Who knew about this quality-time business?" my mother will often ask. "In our day, quality time meant you had food in the refrigerator, the rent was paid for the next month, and no one at the dinner table was getting sued or recovering from surgery."

My parents are not the only people who are confused by the concept of quality time. Many books have been written on the subject in the hopes of explaining to modern parents the damage they can inflict on their children by not allocating time into quality increments. "Raw time is like nonhomogenized milk," explains one child psychologist. "It can make both you and your child sick to your respective stomachs. We now recognize that every moment spent with your child should be as jam-packed with learning, fun, and bonding as humanly possible for psychological health. The proof is in the pudding. Parents didn't begin doling out quality time until the mid-1980s, which explains why so many Baby Boomers are currently in therapy or on medication."

We are the dysfunctional generation, and celebrity dysfunctional families have become the most popular guests on the talkshow circuit, the subjects of bestselling books, and the topics of discussion in anonymous meetings across the country. Everyone, in short, is jumping on the neo-neurotic bandwagon.

I don't mean to brag, but I take great pride in reporting that members of my family have been in the otherly abled psychological forefront for many decades. We were a dysfunctional group long before the term was ever used on national television. For this reason, my grandmother can barely contain herself when she watches *Donahue* or *Oprah*.

"These know-it-alls act like they've invented emotional abuse and addictive behavior," she'll often rant and rage at the television set when I visit her in Miami Beach. "Whole generations of this family were dysfunctional way before television was even invented. Why, you had a great-grandfather, he should rest in peace, who was known throughout Schönhausen as the village alcoholic. Drank like a fish. And my aunt Mavis, your great-great-aunt, was married to a Cossack who beat her senseless once a month. Mavis didn't have low self-esteem, she had *no* self-esteem to have married that moron in the first place.

"And you want to talk nervous breakdowns? We've had relatives in every major world war and foreign conflict who were kept out of service because of a loose screw. None of our men have ever seen combat.

"We've had manic depressives, attempted suicides, and even one bona fide psychotic. Leonard. True, Leonard was a cousin by marriage of your Uncle Morris, but still, we always considered him family. There he sat at every Seder with his automatic rifle, it scared the living daylights out of Great-Grandma Nettie, who was from the Old Country and didn't know from such technology. Nettie made Leonard leave the gun on the seat for Elijah, wrapped in plastic, naturally, because it was so greasy."

If you don't stop Grandma by this point, she gets out the photographs. "Just look in our family album—you'll find weepers, dreamers, nail biters, hysterics, bed wetters, screamers, hypochondriacs, neurotics, womanizers, check bouncers. We got 'em all. Ach! It gives me a pain in my gall bladder when I think about the fortune we could've made if talk shows had been around in my day."

Family pride runs deep in my family, it courses through our blood like my brother-in-law's Corvette on the Garden State Parkway. We have often discussed having a family crest made. It would be shaped like a poker table and contain symbols of the three most prominent genetic trademarks of the family clan: obesity, kleptomania, and agoraphobia.

Parent-child relationships are as troubled in my family as anything you'll see on daytime talk shows. I have several cousins who've moved clear across the continent just to get away from their parents and others who still live at home well into their thirties and forties. Separation anxiety is endemic in our family, and even our family pets tend to hyperventilate during family gatherings.

We gamble, smoke, and lie a lot, especially among ourselves. We spend our time together insulting each other and our time apart being critical of our weaker members.

Most of my blood relatives are in complete denial. We think of ourselves as a happy, close, and fun-loving family, yet every one of us has frequent stomachaches and migraine headaches. We cry easily and often, especially when Grandpa Max joins us for dinner.

Unfortunately, we are given little credit in the media. Despite the thousands of dollars we've spent collectively on psychiatric help, none of us has ever been written up in any scientific journal. Even more disturbing is the lack of attention from the media.

My grandmother would love to share the spotlight with celebrity dysfunctional families such as the Ronald Reagans, the Bing Crosbys, the Joan Crawfords, the Kennedys, and the Windsors of England. She feels that too much hoopla is made over celebrity child-abusers while the ordinary citizens who neglect their children or cause violence to their household pets are never noticed by the press.

"It's very unfair," agrees the publisher of a prominent New York newspaper, "but the public is more interested in the dysfunctions of the rich and famous than in those of Mr. and Mrs. America."

But the public should not be fooled by the headlines. There are successful dysfunctional families in all walks of life. You don't have to be a movie star, president of a country, or the future king of England to live in a dysfunctional family. Your family is just as important and probably as dysfunctional as any other.

"Always remember that blood is thicker than water," says my Aunt Elsie, the overweight kleptomaniac who hasn't left her house in three years, so she's forced to steal from family. It's not as bad as it sounds. When we have Passover dinner with Aunt Elsie and Uncle Abe, we leave our wallets in the car.

BACKLASH OR WHIPLASH?

The Undeclared War Against Single Women and Susan Faludi

In the 1970's single women were encouraged to pursue a career instead of a husband. By the 1990's, they were being assaulted for remaining single and for not having babies. Yes, being a single mother was accepted, even encouraged, by many people in society, with the glaring exception of anyone you knew personally who was a single mother.

The journalist Susan Faludi wrote about the backlash against single women, but she failed to mention the most prevalent physical manifestation of this condition: whiplash. Whiplash, which most victims describe as a severe and persistent pain in the neck, is caused by a single woman's conflicting ambitions to live an adult life but maintain a teenager's body. And maybe have a kid someday.

Several factors have foisted this problem on today's single woman. Radical changes in the women's movement have affected the economic climate, the cultural landscape, and most important, dating patterns between single men and women. These changes can best be documented by a close examination of the two most prominent female icons of the past two decades: Mary Richards and Murphy Brown.

Both of these fictional characters should be well known to all single women. Mary Richards was played by the phenomenally skinny though diabetic Mary Tyler Moore who, in real life, is married to a much younger doctor and lives in New York City. Murphy Brown is played by the former model/photojournalist/serious person Candice Bergen who, in real life, is married to a famous French director, has a young daughter, and commutes between California and France.

Both of these TV characters set precedents for their day. Both Mary and Murphy are independent, single working gals who dress great and interact well with a crew of off-beat coworkers. Both work in television, although Mary worked behind the scenes in the newsroom while Murphy appears in front of the camera. However, Murphy pays a high price for her better job. She's got way fewer boyfriends than Mary, and not even her friends think she deserves one. These are only some of the similarities between Murphy and Mary. The following chart details the contrasts between these two characters, who exemplify the changes women have undergone in the past twenty years.

"As we moved from Mary to Murphy, the image of the working woman changed radically in this country," reports Professor Constance Crueller, who teaches "Women of the Sitcom: An Overview," at Bryn Mawr College. "Mary always called her boss Mr. Grant. She blushed and stammered if she had to ask him for a day off. Conversely, Murphy continually browbeats her boss, and often threatens to deflate his tires.

"Mary always had a flower on her desk as a symbol of her sweetness. Murphy can't keep a secretary, a metaphor for her short temper and unrealistic expectations. By today's standards, Mary Richards would be considered a complete sap; she wouldn't last five minutes in Murphy's newsroom."

SOCIOLOGICAL INDICATORS

Mary Richards	*Murphy Brown*
DECLINE IN MANNERS	
Spunky but good-natured	Spunky but ill-tempered
Stutters when nervous	Wisecracks, insults people when feeling vulnerable
SIGNS OF UPWARD MOBILITY	
Lives in small studio, later moves to one-bedroom apartment	Lives in an elaborate town house
RESULTS OF WOMEN'S ASSERTIVENESS	
Apologizes for everything	Never apologizes
Everyone loves her	Everyone hates her
Easily intimidated	Intimidating
Nice girl	Rhymes with rich
INCREASED REALISM ON TELEVISION	
No vices	Recovering alcoholic, former smoker
Took the pill	Got pregnant

A big part of Murphy's problem with men stems from the so-called Man Shortage Epidemic, which wasn't invented until long after Mary Richards went into syndication.

The epidemic was first recognized in 1986, when the *Stamford Advocate* published results of a Yale study indicating that women who don't marry by the age of thirty had only a 20 percent chance of being wed; their odds went down to 5 percent by thirty-five, and after forty, well, junk those back issue's of *Bride's Magazine* and burn grandma's wedding veil, it isn't going to happen.

The story of the epidemic was picked up by dozens of newspapers, talk shows, magazines, sitcoms, movies, self-help books, syndicated cartoon strips, greeting cards, and mothers of thirty-something women across the nation. The survey caused severe anxiety and panic among single women, sending thousands stampeding to the personal ads, dating services, and whenever possible, down the aisle. The marriage rate increased a whopping 127 percent in the six months following the explosion of publicity about the man shortage.

The women who rushed to the altar (and many of them are currently in divorce proceedings) would later be surprised to discover that the study was, in fact, a complete misinterpretation of statistics. Investigations revealed the numbers were improperly crunched by three lonely statisticians who were hoping to make themselves appear more attractive to the female population in Connecticut. "A desperate woman is more likely to lower her standards," confessed one of the authors of the study. "We weren't out to hurt anyone, we just wanted a date for the Harvard-Yale game." They succeeded brilliantly. Within three months, each young man was involved in a serious relationship with at least two women. One was dating two roommates and flirting with a third.

In reality, there was no man shortage. Marriageable men existed. However, since the advent of cable television, they preferred to stay at home with their remote controls and 107 channels. Contributing to their alleged disappearance were several technological advances, including microwave ovens, fax machines, modems, VCR's, and half-hour delivery service from Domino's Pizza.

In point of fact, women were single because in overwhelming numbers, they were choosing not to marry, even when they had the opportunity. "What's the point of getting married?" asked one single woman from Chicago. "I can pump my own gasoline."

According to a poll by a major magazine, more than half the women in the survey claimed they'd never remarry their current husband if they were given the opportunity (and many begged for the option). In another poll, when asked why they remained unmarried, more than 78 percent of the 60,000 single women surveyed said that instead of marriage, they much preferred their freedom, financial independence, and extra closet space.

It has been proven that marriage is, in fact, much more beneficial to men than women. Many statistics confirm that married men are more emotionally stable and less likely to experience nightmares, nervous breakdowns, or attempts at suicide than bachelors. The reverse is true for women. In general, single women are happier, healthier, and more physically fit than married women. Also, single women generally have nicer clothes, longer vacations, less laundry, and more fun at parties than their married counterparts.

Still, some women chose marriage over the single life-style because, as one prominent psychologist told Sally Jessy, "Having a husband means never having to say you're sorry to your mother again. It's worth it." Sally Jessy agreed.

And so the debate continues to rage among women: Single vs. Married, Career vs. Family, Suits vs. Pants, Cellulite vs. Liposuction, Sweet'n Low vs. NutraSweet, Valium vs. Xanax. Every day women are pulled in ten different directions. The multitude of options has given us a major case of whiplash.

We want to sue.

Many of us have law degrees and are ready to put our hard-won skills to maximum use. The question is: Whom to sue? The three statisticians who created the man shortage? The media that publicized it? The talk-show hosts and writers who continue to take advantage of those hateful statistics? The entire male gender? Just give us a name, we'll get the paperwork in motion.

from THE BOOK OF GUYS

Garrison Keillor

~

DON GIOVANNI

Marriage takes too much out of a man, says the old seducer through a cloud of cigarette smoke. Marriage is an enormous drain on a man's time and energy, it produces continual deficits, it reduces him to silliness and servility, it is the deathbed of romance. Figaro, my friend, a man owes it to himself to stop and consider the three advantages of the single life.

One, if you're single, you can think. Two, you can act. Three, you can feel. Probably there are other advantages, but those three surely are important, yes?

Think about it. There is never a substitute for freedom, and there is no prison so deadly as a life of unnecessities, which is what marriage is. A woman takes over a man's life and turns it to her own ends. She heaps up his plate with stones, she fills his bed with anxiety, she destroys his peace so that he hardly remembers it.

But even a married man knows what he should have done. You should find a cheap place to live—who needs a mansion? You put your money in the bank and you furnish your place as you please, with your own junk and great bargains from auctions. You come and go, you eat when you're hungry, you stay up late, you get drunk as it pleases you, and you have two or three terrific lovers who visit when you invite them and stay about the right length of time.

Enjoy yourself. That's what we're here for.

Some men should have two lovers, some three, it depends on the man, said the Don. Never limit yourself to one: monogamy leads to matrimony, and marriage, my boy, is pure struggle. Of course the single life has problems—having two lovers is a scheduling problem, and three is a real test of a man's organizational ability, and yet those are the very problems a man hopes for, Figaro. Living alone in a cushy old apartment with your friendly Jamaican housekeeper coming on Fridays to put a shine on things, the corner laundry delivering clean clothes on Wednesdays, and your girlfriends dropping in on various evenings, each of them crazy about you, anxious to please—you know how accommodating young women can be when they want to be. Think of having three like that at once, their eyes alight at the sight of you, their lips moist, the flush of desire on their cheeks. Sound good? My, yes. The Don smiled at the thought.

"No woman would accept such an arrangement. You would have to lie to her," said Figaro.

Yes, certainly, said the Don.

"To lie to three women at once? To keep inventing stories about where you went? Is that nice?"

The girls who share my bed want to share my life, said the Don, and that would leave me no life at all.

"But to be so selfish—what if everyone were? What if your parents had been?"

I am selfish, Figaro, because I have a larger capacity for pleasure than other people do. Pleasure is only a hobby to them and to me it is a true vocation: the joy of eating a sumptuous meal in the company of a sharp-tongued woman who secretly adores me—who argues with me and ridicules my politics and my ideas, the things I don't care about, and who, in a couple hours, will lie happily next to me, damp and drowsy, smiling, this is to me the beauty of the male existence. As for my parents, what they did wasn't my responsibility.

Figaro had dropped in to see his old friend at the Sportsman's Bar in Fargo, where the Don was engaged for three weeks to play the piano. Figaro had moved to Fargo with Susanna shortly after their marriage, and he had not laid eyes on the Don since he had attempted to seduce Susanna on their wedding night—one of those cases of mistaken identity in dimly lit places, so Figaro bore no grudge.

The Sportsman was an old dive near the Great Northern yards where the switching crews liked to duck in for a bump of whiskey on their coffee breaks. It was not a place you would bring a woman, Figaro thought, and any woman you might find in there you wouldn't want to know better. The little marquee out front said, "BBQ Beef S'Wich $1.95 Happy Hour 4–6 Two Drinks for Price of One D G'vanni in Hunters Lounge Nitely." When Figaro stepped into the gloom, the cloud of beer and smoke and grease, he heard someone playing "Glow Worm," and recognized the Don's florid glissandos, the tremors and trills, the quavers and dips, the big purple chords rising, the mists, the Spanish moss, the grape arbor in the moonlight, the sighs, the throbbing of the thrush. The Don sat all big and glittery at the keyboard in the rear of the deserted room, in an iridescent silver jacket that picked up every speck of light from the sixty-watt spotlight overhead. The silver threads went nicely with the Don's flowing bleached-blonde hair and the gaudy rings on his fingers, chosen for maximum sparkle. Six rings and six chunks of diamond, a ruby-studded bolero tie, a silver satin shirt with pearl buttons, and silver-and-turquoise earrings.

He looked much the worse for wear, Figaro thought, as if he had been living in these clothes for a number of days, including some rainy ones, but he was full of beans, as always. He told Figaro he would soon be back in New York, where a big recording contract was in the offing, a major label, large sums of cash that he was not at liberty to disclose—he rubbed his fingers together to suggest the heavy dough involved—the people were secretive types, *you* understand, said the Don.

"And you? How are you? Have you found a wife yet?" asked Figaro.

The Don laughed. It was their old joke.

Marriage looks very appealing until you are in the company of married people and then the horrors of the institution cry out to you, said the Don. Marriage is for women, Figaro, ugly women. It makes no sense for men. It never did.

The married guy has to have an airtight explanation for every-thing he does by himself. If he wants to go for a *walk around the block* alone, he has to invent an excuse for not taking his beloved with him. To get up out of his chair and go into the kitchen and run a glass of tap water, he has to announce that to his wife, like a child in the third grade, or else she will say, "Where are you going? To the kitchen? For a glass of tap water? Fine. Why can't you say so? Why do you *always just wander away without saying a word?* You wouldn't treat anybody else that way. How do I know if you're going to the kitchen or going to New Orleans for a week? And it would've been nice if you'd offered to bring *me* something from the kitchen. If you loved me, you'd think of these things. But no. You just get up and walk away. I could be sitting here dying and you'd never notice." And then she bursts into tears, grieving for herself and her future death. This is mar-riage, Figaro.

A single guy can walk around without explaining it to anyone. He can also go to New Orleans. This gives a man a dignified feeling, knowing that you could, it you wanted to, drive somewhere. Or drive *nowhere,* just cruise around with the top down soaking up rays and laying down rubber. Married guys can't go nowhere. There always has to be a plan, a list of errands, a system, a des-tination. Alone, your life is intuitive, like poetry. With a woman, it's a form of bookkeeping.

"So—how long are you in town?" asked Figaro, trying to change the subject, but the Don had more to say.

A home belongs to the oldest woman inhabitant, no matter what. Every day, a man has to get her permission to come in, to use the toilet, to draw oxygen from the air, to keep his things in the closet. The permission is always conditional, and some of her rules are never explained: some secret rules (No Loitering, No Unnecessary Conversation, No Putting Things There, No Whistling, No Guests, We Reserve the Right to Change the Terms of This Agreement) are kept for emergencies.

And a married guy is responsible for *everything,* no matter what. Women, thanks to their having been oppressed all these years, are blameless, free as birds, and all the dirt they do is the result of premenstrual syndrome or postmenstrual stress or menopause or emotional disempowerment by their fathers or low expectations by their teachers or latent unspoken sexual harassment in the workplace, or some other airy excuse. The guy alone is responsible for every day of marriage that is less than marvelous and meaningful.

"Why don't we ever make love anymore?" That is the No. 2 all-time question in the world. No. 1 is: "Why don't we ever talk to each other?" Now, there's a great conversational opener. You're ensconced on the couch, perusing the funny papers, sipping your hot toddy, feeling mellow and beloved, and she plops down full of anger and premenstrual uproar, and says, "Why don't we ever talk to each other? Why do you treat me as if I don't exist?"

You take her hand. "What do you want to talk about, my beloved?"

"You and your utter lack of interest in communicating with me, that's what," she snaps, yanking her hand back.

"My love, light of my life, my interest in you is as vast as the Great Plains. Please. Share with me what is in your heart so that we may draw close in the great duet of matrimony."

But she didn't want to converse, of course, she only meant to strike a blow. "Humph," she says, standing up. "I know you. You are only saying that."

That is marriage, Figaro. A boy's constant struggle to maintain his buoyancy.

"Some of what you say, I suppose, is true," said Figaro, "but a guy needs a wife, someone who cares if you've collapsed in the shower with your leg broken."

Well, your chances of collapsing in the shower are sharply improved by being married, the Don said. Helpless rage is a major cause of falls in the home.

No, marriage is a disaster for a man, it cuts him up and broils his spirit piece by piece, until there is nothing left of him but the hair and the harness.

An unhappy man with heavy eyelids appeared in the doorway to the Lounge, hands on hips, chewing a mouthful of peanuts. He appeared to be an owner or manager of some sort. "You on a break right now, Giovanni? Or is the piano busted?"

The Don turned with the greatest disdain and said, "Oh, Cy. I *thought* it was you."

"I hired you as a piano player, Giovanni, not a philosopher. I'd like to hear less thinking and more tinkling. A word to the wise." The man turned and disappeared.

The Don looked down at the keyboard, plunked a couple notes, got up from the bench, and motioned to a table in the corner. "We can sit there," he said.

"A life without a woman is the lonesomest life I can imagine," Figaro said with a sigh. "I would be miserable without Susanna."

Life *is* lonesome, said the Don, and lonesome isn't bad, compared to desperate. But of course a man should not live without women. Luckily, marriage is not a requirement. Nobody needs monogamy except the unenterprising. Hungry women are everywhere! Lonely housewives who advertise on recipe cards pinned to a bulletin board in the Piggly-Wiggly—wistful ladies at the copier, putting flesh to glass, faxing themselves to faroff officedom—fervid women sending out E-mail invites—hearty gals working out on the weight machine who drop a note in your street shoes—cocktail joints along the freeway, wall-to-wall with women whose lights are on and motors are running!—Figaro, they're out there! Free. No legal contract required. What could be better?

Figaro shook his head. "The life of a libertine ends badly," he said. "You get old, your teeth turn yellow, and you smell like a mutt, and you have to pay women to look at you. Much better to marry, to be faithful, to build a deeper partnership that will hold together through the terrible storms of old age."

My dear Figaro, seduction is an art, to be learned, practiced, adapted, and improvised according to the situation, and, like other arts, it will not desert you late in life.

"Seduction is a lie, and as we get older, we get tired of lies," said Figaro. "We know them all and they're not amusing anymore."

Seduction is a sweet story, and if the listener wants so much to hear it, then it is no lie. Seduction is a mutual endeavor in which I conspire with a woman to give her an opening to do what she wants to do without reminding her that this goes against her principles. A woman's principles and her desires are constantly at war, and if there were no one to seduce a woman, she would have to figure out how to do it herself. Her principles call for her to remain aloof and uninterested until she meets a man who makes her faint. Her desires are otherwise. She wants to say, "That man, there. Unwrap him and send him over here so he can love me." She cannot say this. So I try to help her. I say, *Zerlina, I would like to hold your hand for two minutes and then you can shoot me and I will die a happy man.*

She laughs, but she does not turn away. She rolls her eyes. She says, "Oh, phoo." She gives me her hand.

I say: *The greatest tragedy is to be cut off from intimacy, from touch, which is the most human of languages, Zerlina, and the most honest. There is no lie in a touch, a caress, never. The language of the body is a language of the purest truth.*

She is amused. I put my other hand on her shoulder. She turns and leans against me. "You're something," she says.

Zerlina, I say, there's a bottle of champagne waiting on ice at the Olympia Hotel, and a couple dozen oysters. When we get there, we'll order up a big salad in a wooden bowl, with basil and spinach and fennel and cilantro and radicchio, and we'll have it with olive oil and vinegar and pepper and garlic. Then a steak tartare, with chopped onions and an egg yolk. And then we'll undress quickly without shame, as adults, and jump into the big bed and amuse each other as only adults can do. And afterward, we'll eat an omelet. And then do it again.

Her hand twitches in mine, and I guess that I have touched a chord—"This is the best time of year for oysters," I say in a low voice, "and one should never eat them without erotic plans for later."

She tells me to be real, but even so, she is reaching for her purse, putting on her coat, checking her lipstick. "You're outrageous," she says, and now we are almost to the hotel, and then in the room, she says, "I can't believe I'm actually doing this." But she is. She is. A wonderful occasion, Figaro. The sort of evening that someday, as you lie dying, you will remember and it will bring a smile to your lips.

"You *slept* with her? Zerlina? But she is married to Maseppo," said Figaro. "I can't believe this!"

I may have slept with her, I may not have slept with her, I only mention her as an example. Zerlina, Marilyn, Marlene—what's the difference? A *woman*.

"Having an affair is not the same as marital happiness," said Figaro.

You are right. Marital happiness is briefer and it has a sword hanging over its head. The happiness in marriage is fitful, occasional. It is the pleasure one gets from the absence of the pain of not conforming exactly to the wishes of your wife. A married man walks into the room and his wife looks up and smiles—he is dressed and groomed exactly as she has trained him, his gait is perfect, his personality is champion quality, and he is prepared to converse on topics of her liking, a neat trick it took her years to teach him—and for the duration of her smile, he is happy. But her smile is brief. She spots the flaw: the spiritual emptiness in his eye. She has warned him against emptiness, but there it is. "Why are you looking at me like that?" she hisses. "You look as dim as a dodo." And his happiness is now over for a while. He must think of a way to fill up his spirit.

The man with the heavy eyelids reappeared in the door, an envelope in his hand. "Time to go, Giovanni," he said, setting his big hand on the table. "Yer outta here. You broke the deal. Yer history. The job's over. Move it."

The Don sneered. What a relief to get out of this mausoleum, he said. I am, he said, the greatest romantic pianist of all time. But a romantic pianist in Fargo is like an All-Star shortstop in Paris. Not a priority item.

"Go to hell," said the man, and he stamped his foot on the floor. Figaro looked down. The man had hooves instead of shoes.

The Don stood up. *Gladly, he said, it would be better than looking at your ugly face.*

The man strode to the back door by the piano and opened it, and Figaro saw the orange glow of flames in the basement, fingers of flame licking the doorsill.

"Stop!" he cried. "No! Giovanni! Repent!" He took the Don by the arm. "It's not too late. *Repent!*"

The Don put a hand on Figaro's shoulder. "Believe me," he said, "it's easier simply to go. And compared to marriage, it isn't that bad. Farewell, *mon ami*." And he took off his great silver jacket and gave it to Figaro and walked to the stairs, put his hands on the door frame, and then, with a mighty cry, plunged down into the fiery abyss.

"Your hair smells of smoke," Susanna said to Figaro when he arrived home. "Where were you? In a bar? You stopped in a bar on your way home? I thought you had outgrown that, darling. And what are you going to do with that hideous jacket? My gosh. You can put it in the garage. It reeks of shellfish. I don't want it in the house. Go on. Take it out of here."

So he did. He put the silver jacket on a hanger and hung it on a nail next to the rakes and shovels, and it stayed there for years. Twice she threw it in the trash and twice he retrieved it.

WHAT WE WANTED TO DO
Ron Carlson

What we wanted to do was spill boiling oil onto the heads of our enemies as they attempted to bang down the gates of our village, but, as everyone now knows, we had some problems, primarily technical problems, that prevented us from doing what we wanted to do the way we had hoped to do it. What we're asking for today is another chance.

There has been so much media attention to this boiling oil issue that it is time to clear the air. There is a great deal of pressure to dismantle the system we have in place and bring the oil down off the roof. Even though there isn't much left. This would be a mistake. Yes, there were problems last month during the Visigoth raid, but as I will note, these are easily remedied.

From its inception I have been intimately involved in the boiling oil project—research, development, physical deployment. I also happened to be team leader on the roof last month when we had occasion to try the system during the Visigoth attack, about which so much has been written.

(It was not an "entirely successful" sortie, as I will show. The Visigoths, about two dozen, did penetrate the city and rape and plunder for several hours, but *there was no pillaging*. And make no questions about it—they now know we have oil on the roof and several of them are going to think twice before battering down our door again. I'm not saying it may not happen, but when it does, they know we'll be ready.)

First, the very concept of oil on the roof upset so many of our villagers. Granted, it is exotic, but all great ideas seem strange at first. When our researchers realized we could position a cauldron two hundred feet directly above our main portals, they began to see the possibilities of the greatest strategic defense system in the history of mankind.

The cauldron was expensive. We all knew a good defense was going to be costly. The cauldron was manufactured locally after procuring copper and brass from our mines and it took—as is common knowledge—two years to complete. It is a beautiful thing capable of holding one hundred and ten gallons of oil. What we could not foresee was the expense and delay of building an armature. Well, of course, it's not enough to have a big pot, pretty as it may be; how are you going to pour its hot contents on your enemies? The construction of an adequate superstructure for the apparatus required dear time: another year during which the Huns and the Exogoths were raiding our village almost weekly. Let me ask you to remember that era—was that any fun?

I want to emphasize that we were committed to this program—and we remain committed. But at every turn we've met problems that our researchers could not—regardless of their intelligence and intuition—have foreseen. For instance: how were we to get a 1900-pound brass cauldron onto the roof? When had such a question been asked before? And at each of these impossible challenges, our boiling oil teams have come up with solutions. The cauldron was raised to the roof by means of a custom-designed net and petard including a rope four inches in diameter which was woven on the spot under less than ideal conditions as the Retrogoths and the Niligoths plundered our village almost incessantly during the cauldron's four-month ascent. To our great and everlasting credit, we did not drop the pot. The superstructure for the pouring device was dropped once, but it was easily repaired on site, two hundred feet above the village steps.

That was quite a moment and I remember it well. Standing on the roof by that gleaming symbol of our impending safety, a bright brass (and a few lesser metals) beacon to the world that we were not going to take it anymore. The wind carried up to us the cries of villagers being carried away by either the Maxigoths or the Minigoths, it was hard to tell. But there we stood and as I felt the wind in my hair and watched the sporadic procession of home furnishings being carried out of our violated gates, I knew we were perched on the edge of a new epoch.

Well, there was some excitement; we began at once. We started a fire under the cauldron and knew we would all soon be safe. At that point I made a mistake, which I now readily admit. In the utter ebullience of the moment I called down—I did not "scream maniacally" as was reported—I called down that *it would not be long,* and I probably shouldn't have, because it may have led some of our citizenry to lower their guard. It was a mistake. I admit it. There were, as we found out almost immediately, still some bugs to be worked out of the program. For instance there had never been a fire on top of the entry tower before, and yes, as everyone is aware, we had to spend more time than we really wanted containing the blaze, fueled as it was by the fresh high winds and the tower's wooden shingles. But I hasten to add that the damage was moderate, as moderate as a four-hour fire could be, and the billowing black smoke surely gave further intruders lurking in the hills pause as they considered finding any spoils in our ashes!

But throughout this relentless series of setbacks, pitfalls, and rooftop fires, there has been a hard core of us absolutely dedicated to doing what we wanted to do and that was to splash scalding oil onto intruders as they pried or battered yet again at our old damaged gates. To us a little fire on the rooftop was of no consequence, a fribble, a tiny obstacle to be stepped over with an easy stride. Were we tired? Were we dirty? Were some of us burned and cranky? No matter! We were committed. And so the next day, the first quiet day we'd had in this village in months, that same sooty cadre stood in the warm ashes high above the entry steps and tried again. We knew—as we know right now that our enemies are manifold and voracious and generally rude and persistent—and we wanted to be ready.

But tell me this: where does one find out how soon before

an enemy attack to put the oil on to boil? Does anyone know? Let me assure you it is not in any book! We were writing the book!

We were vigilant. We squinted at the horizon all day long. And when we first saw the dust in the foothills we refired our cauldron using wood which had been elevated through the night in woven baskets. Even speaking about it here today, I can feel the excitement stirring in my heart. The orange flames licked the sides of the brass container hungrily as if in concert with our own desperate desire for security and revenge. In the distance I could see the phalanx of Visigoths marching toward us like a warship through a sea of dust, and in my soul I pitied them and the end toward which they so steadfastly hastened. They seemed the very incarnation of mistake, their dreams of a day abusing our friends and families and of petty arsony and lewd public behavior about to be extinguished in one gorgeous wash of searing oil! I was beside myself.

It is important to know now that everyone on the roof that day exhibited orderly and methodical behavior. There was professional conduct of the first magnitude. There was no wild screaming or cursing or even the kind of sarcastic chuckling which you might expect in those about to enjoy a well-deserved and long delayed victory. The problems of the day were not attributable to inappropriate deportment. My staff was good. It was when the Visigoths had approached close enough that we could see their cruel eyes and we could read the savage and misspelled tattoos that I realized our error. At that time I put my hand on the smooth side of our beautiful cauldron and found it only vaguely warm. Lukewarm. Tepid.

We had not known then what we now know. *We need to put the oil on sooner.*

It was my decision and my decision alone to do what we did, and that was to pour the warm oil on our enemies as they milled about the front gates, hammering at it with their truncheons.

Now this is where my report diverges from so many of the popular accounts. We have heard it said that the warm oil served as a stimulant to the attack that followed, the attack I alluded to earlier in which the criminal activity seemed even more animated than usual in the minds of some of our townspeople. Let me say first: I was an eye-witness. I gave the order to pour the oil and I witnessed its descent. I am happy and proud to report that the oil hit its target with an accuracy and completeness I could have only dreamed of. We got them all. There was oil everywhere. We soaked them, we coated them, we covered them in a lustrous layer of oil. Unfortunately, as everyone knows, it was only warm. Their immediate reaction was also what I had hoped for: surprise and panic. This, however, lasted about one second. Then several of them looked up into my face and began waving their fists in what I could only take as a tribute. And then, yes, they did become quite agitated anew, recommencing their assault on the weary planks of our patchwork gates. Some have said that they were on the verge of abandoning their attack before the oil was cast upon them, which I assure you is not true.

As to the attack that followed. It was no different in magnitude or intensity than any of the dozens we suffer every year. It may have seemed more odd or extreme since the perpetrators were greasy and thereby more offensive, and they did take every stick of furniture left in the village including the pews from the church, every chair in the great hall, and four milking stools, the last four, from the dairy.

But I for one am simply tired of hearing about the slippery stain on the village steps. Yes, there is a bit of a mess and yes some of it seems to be permanent. My team removed what they could with salt and talc all this week. All I'll say now is watch your step as you come and go; in my mind it's a small inconvenience to pay for a perfect weapon system.

So, we've had our trial run. We gathered a lot of data. And you all know we'll be ready next time. We are going to get to do what we wanted to do. We will vex and repel our enemies with boiling oil. In the meantime who needs furniture! We have a project! We need the determination not to lose the dream and we need a lot of firewood. They will come again. You know it and I know it, and let's simply commit ourselves to making sure that the oil, when it falls, is very hot.

Two Shorts

Robin Hemley

~

The Employee's Head

The sign outside the Burger Boy Food-A-Rama said "Male Help Wanted," so I told the manager I was male. He smiled and said he'd give me a dollar for one hour a day after school. Then he fixed me up with a little BBF uniform.

He led me downstairs to Eric, who supervised me packing coleslaw into paper cups. Eric, who sliced meat, showed me his hand missing three fingers.

"The special that day was knuckle sandwich," he said, clearing his throat, and sending a big honker into the ground beef. "Screw them child labor laws, right Sport?"

Eric scared me, so I worked quickly. When I finished two trays of slaw, he handed me a toilet brush. "Go scour out the employee's head."

All these body parts. Knuckle sandwiches, phlegmy beef. Now he wanted me to scour somebody's head.

Eric put his mangled hand, greasy with beef, under my nose. I screamed and wet my pants. It suddenly struck me that maybe that employee's head was mine.

In the bathroom, I dried myself. The walls were covered with writing about heads people wanted to give, but I didn't find the employee's head, which I imagined sat somewhere repeating, "May I take your order?" I wondered how many employees had lost body parts on the job. I wondered what I might lose and what I could live without. I saw myself older, headless and hollow inside, while upstairs happy customers gorged.

An Intruder

The Queen's first thought upon awakening is, "Oh my, not again, and this one's coal black." Her thoughts are not of her own safety. They never are. Her thoughts always settle on the larger ramifications. Like the crows in front of the palace, the Queen's thoughts are ponderous and never take flight. They pace mutely and passively in front of their station.

"I didn't want to wake you," the man says from the foot of the bed.

The man at the foot of her bed has his hair in that extravagant West Indian style. The Prince Consort said once he quite liked that fashion, and might try it out himself if not for the paucity of his hair, but he'd been smashed when he said that.

The man looks nearly fifty, a slender fellow with a beaked nose and a long drawn face. "Young man," she addresses him. Everyone is young to her. You cannot count her age in mortal years. "I am your queen and you are in my bed chambers."

The man stands and bumps his head on the canopy. "I mean no disrespect. I've come here for what belongs to me."

The Queen nods her head as the man speaks each word. His speech is musical. Her hat tips off her head and she straightens it. This is how she always sleeps, fully clothed in a modest dress, her purse by her side, a plain hat on her head. She keeps her body straight when she sleeps. She didn't always sleep this way, but before she did, she frequently had nightmares. Sometimes she'd be walking past the crows in front of the palace, dressed only in a white nightgown, jeered by thousands. Other times, she simply saw herself growing. Or she imagined herself a coin, the face worn thin by the hands and pockets of her people. She enjoys dreams as little as she enjoys free-flying thought. Now that she sleeps like the Queen, fully clothed, her dreams no longer bother her.

"It's entirely possible you're looking for something that's rightfully yours," she says. Best not to alarm him. "But I doubt anything here belongs to you, except in the most general sense. I assume you're a subject of the realm?"

"Yes, Mom, more citizen than you can reckon. I'm your own son, your flesh and blood."

There's not the slightest chance, the most remote possibility that what this man says is true . . . Well, yes, maybe a slight chance. The gardener, of course. Long before she was Queen.

"I just want what's rightfully mine, a mother's love."

She stares at him.

"That's quite impossible," she says.

"I could ask for more, you know. I'm older than the Crown Prince by five years."

These Jamaicans! Next thing you know, her Paki son will want to be acknowledged. And maybe her son from New Jersey. And her daughter from The Gambia. Oh, she was a wild one when she was young, back when the press was more respectful and knew how to keep a secret.

"Are you married?" she asks, hoping to change the subject, but also out of true concern.

"Very happily, Mom," he says, smiling broadly at her. "To the most lovely woman in the world. And I have many children. You'd be proud of them. You can smell the royalty in them. You want to see their pictures?"

She surprises herself by sitting up in bed and saying, "Why yes, I think I do." After all, he is her son, and she's happy that at least one of her line has not botched his marriage. One by one, her son shows her the photos in his wallet. His wallet bulges with photos. She studies each picture closely, looking for the resemblances. She wishes she was young again. She wishes she'd set a better example.

Of course, acknowledgment is out of the question. It would only be an embarrassment and a burden for her, the nation, and even her Jamaican son and his family. Tonight, she will give him a mother's attention, a mother's ear, a mother's love. But in the morning he will have to go. She will ring for the guards and they will take the man away. But what if they don't respond? Lately, they've been slowing down, have become unreliable.

She lies back, just as her son is saying, "And this is little Betsy..."

She closes her eyes and says, "You were a mistake, weren't you? One of many. I should have known you'd find your way here sooner or later."

"All I'm asking for is what's rightfully mine," he says, "just a bit of your time, a little company." And then he prattles on with his photos. "And this is little Henry. And this is Ethelbert, my oldest, and Johnny. He's a troublemaker." How many children can one man have? "And this is little Mary. Mom! Mom! Don't you want to see young Richard, my favorite...?"

DRUG ADDICT

Harold Jaffe

~

You know what's a real up?

Enemas?

No, not enemas. Shopping malls.

Are they a *real* up or a so-so up?

That depends on whether it's a city or suburban mall. Whether it's open-air or enclosed. Whether it's a theme mall or just regular. How much money you got to spend...

What flavor muzak they pipe in?

Right. That too.

I know a better up than shopping malls. Fast freeway driving.

No shit. I get a hard-on when I pull on the freeway and accelerate real fast to seventy.

Uh-huh. How's about we shave our heads, change into camo, kick some queer boy's ass, *then* pull on the freeway and accelerate real fast to seventy?

Now you're cookin'.

[Pause]

You know what's a real down?

Doing your taxes. Reading the papers. Watching TV. Going to

work. Getting anything repaired. Seeing the doctor. Breathing the air. Making love . . .

What?

I thought I could slip that one by you. Actually, with the right condom and the right gal, making love, fucking, balling, what have you, is still A-OK.

When you say "right gal" I don't guess you're talkin' 'bout feminists?

'Bout what?

Feminists. Like . . . what's her name? Thatcher. From over there in England?

Thatcher? With the hair?

Right.

No, I wasn't talking 'bout her.

[Pause]

Well, what you want to do?

When do you mean? Now?

Sure.

Do you have your Marlboro pack-sized calculator on you?

Damn right.

Well let's count. Keeps you sharp.

Okay. How many homeless did we see?

Since we started walking, you mean? I'd guess about 39. Are we counting bag-ladies? Or is that a separate category?

No, they count. Bag-ladies.

Then make it 49.

I'll round it off to 50. How many folks did we see that averted their eyes?

That didn't care to look at us, you mean? Hmm. I'd say about 17.

How many houses we pass have panels out front that say they're electronically protected against trespassers?

Shoot. That'd be 'bout every house we seen. Maybe 39.

Okay, call it 40 houses electronically protected against tres-passers. That'd make about 130 folks in those houses. Now how many those folks do you estimate are watching a sitcom or sports or so-called news on their color TV?

You mean right now? I'd say every damn one.

Right. Of those 130 watching sitcoms, sports or so-called news on their color TV, let's say 80 are spouses of varying ages. Which makes 40 pairs, okay? Now how many of those 40 pairs made love at least once this last month in some position that wasn't the missionary?

Like what do you mean?

Side by side. Gal on top. Horsey . . .

Hell. I'd say 2 out of 40 did it at least once last month in some position that wasn't the missionary. Check that. Make it 1 out of 40.

1 pair out of 40. Hang on just a minute. Gives us a grand total of 277.

277 what?

What the hell difference does it make?

Are you sure of those numbers?

You kidding? Take a look at this calculator. What does it say?

Where? There? It says General Electric.

American technology, partner. We're back in the fray, and you know what? We gonna drive them Japs back to their drawing boards.

Which reminds me. What did the Japanese bride get on her wedding night that was long and hard?

Well, it sure as hell wasn't . . .

A new name.

Right. Those long damn names full of vowels.

[Long pause]

Who won the Rams game?

The Bears. Won by a safety. 19–17.

[Pause]

I'm sure glad we got Gretzky.

Yeah.

They say he's lost a step.

Naw. He's only, what? 32?

Right. But with a whole lotta miles on his wheels.

[Pause]

Magic Johnson's the same age.

That's right.

Shoot. Hard to believe, ain't it? I remember when he was a fresh-faced kid out of Michigan State.

Talk about miles. Magic has some kind of big miles on his pins, don't he?

You got that right.

[Pause]

Hey, the salaries they get, they can't complain.

Sheeit. Magic makes more in a single game than most working stiffs make in a year.

And working ain't no game.

Ha! You got that right.

[Pause]

You know something. I felt a drop. I think it's gonna rain.

Real rain or acid rain?

Good question. Let's head back, huh?

You feel like gettin' high?

Yeah.

I got me a fifth of Jack Daniels and a carton of Marlboros, hard pack. Back at the apartment.

Your apartment?

Yeah. You interested?

You got today's *Wall Street Journal?*

Yeah, I do. You interested?

Your color TV ain't on the fritz, is it?

Hell no.

You got your Colt Delta Elite 10mm cleaned/oiled/ready to fire?

Damn right. What you have in mind? Draping the *Wall Street Journal* over the color TV and firing at it from between our legs?

Sounds good. Why don't we suck on your Jack for a little and see what comes up.

From BEAM ME UP, SCOTTY
Michael Guinzburg

~

"My name is Ed, and I'm a stupid stinking drug addict and alcoholic."

"Hi, Ed!" chorused the joyous recovering boozers and addicts.

"I got out of detox today. My fucking wife has taken off. I thought if I got clean, things would get better. But I feel like fried dogshit on a bun. I want to drink or do some dope or smoke some crack so bad I can taste it. The bitch stole my kids. I'd like to kill her."

"Thanks for sharing that, Ed," chirped Miss Happy-face with a shit-eating grin. "It gets better. Give time time. Keep it simple, stupid. Easy does it. One day at a time. Get a sponsor, someone you can talk with about those feelings. Don't stuff them. Keep coming back. The HDA Center has meetings all day and night.

About your wife? Don't beat yourself up about it. Listen to learn and learn to listen."

I listened. People spilling their guts: pain, hope, doubt, joy, dreams, demons—psychotherapy for the psychotic masses. When the hour was up we all linked hands and prayed. The AC/DC currents of hope and despair flowed through me.

Between meetings the anonymous boozers and junkies welcomed me. "Thanks for sharing." "You're in the right place." "Take my phone number." "Keep coming back." "Don't stuff those feelings." "Have some coffee." Fuckups of all ages, all races, all manner of dress and demeanor, thanked me for my honesty and told me, "Don't beat yourself up about it." "Give time time." "Hang in there." I was overwhelmed. Who the fuck was I? Just some piece of shit scraped off the street. Warm hands pressed mine. An old guy smiled. A beautiful brunette, straight from a girlie magazine, crushed me to her bountiful breast, whispered, "I know how you feel." It had been ages since I felt so safe, so warm, so at home. So I stayed, through the afternoon and long into the night, soaking up meetings like a Miami codger takes the sun, studying the faces, downing coffee, smiling at strangers.

"My name is Myron," said the speaker leading the last meeting of the night, a middle-aged man in a tasteful tweed skirt and a white silk blouse, "and I'm a grateful recovering alcoholic."

"Hi, Myron!" we chimed.

"Alcohol is one of the hardest drugs of all, and I let it beat me up for twenty-five years. I've always been a woman inside. I've known that since I was two. I thought like a woman, felt like a woman, had a woman's intuition and emotions, but I lived in a man's body. Now I take hormones and go to therapy to prepare myself for the eventual operation. When I get this silly old troublemaker between my legs chopped off, then I'll be happy and proud to call myself Myra. Of course it will cost a bundle, so I'm saving up, one day at a time."

Yes, I thought, yes! This is beautiful. A man who feels like a woman and has the balls to do something about it! What a glorious program! It allows people to be who they really are. Yes! And no one is laughing. Not that rough-looking fuck over there with the black hair and the permanent five o'clock shadow who looks like he wouldn't know a feeling if it kicked him in the crackers—he's nodding right along. And those bikers in the front row, they're down with Myron too. And that sweet thang who hugged me earlier—she's crying! And that filthy red-haired guy in the corner who was muttering all through the last meeting— he's quiet now, listening. The old lady; the bald-headed guy with the briefcase; the Native American with his cowboy hat and shit- kicker boots; the yuppie couple over there with the matching corduroys and button-down shirts; the black woman with the dreadlocks; the—

"Growing up as Myron was no fun. It felt all wrong. Other boys played ball; I played house. I was different. Little girls teased me. My father beat me. I became withdrawn. I played with my sister's dolls and dressed in my mother's clothes. When I was twelve I was raped. I felt worthless, horrible. That night I discovered al- cohol, and it helped the pain. From the beginning I drank to get drunk. I loved the warm glow, the feeling of safety. When I was loaded it was okay to be Myra. With others I had to wear a mask.

"At nineteen I got married. I functioned as a man physically, and yeah, I enjoyed it; but the booze was always there. I was drunk all the time. Had three kids, my own dress shop; but trouble was nipping at my heels. One night my wife came to the shop and found me passed out, wearing a lovely little yellow number from the spring line. Divorce, humiliation: the works. I drank more and more, went over that invisible line and kept on falling deeper and deeper into the abyss. I was so numb I didn't even know I was in pain. My real feelings were stuffed so deep and I was in such denial that if you told me I had a problem I'd laugh in your face. For years I lived on the Bowery in a so-called room. A cage with walls. I drank wine and vodka. Gave blowjobs for cash. Finally I couldn't even do that without throwing up, so I ended up on the street, living in a cardboard box. Couldn't afford vodka or wine, so I drank gasoline. That's right, gas. High-octane, regular, unleaded—I cherished them all. I hung around the pumps and begged. I mixed my gas with ginger ale, called my cardboard box the Gas Chamber. Y'see, I was raised Jewish and I thought that was funny. Ha ha ha. That box was my personal Auschwitz, my prison, my coffin, where I was slowly fucking killing myself. Nu- merous times the cops picked me up, freezing or puking or bleed- ing or comatose, and they'd drag me fighting and screaming and complaining to countless emergency rooms to have my stomach pumped out. And every time, I figured it was the ginger ale. I was allergic to ginger ale. Never once did this recovering gasoholic conceive that the problem might just be the gas. Christ. My cousin

Bernie was the only member of my family who kept in touch. He'd come by my box and beg me to get help. 'Myron, Myron, what's a nice Jewish boy from the Bronx doing this for? To shame your parents?' He'd give me twenty bucks. I'd buy some panty hose, some lipstick, some vodka, and have plenty left over to keep my motor running for a week. . . ."

The feeling of warmth in the room was like an electric blanket. Faces all happy and rapt with attention—even sad-eyed mumblers were grooving to Myron's solo—heads nodding up and down with identification like those little plastic dogs in the rear windows of cars. It didn't take a rocket scientist to figure out that Myron's story was touching them all in some special way. The details were unique, but the emotions that drove him to the Gas Chamber were universal. Feeling different—unloved, rejected, violated, terrorized, hopeless, helpless, despondent—and then the denial that a problem existed. That was a syndrome I knew only too well. The denial. When Michelle badgered me to get help and I'd tell her to get out of my face, that the problem was hers; when I got booted from the newspaper for one too many screw-ups; when I worked as a messenger and crashed the bike into a parked car or some faceless business suit crossing the street and I blamed it on traffic instead of the Lenny Bias-sized hit of crack I'd just sucked down; when I stole the kids' lunch money for a single vial of rock, then came back later that day and pawned their Nintendo box; when I ended up employed as a mopboy in a Times Square peepshow, swabbing semen from the floor for minimum wage, blaming society for my situation—when I did all that and still got sky-high, still kept stoking my head with cokedopeboozeweed and refused to admit that I was anything but normal, that was the hell of compulsion, the horror of obsession: that was denial. I'd become a dumb junkie, a blackout drinker, a loser.

I'd been on a mission, a long mission, and when I came to, the boys were sobbing and Michelle was yelling. I had no idea what I'd done, so I sat there and smoked a fat joint laced with crack and heroin, guzzled a warm flat beer, tried to block the awful noise of their lamentations out of my ears and piece together the preceding days. I couldn't remember. I was blank and filled with fear. As the substances played pinball in my brain, thrilling and chilling, zipping and zapping, the boys' moans got louder, more horrible, pounding at my weary brain like Muhammad Ali jabs and Joe Frazier hooks. Michelle's voice speared my head like a red-hot knitting needle inserted from ear to ear. I looked into their eyes and saw hate, misery, and fear. My heart ached. God help me, what had I done?

"My name is Ed," I said when Myron opened the meeting up to the floor, "and I'm a stupid stinking drug addict and alcoholic."

"Hi, Ed!"

"My wife is gone. She was right to leave. I was a mess. On the pipe 24/7. A dope-sniffing stemsucking crackerjack. The lowest form of life on the planet. I don't blame her for splitting. But I'm clean and sober now. Why can't it be a Hollywood ending? I don't understand. I miss my boys. I feel like taking some motherfucker by the throat and squeezing till his eyes pop right the fuck out."

"Listen, Ed." Myron spoke soothingly, like a mother, like a father, like a mother and father wrapped up in one. "Don't beat yourself up about it. You weren't in your right mind when you did all those things. The disease transformed you. You weren't responsible for your actions. Everyone in this room has done shit high we're not proud of." Heads bobbed. "I myself once siphoned gas from an ambulance on call. I stood there fifty feet away, gassing up on a Mobil martini, watching the paramedics wheel some poor bleeding fish out." He coughed nervously. "Ed, they couldn't start the vehicle. The guy maybe died. I don't know. I took off. A sober night doesn't go by I don't think about that man, pray for him, beg God's forgiveness. Look, by working The Program we learn to live with the past. Your wife is angry. With good reason. My own family, all except Cousin Bernie, took twenty-five years to forgive me; six of those years I was clean. You gotta give time time. Last month my youngest son was married, and I got invited. An Orthodox Jewish wedding, and they let me sit with the women. I wore a secondhand Halston and no one batted an eyelash. They forgave me, and now they accept me, for who I am, for what I was. You've been wandering in the woods for so long, you expect to find your way out in an instant? Give time time, Ed. Easy does it. Keep coming back. Hang in there. Take the toilet paper out of your ears and listen."

I listened. I'd been listening for hours. Rich people, poor people ("from Park Avenue to park benches," "from Yale to jail"), happy people, sad people ("from pink cloud to black shroud"). People who had conquered fear ("F-E-A-R, the active alcoholic's prime directive: Fuck Everything And Run"). People who wanted to kill, wanted to commit suicide, wanted to earn fortunes, or were content with nothing. People who lived with AIDS and wanted to die with dignity. People who loved, people whose hearts were breaking, who were jealous, angry, elated, deflated, constipated. Here was the human condition, every emotion and situation imaginable, and people were exulting in it. Living it sober. Sober! A word I once considered the filthiest in the English language. People living sober, people dying sober. It was beautiful, it was heartwarming, it was amazing—it was time for a drink.

Just one whiskey, I thought, as I filed with the penitents out of the church basement into the cold. Just one whiskey.

I felt a tap on the shoulder. Myron.

"It's the first one that gets you drunk."

"Mind your own business," I spat back. "The first will take the edge off. The sixth might get me drunk."

"Calm down, honey. Listen to me. You take that first drink you'll be back sucking a crackstem in no time. If you don't take the first drink you can't get loaded."

"Maybe I want to get loaded. It's not every day your wife kidnaps your kids and bolts. I deserve to get shit-faced. I want it. I need it."

"I don't think so." He circled my shoulders with his strong arm. "Why did you come to HDA?"

"Beats me."

"Drugs beat you. Booze beat you. Used you as a doormat. Walked all over you and wiped streetshit onto your soul. Are you sick and tired of getting beat? Sick and tired of being sick and tired? You want to gain your family's respect? Maybe win them back?"

I nodded through the tears.

"Then come for coffee."

Eight cups of coffee later I had to piss like a racehorse. Myron sure could rap. Made a used car salesman seem downright shy, he was so enthusiastic about The Program. Peppering me with slogans and philosophy, he related the history of Hard Drugs Anonymous, its principles and practices, from the first historic meeting in Paynesville, Ohio, back in '34, between Big Jim Williams, the pro wrestler, and Farmer Rob Jones, a simple country boy who'd found he just couldn't get the crop in while zooted on morphine. The two alcoholic addicts had picked up their habits and their friendship in the hospital after being wounded in WWI, and almost two decades of shooting dope later (Farmer Rob was fond of claiming he was "the only fella in the Midwest who could find a needle in a haystack"), they desperately wanted to get clean. They'd tried every known remedy for addiction, taken all the cures, and still couldn't kick; but there, in that humble Ohio barn, midst a symphony of clucking chickens and oinking pigs, they realized that together—"We can do what I cannot"—through mutual support, one addict helping another, they could scrape the massive monkey off their backs and keep it away forever by just plain talking it to death.

*   *   *

His handshake was firm, his smile white. His little breasts budded against the white silk blouse. And you know, maybe if I had listened a little better, taken the toilet paper out of my ears and really listened, if I hadn't been so impressed with what a good-looking woman Myron was for a man his age, maybe if I had drunk less coffee or just simply used the restaurant's bathroom, or ducked around the corner into a bar and banged back a bunch of boilermakers, then maybe, just maybe, the next few days might have broken differently.

"Sure, Myron. And thanks," I said, trying to figure out his bra size.

EXCERPTS FROM NOVELS

and

OTHER LONGER WORKS

from OPERATION SHYLOCK

Philip Roth

～

I AM PIPIK

George's was one of half a dozen stone houses separated by large patches of garden and clustered loosely around a picturesque old olive grove that stretched down to a small ravine—originally, during Anna's early childhood, this had been a family compound full of brothers and cousins but most of them had emigrated by now. There was a biting chill in the air as it was getting to be dusk, and inside the house, in a tiny fireplace at the end of the narrow living room, a few sticks of wood were burning, a pretty sight but without effect against the chill pervasive dankness that went right to one's bones. The place was cheerily fixed up, however, with bright textiles splashed about on the chairs and the sofa and several rugs with modernistic geometric designs scattered across the uneven stone floor. To my surprise I didn't see books anywhere—maybe George felt his books were more secure at his university office—though there were a lot of Arabic magazines and newspapers strewn atop a table beside the sofa. Anna and Michael wore heavy sweaters as we sat close to the fire drinking our hot tea, and I warmed my hands on the cup, thinking, This above-ground cellar, after Boston. The cold smell of a dungeon on top of everything else. There was also the smell of a kerosene heater burning—one that might not have been in the best state of repair—but it seemed to be off in another room. This room opened through multi-paned French doors onto the garden, and a four-bladed fan hung by a very long stem from an arched ceiling that must have been fifteen feet high, and though I could see how the place might have its charm once the weather grew warm, right now this wasn't a home to inspire a mood of snug relaxation.

Anna was a tiny, almost weightless woman whose anatomy's whole purpose seemed to be to furnish the housing for her astonishing eyes. There wasn't much else to her. There were the eyes, intense and globular, eyes to see with in the dark, set like a lemur's in a triangular face not very much larger than a man's fist, and then there was the tent of the sweater enshrouding the anorexic rest of her and, peeping out at the bottom, two feet in baby's running shoes. I would have figured as a mate for the George I'd known a nocturnal creature fuller and furrier than Anna, but perhaps when they'd met and married in Boston some two decades back there'd been more in her of the sprightly gamine than of this preyed-upon animal who lives by night—if you can call it living—and during the day is gone.

Michael was already a head taller than his father, an excruciatingly skinny, delicate brunette with marbleized skin, a prettyish boy whose shyness (or maybe just exasperation) rendered him mute and immobile. His father was explaining that Diasporism was the first original idea that he had heard from a Jew in forty years, the first that promised a solution based on honest historical and moral foundations, the first that acknowledged that the only just way to partition Palestine was by transferring not the population that was indigenous to the region but the population to whom this region had been, from the start, foreign and inimical . . . and all the while Michael's eyes remained rigidly fixed on some invisible dot that compelled his entire attention and that was situated in the air about a foot above my knee. Nor did Anna appear to take much hope from the fact that Jewry's leading Diasporist was visiting her home for tea. Only George, I thought, is so far gone, only he is so crazily desperate . . . unless it's all an act.

Of course George understood that such a proposal would be received with nothing but scorn by the Zionists, whose every sacrosanct precept Diasporism exposed as fraudulent; and he went on to explain that even among Palestinians, who should be my ardent advocates, there would be those, like Kamil, lacking the imagination to grasp its political potential, who would stupidly misconstrue Diasporism as an exercise in Jewish nostalgia—

"So that was his take," I said, daring to interrupt the unbridled talker who, it occurred to me, perhaps with his voice alone had reduced his wife to little more than those eyes and battered his son into silence. "A nostalgic Jew, dreaming Broadway dreams about a musical-comedy shtetl."

"Yes. Kamil said to me, 'One Woody Allen is enough.' "

"Did he? In the courtroom? Why Woody Allen?"

"Woody Allen wrote something in *The New York Times,*" George said. "An op-ed article. Ask Anna. Ask Michael. They read it and couldn't believe their eyes. It was reprinted here. It ranks as Woody Allen's best joke yet. Philip, the guy isn't a shlimazl just in the movies. Woody Allen believes that Jews aren't capable of violence. Woody Allen doesn't believe that he is reading the papers correctly—he just can't believe that Jews break bones. Tell us another one, Woody. The first bone they break in defense— to put it charitably; the second in winning; the third gives them pleasure; and the fourth is already a reflex. Kamil hasn't patience for this idiot, and he figured you for another. But it doesn't matter in Tunis what Kamil thinks in Ramallah about Philip Roth. It hardly matters any longer in Ramallah what Kamil thinks about anything."

"Tunis?"

"I assure you that Arafat can differentiate between Woody Allen and Philip Roth."

This was surely the strangest sentence I had ever heard spoken in my life. I decided to top it. If this is the way George wants to play it, then this is the way we shall go. I am not writing this thing. They are. I don't even exist.

"Any meeting with Arafat," I heard myself telling him, "must be completely secret. For obvious reasons. But I *will* meet with him, any place and any time, Tunis or anywhere, and tomorrow is none too soon. It might be communicated to Arafat that through the good offices of Lech Walesa it's likely that I'll be meeting secretly at the Vatican with the Pope, probably next month. Walesa is already committed to my cause, as you know. He maintains that the Pope will find in Diasporism not only a means of resolving the Arab-Israeli conflict but an instrument for the moral rehabilitation and spiritual reawakening of all of Europe. I am myself not as sanguine as he is about the boldness of this pope. It's all well and good for His Holiness to be pro-Palestinian and to berate the Jews for appropriating property to which they have no legal right. It's something else again to espouse the corollary of this position and to invite a million-plus Jews to consider themselves at home in the heart of Western Christendom. Yes, it would be something if the Pope were to call upon Europe publicly and openly to invite its Jews to return from their exile in Israel, and for him to mean it; if he were to call on Europe to confess to its complicity in their uprooting and destruction; if he were to call on Europe to purge itself of a thousand years of anti-Semitism and to make room in its midst for a vital Jewish presence to multiply and flourish there and, in anticipation of the third millennium of Christianity, to declare by proclamation in all its parliaments the right of the Jewish uprooted to resettle in their European home-land and to live as Jews there, free, secure, and welcome. That would be simply wonderful. But I have my doubts. Walesa's Polish pope may even prefer Europe as Hitler passed it on to his Eu-ropean heirs—His Holiness may not really care to undo Hitler's little miracle. But Arafat is another matter. Arafat—" On I went, usurping the identity of the usurper who had usurped mine, heedless of truth, liberated from all doubt, assured of the indis-putable rightness of my cause—seer, savior, very likely the Jews' Messiah.

So this is how it's done, I thought. This is how they do it. You just say everything.

No, I didn't stop for a very long time. On and on and on, obeying an impulse I did nothing to quash, ostentatiously free of uncer-tainty and without a trace of conscience to rein in my raving. I was telling them about the meeting of the World Diasporist Con-gress to take place in December, fittingly enough in Basel, the site of the first World Zionist Congress just ninety years ago. At that first Zionist Congress there had been only a couple of hundred delegates—*my* goal was to have twice that many, Jewish dele-gations from every European country where the Israeli Ashkenazis would soon resume the European Jewish life that Hitler had all but extinguished. Walesa, I told them, had already agreed to ap-pear as keynote speaker or to send his wife in his behalf if he concluded that he could not safely leave Poland. I was talking about the Armenians, suddenly, about whom I knew nothing. "Did the Armenians suffer because they were in a Diaspora? No, because they were *at home* and the Turks moved in and massacred them *there.*" I heard myself next praising the greatest Diasporist of all, the father of the new Diasporist movement, Irving Berlin. "People ask where I got the idea. Well, I got it listening to the radio. The radio was playing 'Easter Parade' and I thought, But this is Jewish genius on a par with the Ten Commandments. God gave Moses the Ten Commandments and then He gave to Irving Berlin 'Easter Parade' and 'White Christmas.' The two holidays that celebrate the divinity of Christ—the divinity that's the very heart of the Jewish rejection of Christianity—and what does Irving Berlin brilliantly do? He de-Christs them both! Easter he turns into a fashion show and Christmas into a holiday about snow. Gone is the gore and the murder of Christ—down with the crucifix and up with the bonnet! *He turns their religion into schlock.* But nicely! Nicely! So nicely the goyim don't even know what hit 'em. They love it. *Everybody* loves it. The Jews especially. Jews loathe Jesus. People always tell me Jesus is Jewish. I never believe them. It's like when people used to tell me Cary Grant was Jewish. Bull*shit.* Jews don't want to *hear* about Jesus. And can you blame them? So—Bing Crosby replaces Jesus as the beloved Son of God, and the Jews, the *Jews,* go around whistling about Easter! And is that so disgraceful a means of defusing the enmity of centuries? Is anyone really dishonored by this? If schlockified Christianity is Christianity cleansed of Jew hatred, then three cheers for schlock. If supplanting Jesus Christ with snow can enable my people to cozy up to Christmas, then let it snow, let it snow, let it snow! Do you see my point?" I took more pride, I told them, in "Easter Parade" then in the victory of the Six Day War, found more security in "White Christmas" than in the Israeli nuclear reactor. I told them that if the Israelis ever reached a point where they believed their survival depended not merely on breaking hands but on dropping a nuclear bomb, that would be the end of Judaism, even if the state of Israel should survive. "Jews as Jews will simply disappear. A generation after Jews use nuclear weapons to save themselves from their enemies, there will no longer be people to identify themselves as Jews. The Israelis will have saved their state by destroying their people. They will never survive morally after that; and if they don't, why survive as Jews at all? They barely have the wherewithal to survive morally now. To put all these Jews in this tiny place, surrounded on all sides by tremendous hostility—how *can* you survive morally? Better to be marginal neurotics, anxious assimilationists, and everything else that the Zionists despise, better to *lose* the state than to lose your moral being by unleashing a nuclear war. Better Irving Berlin than Ariel Sharon. Better Irving Berlin than the Wailing Wall. Better Irving Berlin than Holy Jerusalem! What does owning *Jerusalem,* of all places, have to do with being Jews in 1988? Jerusalem is by now the *worst* thing that could possibly have happened to us. *Last* year in Jerusalem! Next year in Warsaw! Next year in Bucharest! Next year in Vilna and Cracow! Look, I know people call Diasporism a revolutionary idea, but it's *not* a revolution that I'm proposing, it's a *retroversion,* a turning back, the very thing Zionism itself once was. You go back to the crossing point and cross back *the other way.* Zionism went back too far, that's what went wrong with Zionism. Zionism went back to the crossing point of the dispersion—Diasporism goes back to the crossing point of *Zionism.*"

My sympathies were entirely with George's wife. I didn't know which was more insufferable to her, the fervor with which I presented my Diasporist blah-blah or the thoughtfulness with which George sat there taking it in. Her husband had finally stopped talking—only to listen to this! Either to warm herself or to contain herself she'd enwrapped herself in her own arms and, like a woman on the brink of keening, she began almost imperceptibly rocking and swaying to and fro. And the message in those eyes of hers couldn't have been plainer: I was more than even she could bear, she who had by now borne everything. *He suffers enough without you. Shut up. Go away. Disappear.*

All right, I'll address this woman's fears directly. Wouldn't Moishe Pipik? "Anna, I'd be skeptical too if I were you. I'd be thinking, just as you are, This writer is one of those writers with no grasp on reality. This is all the nonsensical fantasy of a man who understands nothing. This is not even literature, let alone politics, this is a fable and a fairy tale. You are thinking of the thousand reasons why Diasporism can only fail, and I am telling you that I know the thousand reasons, I know the *million* reasons. But I am also here to tell you, to tell George, to tell Kamil, to tell whoever here will listen that it cannot fail *because it must not fail,* because the absurdity is not Diasporism but its alternative: Destruction. What people once thought about Zionism you are now thinking about Diasporism: an impossible pipe dream. You are thinking that I am just one more victim of the madness here that is on both sides—that this mad, crazy, tragic predicament has engulfed my sanity too. I see how miserable I am making you by exciting expectations in George that you know to be utopian and beyond implementation—that George, in *his* heart of hearts, knows to be utopian. But let me show you both something I received just a few hours ago that may cause you to think otherwise. It was given to me by an elderly survivor of Auschwitz."

I removed from my jacket the envelope containing Smilesburger's check and handed it to Anna. "Given to me by someone as desperate as you are to bring this maddening conflict to a just and honorable and workable conclusion. His contribution to the Diasporist movement."

When Anna saw the check, she began to laugh very softly, as though this were a private joke intended especially for her amusement.

"Let me see," said George, but for the moment she would not relinquish it. Wearily he asked her, "Why do you laugh? I prefer that, mind you, to the tears, but why do you laugh like this?"

"From happiness. From joy. I'm laughing because it's all over. Tomorrow the Jews are going to line up at the airline office to get their one-way tickets for Berlin. Michael, look." And she drew the boy close to her to show him the check. "Now you will be able to live in wonderful Palestine for the rest of your life. The Jews are leaving. Mr. Roth is the anti-Moses leading them out of Israel. Here is the money for their airfare." But the pale, elongated, beautiful boy, without so much as glancing at the check in his mother's hand, clenched his teeth and pulled away violently. This did not stop Anna, however—the check was merely the pretext she needed to deliver *her* diatribe. "Now there can be a Palestinian flag flying from every building and everybody can stand up and salute it twenty times a day. Now we can have our own money, with Father Arafat's portrait on our very own bills. In our pockets we can jingle coins bearing the profile of Abu Nidal. I'm laughing," she said, "because Palestinian Paradise is at hand."

"Please," George said, "this is the royal road to the migraine." He motioned impatiently for her to hand him my check. Pipik's check.

"Another victim who can't forget," said Anna, meanwhile studying the face of the check with those globular eyes as though there at last she might find the clue to why fate had delivered her into this misery. "All these victims and their horrible scars. But, tell me," she asked, and as simply as a child asks why the grass is green, "how many victims can possibly stand on this tiny bit of soil?"

"But he *agrees* with you," her husband said. "That is why he is *here*."

"In America," she told me, "I thought I had married a man who had left all this victimization behind, a man of cultivation who knew what made life rich and full. I didn't think I had married another Kamil, who can't start being a human being until the occupation is over. These perpetual little brothers, claiming they can't live, they can't breathe, because somebody is casting a shadow over them! The moral childishness of these people! A man with George's brain, strangling on spurious issues of *loyalty!* Why aren't you loyal," she cried, wildly turning on George, "to your *intellect?* Why aren't you loyal to *literature?* People like you"—meaning me as well—"run for their *lives* from backwater provinces like this one. You ran, you were *right* to run, both of you, as far as you could from the provincialism and the egocentricity and the xenophobia and the lamentations, you were not poisoned by the sentimentality of these childish, stupid ethnic mythologies, you plunged into a big, new, free world with all your intellect and all your energy, truly free young men, devoted to art, books, reason, scholarship, to *seriousness*—"

"Yes, to everything noble and elevated. Look," said George, "you are merely describing two snobbish graduate students—and we were not so pure even then. You paint a ridiculously naive portrait that would have struck us as laughable even then."

"Well, all I mean," she answered contemptuously, "is that you couldn't possibly have been as idiotic as you are now."

"You just prefer the high-minded idiocy of universities to the low-minded idiocy of political struggle. No one says it isn't idiotic and stupid and perhaps even futile. But that is what it's like, you see, for a human being to live on this earth."

"No amount of money," she said, ignoring the condescension to address me again about my check, "will change a single thing. Stay here, *you'll* see. There is nothing in the future for these Jews and these Arabs but more tragedy, suffering, and blood. The hatred on both sides is too enormous, it envelops everything. There is no trust and there will not be for another thousand years. 'To live on this earth.' Living in Boston was living on this earth—" she angrily reminded George. "Or isn't it 'life' any longer when people have a big, bright apartment and quiet, intelligent neighbors and the simple civilized pleasure of a good job and raising children? Isn't it 'life' when you read books and listen to music and choose your friends because of their qualities and not because they share your roots? Roots! A concept for *cavemen* to live by! Is the survival of Palestinian culture, Palestinian people, Palestinian heritage, is that really a 'must' in the evolution of humanity? Is all that mythology a greater must than the survival of my son?"

"He's going back," George quietly replied.

"When? *When?*" She shook the check in George's face. "When Philip Roth collects a thousand more checks from crazy Jews and the airlift to Poland begins? When Philip Roth and the Pope sit down together in the Vatican and solve our problems for us? I will not sacrifice my son to any more fanatics and their megalomaniacal fantasies!"

"He will go back," George repeated sternly.

"Palestine is a lie! Zionism is a lie! Diasporism is a lie! The biggest lie yet! I will not sacrifice Michael to more lies!"

George phoned to downtown Ramallah for a taxi to come to his house to drive me to Jerusalem. The driver was a weathered-looking old man who seemed awfully sleepy given that it was only seven in the evening. I wondered aloud if this was the best George could do.

First George told him in Arabic where to take me, then, in English, he said, "He's used to the checkpoints, and the soldiers there are familiar with him. You'll get back all right."

"To me he looks a little the worse for wear."

"Don't worry," George said. He had wanted, in fact, to take me back himself, but in their bedroom, where Anna had gone to lie down in the dark, she had warned George that if he dared to go off in the evening to drive to Jerusalem and back, neither she nor Michael would be there when he returned, *if* he returned and didn't wind up beaten to death by the army or shot by vigilante Jews. "It's the migraine talking," George explained. "I don't want to make it worse."

"I'm afraid," I said. "I already have."

"Philip, we'll speak tomorrow. There are many things to discuss. I'll come in the morning. I want to take you somewhere. I want you to meet someone. You will be free in the morning?"

I had arranged a meeting with Aharon, I had somehow to get to see Apter, but I said, "For you, yes, of course. Say goodbye to Michael for me. And to Anna. . . ."

"He's in there holding her hand."

"Maybe this *is* all too much for him."

"It does begin to look that way." He closed his eyes and pressed his fingers to his forehead. "My *stupidity*," he moaned. "My fucking stupidity!"

At the door he embraced me. "Do you know what you're doing? Do you know what it's going to mean for you when the Mossad finds out you've met with Arafat?"

"Arrange the meeting, Zee."

"Oh, you're the best of them!" he said emotionally. "The very best!"

Bullshit artist, I thought, actor, liar, fake, but all I did was return the embrace with no less fervent duplicitousness than was being proffered.

To circumvent the Ramallah roadblocks, which still barred the entrance to the city center and access to the telltale bloodstained wall, the taxi driver took the circuitous route through the hills that George had used earlier to get home. There were no lights to be seen anywhere once we were headed away from the complex of stone houses at the edge of the ravine, no cars appeared on the hillside roads, and for a long time I kept my eyes fixed on the path cut by our headlamps and was too apprehensive to think of anything other than making it safely back to Jerusalem. Shouldn't he be driving with his brights on? Or were those feeble beams the brights? Going back with this old Arab, I thought, had to be a mistake but so was coming out with George, so, surely, was everything I had just said and done. This little leave I had taken not merely of my senses but of my life was inexplicable to me—it was as though reality had stopped and I had gotten off to do what I did and now I was being driven along these dark roads to where reality would be waiting for me to climb back on board and resume doing what I used to do. Had I even been present? Yes, yes, I most certainly had been, hidden no more than an inch or two behind that mild exercise in malicious cynicism. And yet I could swear that my carrying-on was completely innocent. The lengths I had gone to to mislead George hadn't seemed to me any more underhanded than if we'd been two children at play in a sandpile, no more insidious and about as mindless—for one of the few times in my life I couldn't really satirize myself for thinking too much. What had I yielded to? How did I get here? The rattling car, the sleepy driver, the sinister road . . . it was all the unforeseen outcome of the convergence of my falseness with his, dissimulation to match dissimulation . . . unless George hadn't been dissimulating, *unless the only act was mine!* But could he possibly

have taken that blather seriously about Irving Berlin? No, no—
here's what they're up to: They're thinking of the infantile idealism
and immeasurable egoism of all those writers who step momentarily onto the vast stage of history by shaking the hand of the
revolutionary leader in charge of the local egalitarian dictatorship;
they're thinking of how, aside from flattering a writer's vanity, it
lends his life a sense of significance that he just can't seem to get
finding the mot juste (if he even comes anywhere close to finding
it one out of five hundred times); they're thinking that nothing
does that egoism quite so much good as the illusion of submerging
it for three or four days in a great and selfless, highly visible cause;
they're thinking along the lines that Shmuel the lawyer had been
thinking when he observed that it might just be that I'd come
round to the courtroom in the clutches of "the world's pet victims" to beef up my credentials for the big prize. They're thinking
of Jesse Jackson, of Vanessa Redgrave, smiling in those news photographs arm in arm with their leader, and of how, in the public-
relations battle with the Jews, which well might decide more in
the end than all of the terrorism would, a photograph in *Time*
with a celebrity Jew might just be worth ten seconds of the
leader's precious time. Of course! They're setting me up for a
photo opportunity, and the looniness of my Diasporism is incon-
sequential—Jesse Jackson isn't exactly Gramsci either. Mitterrand
has Styron, Castro has Márquez, Ortega has Pinter, and Arafat is
about to have me.

No, a man's character isn't his fate; a man's fate is the joke that
his life plays on his character.

We hadn't yet reached the houses sporting their Eiffel Tower
TV antennas but we were out of the hills and on the main road
south to Jerusalem when the taxi driver spoke his first words to
me. In English, which he did not pronounce with much assurance,
he asked, "Are you a Zionist?"

"I'm an old friend of Mr. Ziad's," I replied. "We went to university together in America. He is an old friend."

"Are you a Zionist?"

And who is *this* guy? I thought. This time I ignored him and
continued looking out the window for some unmistakable sign,
like those TV aerials, that we were approaching the outskirts of
Jerusalem. Only what if we weren't anywhere near the road to
Jerusalem but on the road to somewhere else? Where were the
Israeli checkpoints? So far we hadn't passed one.

"Are you a Zionist?"

"Tell me," I replied as agreeably as I could, "what you mean by a Zionist and I'll tell you if I'm a Zionist."

"Are you a Zionist?" he repeated flatly.

"Look," I snapped back, thinking, Why don't you just say no? "what business is that of yours? Drive, please. This is the road to Jerusalem, is it not?"

"Are you a Zionist?"

The car was now perceptibly losing speed, the road was pitch-black, and beyond it I could see nothing.

"Why are you slowing down?"

"Bad car. Not work."

"It was working a few minutes ago."

"Are you a Zionist?"

We were barely rolling along now.

"Shift," I said, "shift the car down and give it some gas."

But here the car stopped.

"What's going on!"

He did not answer but got out of the car with a flashlight, which he began clicking on and off.

"Answer me! Why are you stopping out here like this? Where are we? Why are you flashing that light?"

I didn't know whether to stay in the car or to jump out of the car or whether either was going to make any difference to whatever was about to befall me. "Look," I shouted, leaping after him onto the road, "did you understand me? I am George Ziad's *friend!*"

But I couldn't find him. He was gone.

And this is what you get for fucking around in the middle of a civil insurrection! This is what you get for not listening to Claire and not turning everything over to lawyers! This is what you get for failing to comply with a sense of reality like everyone else's! *Easter Parade!* This is what you get for your bad jokes!

"Hey!" I shouted. "Hey, you! Where are you?"

When there was no reply, I opened the driver's door and felt around for the ignition: *he'd left the keys.* I got in and shut the door and, without hesitating, started the car, accelerating hard in neutral to prevent it from stalling. Then I pulled onto the road and tried to build up speed—there must be a checkpoint *somewhere!* But I hadn't driven fifty feet before the driver appeared in the dim beam of the headlights waving one hand for me to stop and clutching his trousers around his knees with the other. I had to swerve wildly to avoid hitting him, and then, instead of stopping to let him get back in and drive me the rest of the way, I gunned the motor and pumped the gas pedal but nothing was able to get the thing to pick up speed and, only seconds later, the motor conked out.

Back behind me in the road I saw the flashlight wavering in the air, and in a few minutes the old driver was standing, breathless, beside the car. I got out and handed him the keys and he got back in and, after two or three attempts, started the motor, and we began to move off, jerkily at first, but then everything seemed to be all right and we were driving along once again in what I decided to believe was the right direction.

"You should have said you had to shit. What was I supposed to think when you just stopped the car and disappeared?"

"Sick," he answered. "Stomach."

"You should have told me that. I misunderstood."

"Are you a Zionist?"

"Why do you keep *asking* that? If you mean Meir Kahane, then I am not a Zionist. If you mean Shimon Peres..." But why was I favoring with an answer this harmless old man with bowel problems, answering him seriously in a language he understood only barely... where the hell *was* my sense of reality? "Drive, please," I said. "Jerusalem. Just get me to Jerusalem. And without talking!"

But we hadn't got more than three or four miles closer to Jerusalem when he drove the car over to the shoulder, shut off the engine, took up the flashlight, and got out. This time I sat calmly in the back seat while he found himself some spot off the road to take another crap. I even began to laugh aloud at how I had exaggerated the menacing side of all this, when suddenly I was blinded by headlights barreling straight toward the taxi. Just inches from the front bumper, the other vehicle stopped, although I had braced for the impact and may even have begun to scream. Then there was noise everywhere, people shouting, a second vehicle, a third, there was a burst of light whitening everything, a second burst and I was being dragged out of the car and onto the road. I didn't know which language I was hearing. I could discern virtually nothing in all that incandescence, and I didn't know what to fear more, to have fallen into the violent hands of marauding Arabs or a violent band of Israeli settlers. "English!" I shouted, even as I tumbled along the surface of the highway. "I speak English!"

I was up and doubled over the car fender and then I was yanked and spun around and something knocked glancingly against the back of my skull and then I saw, hovering enormously overhead, a helicopter. I heard myself shouting, "Don't hit me, God damn it, I'm a Jew!" I'd realized that these were just the people I'd been looking for to get me safely back to my hotel.

I couldn't have counted all the soldiers pointing rifles at me even if I could have managed successfully to count—more soldiers even than there'd been in the Ramallah courtroom, helmeted and armed now, shouting instructions that I couldn't have heard, even if their language was one I understood, because of the noise of the helicopter.

"I hired this taxi in Ramallah!" I shouted back to them. "The driver stopped to shit!"

"Speak English!" someone shouted to me.

"THIS IS ENGLISH! HE STOPPED TO MOVE HIS BOWELS!"

"Yes? Him?"

"The driver! The Arab driver!" But where was he? Was I the only one they'd caught? *"There was a driver!"*

"Too late at night!"

"Is it? I didn't know."

"Shit?" a voice asked.

"Yes—we stopped for the driver to shit, he was only flashing the flashlight—"

"To shit!"

"Yes!"

Whoever had been asking the questions began to laugh. "That's all?" he shouted.

"As far as I know, *yes*. I could be wrong."

"You are!"

Just then one of them approached, a young, heavyset soldier, and he had a hand extended toward mine. In his other hand was a pistol. "Here." He gave me my wallet. "You dropped this."

"Thank you."

"This is quite a coincidence," he said politely in perfect English, "I just today, this afternoon, finished one of your books."

*   *   *

Thirty minutes later, I was safely at the door of my hotel, chauf-
feured there in an army jeep by Gal Metzler, the young lieutenant
who that very afternoon had read the whole of *The Ghost Writer.*
Gal was the twenty-two-year-old son of a successful Haifa man-
ufacturer who'd been in Auschwitz as a boy and with whom Gal
had a relationship, he told me, exactly like the one Nathan Zuck-
erman had with *his* father in my book. Side by side in the jeep's
front seats, we sat in the parking area in front of the hotel while
Gal talked to me about his father and himself, and while I was
thinking that the only son I'd seen yet in Greater Israel who was
not in conflict with his father was John Demjanjuk, Jr. There there
was only harmony.

Gal told me that in six months he would be finishing four years
as an army officer. Could he continue to maintain his sanity that
long? He didn't know. That's why he was devouring two and three
books a day—to remove himself every minute that he possibly
could from the madness of this life. At night, he said, every night,
he dreamed about leaving Israel after his time was up and going
to NYU to study film. Did I know the film school at NYU? He
mentioned the names of some teachers there. Did I know these
people?

"How long," I asked him, "will you stay in America?"

"I don't know. If Sharon comes to power . . . I don't know. Now
I go home on leave, and my mother tiptoes around me as though
I'm somebody just released from the hospital, as though I'm crippled or an invalid. I can stand only so much of it. Then I start
shouting at her. 'Look, you want to know if I personally beat
anyone? I didn't. But I had to do an awful lot of maneuvering to
avoid it!' She's glad and she cries and it makes her feel better. But
then my father starts shouting at the two of us. 'Breaking hands?
It happens in New York City every night. The victims are black.
Will you go running from America because they break hands in
America?' My father says, 'Take the British, put them here, face
them with what we are facing—they would act out of morality?
The Canadians would act out of morality? The French? A state
does not act out of moral ideology, a state acts out of self-interest.
A state acts to preserve its existence.' 'Then maybe I prefer to be
stateless,' I tell him. He laughs at me. 'We tried it,' he tells me. 'It
didn't work out.' As if I need his stupid sarcasm—as if half of me
doesn't believe exactly what *he* believes! Still I have to deal with

women and children who look me in the eyes and scream. They look at me ordering my troops to take away their brothers and their sons, and what they see is an Israeli monster in sunglasses and boots. My father is disgusted with me when I say such things. He throws his dishes on the floor in the middle of the meal. My mother starts crying. *I* start crying. I cry! And I never cry. But I love my father, Mr. Roth, so I cry! Everything I've done in my life, I've done to make my father proud of me. That was why I became an officer. My father survived Auschwitz when he was ten years younger than I am now. I am humiliated that I can't survive this. I know what reality is. I'm not a fool who believes that he is pure or that life is simple. It is Israel's fate to live in an Arab sea. Jews accepted this fate rather than have nothing and no fate. Jews accepted partition and the Arabs did not. If they'd said yes, my father reminds me, they would be celebrating forty years of statehood too. But every political decision with which they have been confronted, invariably they have made the wrong choice. *I know all this.* Nine tenths of their misery they owe to the idiocy of their own political leaders. *I know that.* But still I look at my own government and I want to vomit. Would you write a recommendation for me to NYU?"

A big soldier armed with a pistol, a two-hundred-pound leader of men whose face was darkly stubbled with several days' whiskers and whose combat uniform foully reeked of sweat, and yet, the more he recounted of his unhappiness with his father and his father's with him, the younger and more defenseless he had seemed to me. And now this request, uttered almost in the voice of a child. "So—" I laughed—*"that's* why you saved my life out there. That's why you didn't let them break my hands—so I could write your recommendation."

"No, no, *no,*" he quickly replied, a humorless boy distressed by my laughter and even more grave now than he'd been before, "no—no one would have hurt you. Yes, it's there, of course it's there, I'm not saying it's not there—some of the boys *are* brutal. Most because they are frightened, some because they know the others are watching and they don't want to be cowards, and some because they think, 'Better them than us, better him than me.' But no, I assure you—you were never in real danger."

"It's you who's in real danger."

"Of falling apart? You can tell that? You can see that?"

"You know what I see?" I said. "I see that you are a Diasporist

and you don't even know it. You don't even know what a Diasporist is. You don't know what your choices really are."

"A Diasporist? A Jew who lives in the Diaspora."

"No, no. More than that. Much more. It is a Jew for whom
authenticity as a Jew means living in the Diaspora, for whom the
Diaspora is the normal condition and Zionism is the abnormal-
ity—a Diasporist is a Jew who believes that the only Jews who
matter are the Jews of the Diaspora, that the only Jews who will
survive are the Jews of the Diaspora, that the only Jews who *are*
Jews are the Jews of the Diaspora—"

It would have been hard to say where I found the energy after
what I'd been through in just forty-eight hours, but suddenly here
in Jerusalem something was running away with me again and there
seemed to be nothing I had more strength for than this playing-
at-Pipik. That lubricious sensation that is fluency took over, my
eloquence grew, and on I went calling for the de-Israelization of
the Jews, on and on once again, obeying an intoxicating urge that
did not leave me feeling quite so sure of myself as I may have
sounded to poor Gal, torn in two as he was by the rebellious and
delinquent feelings of a loyal, loving son.

from ROAD SCHOLAR
Andrei Codrescu

~

CARLESS IN AMERICA

All my life I had two claims to fame: I was born in Transylvania
and I didn't drive a car.

The first fact made people naturally assume that I didn't *need*
to drive because I could always use bats. I can, but it's a hassle
to harness the bats every time you need a quart of milk. Try
parking bats outside the Safeway! My life would have been much
simpler, I think, if I had learned how to drive when I came to
America. An American without a car is a sick creature, a snail that

has lost its shell.* Living without a car is the worst form of destitution, more shameful by far than not having a home. A carless person is a stationary object, a prisoner, not really a grownup. A homeless person, by contrast, may be an adventurer, a vagabond, a lover of the open sky. The only form of identification an American needs is a driver's license.

Time and time again I stood humiliated before a bank clerk who would not admit to my existence because a passport meant nothing to her. Over and over I've had to prove my existence to petty clerks and policemen for whom there was only one valid form of ID. Driven to despair, I wrote my first autobiography, *The Life and Times of an Involuntary Genius,* at age twenty-three for the sole reason of having my picture on the cover. Whenever a banker asked to see "some identification," I pulled the book from my mirrored Peruvian bag and pointed to the cover. More often than not, it was not enough. "What we mean is," the flustered interpreters of rules and upholders of reality would insist, "we want to see some *proper* ID!" Books have never been proper to those in charge of upholding the status quo.

One very late night in California my friend Jeffrey Miller and I got lost on a country road somewhere above the Pacific Ocean. The sky was pierced by so many stars we thought we were on a cosmic stage with the ocean roaring below us. We stopped because we were tired and awed. Suddenly, the lights of something unearthly and huge were upon us. It was a California Highway Patrol cruiser, its blue light flashing. Jeff stopped slowly, as if he were reluctant to surrender to the intense light, which might be an alien craft. The officer asked Jeff for his ID, which my friend fished with some difficulty either from the depths of his fascinating glove compartment, which was his portable office, or from one of his pockets, which was equally cluttered with napkins full of poetry, pencil nubs, lucky stones, and, undoubtedly, Ritz crackers in case of shipwreck. Jeffrey believed every journey was final, and that one must be prepared.

The officer then turned to me. "Your license!" "I don't drive," I said. He heard that. He also heard the foreign "r" in the word "drive," and was alerted to the possibility of a potential illegal

*That's why one of the biggest gas companies is called Shell: it feeds Americans' exoskeletons.

alien. I pulled out my book. "I wrote this. See, that's my picture!" The cop took the book back to his cruiser and started reading. He read and read. Eons passed. The stars in the sky changed. Jeff and I slept and woke, grew old, died, and came back. At long last, the officer returned from the deeps of time, and tapped my face on the cover with a thoughtful trigger finger. "Anybody can fake a pitcher like this!" he said. "If they could," I argued wearily, "would they bother to write a book to go with it?" "It's OK," he said, "*this time!*" Well, it was OK that time, and Jeff and I went on our way. I immediately wrote another autobiography, for that California cop. In that book, called *In America's Shoes,* which also sports my face on the cover, I told the above story—just in case we met again.

My adventures in the land of those without drivers' IDs would fill several books. Lost souls live in that world: illegal aliens, space aliens, the crazy, the stubborn, handicapped pedestrians of every stripe. The truth is that an American without a driver's license doesn't have an identity.

I tried to learn. Three times. The first time was in 1967, in my wife Alice's old Ford station wagon, a frightening vehicle that would have been rejected by Rent-a-Wreck if Rent-a-Wreck had been around in 1967. Our friend Jan Herman, who gave it to her, didn't think that the clunker would last twenty-four hours. It did in fact last almost a year, even after it had its tires slashed on the Lower East Side of New York, its windows broken in Detroit during the '67 riots, and a garbage bag dropped on it from the fifth floor of a tenement in Harrisburg, Pennsylvania. The thing was made to suffer and withstand disasters: if it had been human it would have been a saint. I was still a brand-new American then, filled with the desire to become motorized. We headed for the Palisades of New Jersey, those sheer cliffs just outside of Manhattan, on a beautiful sunny day. Alice showed me the brake, the gas pedal, and the wheel, and then settled back confidently as I drove straight to the edge of the precipice— and would have driven over if she hadn't quicker than Zorro speared the brake.

The second time I tried was in a church parking lot in California on a Tuesday in 1973. There were no cars in the lot except the reverend's black Oldsmobile neatly stashed in the shadow of a walnut by the church wall. I did great that time. I turned, I backed out, I revved, and then I headed helplessly for the reverend's car and bashed the door on the driver's side. I think I was possessed. It's the only explanation. The devil likes cars and is especially fond of new drivers. Give him one in a church parking lot and he has an orgasm.

The third time I actually drove. In 1975, Alice's yellow Vega was the snazziest car in Monte Rio, California, a little town filled with shady people where the population thought that food stamps were the official U.S. currency. The Vega, of course, was not really a car but a lemon, a real piece of American junk, probably *the* piece of junk that finally got everybody buying Japanese cars. Anyway, I got in it and drove out of Monte Rio on a lovely curving back road following a stream on a beautiful morning, and I was actually *enjoying* it! The leaves made pretty patterns with light on the windshield, the world was peaceful and playful, and I drove right into the stream. I had gotten so confident I forgot to steer.

It was at that point that I decided cars and I were not meant for each other. Neither concentration nor relaxation, neither will nor dreaming worked for me. I was doomed to be what I had always—happily—been: a pedestrian.

ALTERNATIVE TRANSPORTS

I left Transylvania by air in 1965 and got to America in 1966 (it was a long flight!) at just about the time that my generation was piling into VW vans and striking out for the Wild West (again). I went along and lived in a lot of places, among them Detroit, New York, Chicago, and San Francisco. Now I live in New Orleans. I rode along to all these places, the passenger *par excellence.* I was *The* Passenger. I knew exactly what was expected of me. I knew how to entertain at just the right speed. I was not a backseat driver, and my remarks were geared to the driver's moods like a violin to a heartbreak.

Being The Passenger for years was immensely beneficial. At the end of a party, for instance, while my unsteady contemporaries headed for their many cars, I could pick and choose my ride. If I picked the most beautiful woman leaving, alone like everyone else, in her isolated bubble of plastic and glass, can anyone blame me? As folks headed for the sadness of the parking lot, each one to his or her own car, I felt the loneliness. I was a most welcome passenger. I was the one you could give a ride to. I was also the one left, occasionally, standing by the side of the road. Of these occasions I rarely speak though I have some really dark-night-of-the-soul memories that I *could* reveal someday if I find the right therapist.

There were also delicate situations in certain rude places out West where it got rough. To some of them dudes drinking dusty beer in the desert, a nondriving man was a distinct freak of nature, a thing created for cruel entertainment, something effeminate and unnatural made to be prodded with sticks. I had to brave their ridicule and incomprehension now and then, it's true, but it was a small price to pay for the pleasure of being the Consummate Passenger and the Perfect Pedestrian. Being both carless and un-identifiable I began to identify with my Saintly Condition, which called for capitals. One does not really suffer unless one Suffers.

Later, in the seventies, when it became fashionable to not drive because of the environmental horror that is the car, I could have (and occasionally did) claim I was taking a stand. In my own way I was. I walked everywhere and took public transportation when I couldn't mooch a ride. In truth, it was something other than a stand that underlay my handicap, namely:

My Mother

When my mother came to America at age forty-four, she got her driver's license and a huge used Pontiac. Instantly, she became a very great menace, one of those little ladies who can barely see over the dashboard. She never drove over thirty miles an hour, and it is only by the grace of God that many drivers in her vicinity are alive today. One of the most harrowing experiences of my life was when I went to visit her with my son Tristan at the time she was trying to buy a new car. After intimidating a huge, self-confident salesman who became a mass of jelly before her bound-less ignorance and energetic suspicion, she drove this used Cad-illac out of the dealership onto the freeways of Florida with my son and me inside. She had no idea what most of the buttons and gears were for because she was used to her old car. While com-plaining the whole time that she'd been swindled and that the car didn't work, she drove in reverse, she made U-turns on the expressway, and she missed her exits. My son and I were reduced to raw nerves by the experience. I'm sure she gave her grandson a permanent complex. We went back to the dealership eight times.

She raged about the defective machine but each time she allowed herself to be persuaded there was nothing wrong with the car and tried again. The sixth time we went back, the huge salesman hid from her in a bathroom and submitted his tearful resignation through the door. The owner of the company had to be called in to personally reassure my mother that the car was fine.

In the end, she returned the Cadillac anyway, and got her old car back. The Pontiac, even though it didn't work very well, was her friend. She was proud of it. For ten years she had sent our relatives in Romania pictures of herself with the car: Mother with her hand on the roof of her car. Mother at the wheel. Mother sitting on the hood of her car. For about a year after she learned to drive, Mother had a big sign in the back window: CAREFUL! BEGINNER! Fortunately, people took her at her word and avoided her. A fierce, tiny human being with a bright red permanent barely visible above the dash of her American machine, she was like a determined time traveler who had come from the Middle Ages to experience the modern world, and experience it she did. Never mind the terror she spread around her on freeways and streets. In spite of it, I admired her courage. It takes guts to come to a foreign land in your middle age and become one of the armored natives.

Curiously enough, my father, who divorced my mother when I was only six months old, was a superdriver. He drove so fast on the cobblestone streets of my childhood my neighbors had no pets.

My Father

My father's big black Packard scared our neighbors in Sibiu, Romania. There were only six cars in town and my father had one. He also wore a black leather jacket. When he passed people bowed their heads in fear and whispered. When he was gone, they spat and crossed themselves. In those days, at the height of Stalinist terror, the man in the car was the one who came to take you away: he took you away in his car and you never came back again.

My father took me in his car but he always brought me back to my mother on Sunday night. Every Saturday, from age six to nine, I got in my father's black car to the pointed envy and fear of our neighbors, and took off to visit his girlfriends. I waited for him in the car, behind the wheel, not moving, while my father was in a building somewhere, and fantasized about driving the black car. When my father came back, smelling of cheap cologne and a strange carnal odor that took me years to identify, I was exhausted. I had driven thousands of miles through the crooked streets of our medieval burg and I had received the frightened tribute of every citizen who had ever slighted me in the least. I had also magnanimously given rides to every person who had ever been nice to me. My father never suspected a thing because I was sure to set back the odometer. I was such a good imaginary driver, I saw no point in actually driving. But one time I did drive. My father had left the key in the ignition. I got behind the wheel, released the brake, and rolled straight into the window of a hat store. When my father came back I was shaking helplessly in the driver's seat under a mountain of hats. He never left the key in after that. After that, I never wore a hat.

Cars were as rare as swans in Sibiu. As they navigated the twisted streets, the pedestrians watched them with the same kind of dread with which they had once watched the carriages of Transylvanian nobles. The cars of the fifties, like the coaches of the sixteenth century, stopped for no one. The plebes took the bus or rode honest bicycles, which had come through the war. Waiting for the bus in the rain, I would watch the depressing river of bicycles streaming to work, and I could see myself on the back of a swan. My white bird would glide over the gray river of bikes, then soar over the towers of the Teutsch cathedral, skirt the silvery roofs of Sibiu and land in the schoolyard just as the bell rang.

I rode a swan to school (though most of my Transylvanian schoolmates used the traditional bats) until my swan died; then I took the ancient streetcar, which, like the Victorian streetlights, was said to be "the oldest in Europe." This venerable tram groaned its way up the hills so slowly we jumped on its back and rode gratis. Now and then an old conductor, the oldest in Europe, dressed in a threadbare uniform that predated the Hapsburgs, would attempt to shoo away the cluster of children perched on the back of his ancient tram. It was a futile gesture, as he well knew. Only rain and snow kept us off. And it rained and snowed a lot. All through my childhood it rained and snowed without surcease.

Mostly, I walked. The town was full of ghosts and they liked to walk with me and tell me stories. The lower part of the town, where we lived, was linked to the upper by a drawbridge known as "the liars' bridge." On this bridge, lovers lied to each other, and then died of sorrow. Whenever I crossed it, I was besieged by whispers and agonized laments. One night, while I had been wandering in the rain through the alleys of the upper town like a wet cur, I found that the liars' bridge had been raised, and I couldn't return home. I spent the night inside a dry fountain full of damp autumn leaves in a deserted square. A titan embracing a nymph above me protected me from the rain. I traveled farther that night than I ever did using any means of locomotion. I visited places no rockets ever reached. Our speed-driven *fin-de-siècle* has little to tell a child hidden in a fountain in the rain in one of Europe's oldest cities, flying through time wrapped in his thoughts like a black cloak.

from MAD MONKS
ON THE ROAD
Michael Lane and Jim Crotty

~

THE McCAULEY MOVING AND STORAGE TRUCK ARRIVED AT eight o'clock on a sunny Friday morning in San Francisco's Castro District. Making a fatal crash into the concrete retaining wall, it sent a thunderous roar up the canyon of Nineteenth Street. Mrs. Klein's gray cat was flattened under the wheels. It was quite fatal.

Michael Monk jumped awake at the thunderous roar, bumping his head on the oven door. One day left to move and the damn electric heat had been cut, forcing the once upwardly mobile and now penniless Michael to sleep beneath his antique Wedgewood stove for warmth. Everything seemed to be working *against* a smooth departure.

Boxes were piled all over the kitchen in an orgy of cardboard, tape and bubble wrap. Some sat half-assembled, a dozen more leaned against the sliding glass door to the patio.

Half-asleep on a makeshift bed, buried in piles of unpacked books, tapes and bags of papers, Jim lay snoring.

Michael reached for the oven door handle to help himself up as Nurse, the cat, leapt from a towering stack of boxes, leaving them teetering dangerously to the left.

"Nurse, no, watch it, stay..." The boxes sagged against the wall, spilling precious first editions to the hard parquet floor.

The McCauley team angrily banged on the large front door. The banging entered Michael's skull like a jackhammer.

Michael abruptly stood up, his legs trapped in twisted trousers, and hobbled to the oak door to greet the impatient movers.

"Fifteen tons of dynamite, that's what it's gonna take to get your piano outta here... fifteen tons!" Mr. McCauley of McCauley Moving and Storage bellowed in a raspy growl as he stood outside the door in his kelly green overalls, with fifty feet of rope in his left fist and a wooden dolly at his side.

Mr. McCauley had a piano to move.

"This one's gonna cost you, lad. Didn't say they were *outside* now, did ya? When we ran our estimate, we took your stairs to be *inside.* Gonna have to charge you extra, lad, and even more if one of my lads gets hurt."

Behind Mr. McCauley stood five other brutes of similar height and burly build in their green MCCAULEY overalls, sporting crooked smirks and stifled groans. They were casing the joint, smacking gum, chewing on toothpicks, puffing on roll-your-owns, their beady eyes darting left and right. The strong man, a seven-foot Goliath, sneered at the eighty-five wooden stairs that led up to Michael's "Swiss Family Tree House." Meanwhile, the freckled one, the only redhead of the bunch, was taking a leak on the exotic ferns Mike had planted. All six pairs of green eyes were upon Michael, who stood inside the door rubbing his swollen head.

Michael looked at the McCauley team. The McCauley team looked at Michael. They looked like the Irish Mob—big arms, bruises and cuts. Mr. McCauley had a black eye and a missing right finger.

"Like, how much extra?" Michael inquired.

"Double."

Michael considered the dynamite.

Mr. McCauley considered calling the whole thing off until he remembered the retaining wall below. Not to mention the dead cat.

"Listen, we had a little mishap. It got kind of messy down there. I think someone's gonna be mad. You take care of it and we'll stick to our quote. Deal?" Mr. McCauley stuck out his hand, waiting impatiently.

"What sort of mess?"

"It's a dead cat, that's wut it is," blurted the redhead, who'd left his fly open.

"A cat?" Michael's eyes bulged. He flew through the movers like hot grease, brushing the seven-foot Goliath against the rail, taking the steps four at a time, sliding over the slick, moss-covered stairs, banging his hips at the turns.

Down at the bottom the twenty-foot McCauley truck was angled in off the street, across the sidewalk and into the ivy where it had taken a sizable chuck of concrete off the retaining wall. There at Michael's feet lay a cat. A flat cat at that.

"Oh, thank God, it's the Klein cat," said Michael, picking its flattened remains up by the paws. "Thank God it's not Nurse or Nurse's Aide!"

Mrs. Klein was just then coming out the front door for her morning *Chronicle.* Without thinking, Michael ditched the cat in a trash can before Mrs. Klein started screaming her bloody head off. This time, for a change, she'd have an excuse.

For the first time that week Michael laughed.

Mrs. Klein looked up and cast her predictable morning scowl his way. This was one neighbor he wasn't going to miss.

"Wait till she gets a load of this!" Michael thought as he passed the trash can heading back up.

At the top of the stairs, the McCauley team was bumbling out the door with the upright piano turned on its end.

"Hey, watch it, watch it! The leg's about to . . ."

The glass window on the porch shattered across the ferns, the sound echoing down the street. *Of course, it had to be the window with the beveled edges and rounded corners,* Michael appraised bitterly, the window he'd replaced only a month earlier when Jim insisted that the water bed be removed. Michael strained to peek inside and could see where the McCauley monsters had removed a white Corinthian pillar to extract the piano and scraped a freshly painted wall. Glass crunched under the movers' feet, each crunch a painful spike into Michael's fragile nervous system.

"Sorry 'bout that, lad, just send us the bill," Mr. McCauley grunted under his breath. "I should never have agreed to this." He grunted some more, attempting to get the piano around another tight corner.

McCauley's men were now heading for the big drop of stairs, but not before they took out the porch's other window with a loud crash, trampling through the ferns as the two lead men slipped on the wet wood.

"Shiiiiiiiit!"

Just then the phone rang... *next door.* Michael's phone had long since been shut off. Any minute now the neighbor would be poking his head out the window to assess the latest damage and report back to the landlord. It was the neighborhood buddy system that always seemed to work against Mike and Jim.

"Just get it out of here!" Michael barked at the men in green.

"Ayyyyyyyyeeeiieeieieeeeeeeee!" It was Mrs. Klein, letting out a bloodcurdling scream from down below. "My baby, my baby, *who killed my baby!"*

"Michael, Michael, Donald wants to know if they have insurance," the deceptively sweet neighbor asked from next door, phone in hand.

Mr. McCauley's seven-foot giant panicked when he heard Mrs. Klein's anguished wail. His big frame slipped and he fell down the top flight, landing on his back. The piano headed over the guardrail and then got lodged against a eucalyptus tree.

"I hope you have insurance!" Mr. McCauley warned as the other four movers valiantly struggled to pull Michael's upright piano back onto the stairs.

"Who ran over my cat, my baby... *you'll pay for this!"* Mrs. Klein curdled the air, her voice getting closer.

"Are they affiliated with Worldwide?" the neighbor asked from next door, still on the phone.

"Mike, where's the pressure cooker?" A puffy-eyed Jim leaned out the window. "I can't find the pressure cooker. Which box has the kitchen stuff?"

"My cat, my baby—*I'll have your balls!"* Mrs. Klein was advancing up the steps, huffing and sobbing while still managing to puff on a cigarette out of the corner of her mouth, her eyes filled with pure hate and vengeance.

"You sonnabitch, who the hell did this to my cat!" She carried the bloody mess in her left hand like a purse, while still in her dingy housecoat, clutching a Danish with her right hand, the newspaper rolled under her arm.

"Hey, lady, I wouldn't come up here, this is a heavy load!" Mr. McCauley shouted.

"*I want the balls of the coward that ran down my baby!* Just let me have the son of a bitch. I'm gonna sink my teeth into every one of you!" she shrieked toward the Irish lads.

"Michael, Donald wants to know if the insurance covers..."

"Someone's going to have to pay for my man...," sang McCauley.

"Gimme that rope, I'm gonna string you all up by the balls..."

"Where's the pressure..."

"*Shuuuuuuuuut uuuuuuup!* Shut up! Everyone. Shut the fuck up! And get that piano out of here before I take your fifteen tons of dynamite, McCauley, and blow the goddamn block off the map! I don't, I don't want to hear it. Everyone, get moving... *now!*"

Michael stood panting at the top of the stairs, foaming at the mouth, his eyes bulging out of their sockets.

All eyes were upon him, waiting for the next explosion.

"But the pressure cooker, where is the pressure cooker...?" Jim's voice trailed, echoing across the street.

By the time the cops led a frothing, hysterical Mrs. Klein back to her house, the McCauley movers had the piano in the truck. Mr. McCauley wasn't happy about the citation for the damaged wall, but that "tall, skinny bloke" had sent the fear of God into McCauley's Irish heart, and so he carted the piano off with his bruised and grumbling men.

Meanwhile, Jim was inside busily stuffing old high-school debate papers into boxes, labeling them by year, as Michael silently threw out the same papers, which Jim in turn recovered and repacked and Michael again threw out and Jim again salvaged. There had been an ongoing battle of the bulge to stick to the plan and discard useless junk and keep to the essentials for the move.

"C'mon, Jim, you don't need this."

"Are you crazy? You never know when I'll be called upon to debate reverse bail reform and pretrial detainers."

The move was not going as planned. For that matter, nothing had been going as planned for nearly a year. And now everyone was in an uproar. Not one friend approved of the departure.

In fact, no one in the entire megalopolis of San Francisco wanted

Mike or Jim to leave. That is, no one except Uncle Jack, who was probably the only person in the entire state of California who would breathe a sigh of relief when the self-proclaimed "Monks" finally hit the highway.

THE BIG ROCK SAT ON THE MONK BED IN THE BACK OF THE Monkmobile, adding another three hundred pounds to the rear axle. After considerable effort the Monks and Mr. Burris had conquered the stone with the backhoe's assistance and delivered it through the back window of the Bounder.

Kaplunk. It rocked the tires as we pulled off the mountain to find shelter for the night. Back at Denby Point we felt as if we were in Crystal Heaven with our big giant quartz sage in back.

"So what are we going to do with it, sell it to one of these roadside gentlemen?" Mr. Burris was already planning an early retirement back to New Mexico.

"Heck, I don't know. I sort of like it back there. It's very grounding," said Gemini Jim, smiling.

"My God. Do you realize how much this thing must be worth? We'd better keep our mouths shut or we're going to have every dealer in the world hot on our tail," Michael Monk added. Besides, Mike had other plans. *Maybe this big rock will fetch a nice price from the museums.*

The next morning, we decided to hit the road for Memphis and take Mr. Burris to see the King. If anything, we knew we'd better get outta town before the news spread. Despite ourselves, we knew we'd feel compelled to gab about our big find.

As we drove Bounder out of the safe refuge of Denby Point campground, the Monks decided to go for a drive down to the lake. But Michael Monk, a little waterlogged from a morning swim, misjudged the turn. Bounder was soon resting across a ditch, wheels wedged into the culvert, blocking the road.

One by one over the next few hours most of the town strolled by to take a look and offer their two cents worth of advice. It was the general consensus that something "ought be done 'bout that turn." It was also the general consensus that it'd take a "purty big rig" to haul Bounder out.

Just then, while the Monks were in heated debate about how to get a tow, up drove a local mechanic. His name was Elroy and he pulled up alongside in his oversize tow truck, chewing on a straw. He leaned back shaking his head and yelled in a dry, throaty cackle from across the road, "Well, if that don't beat all. Looks like you fellers got yourself in a pickle. Where'n da hell ya'll learn to drive?"

After tugging the Bounder out of the ditch, Elroy had us shove her in park, so he could detach the load from his truck. "What in the hell are ya'll dragging around in thar? A pile of rocks?"

"How'd you know?" Jim volunteered.

Mike cast a furtive look toward Jim, but it was too late. The Mouth was about to *blab.*

"We found the biggest piece of quartz you ever seen!"

"Oh, you did?" Elroy squinted from Mike to Jim.

Jim was about to show Elroy to the door when Michael Monk interjected, "But there wasn't a thing we could do, so we just left it on—"

"The bed. It's sitting right back there." Jim could never tell a lie and led Elroy around the side and pointed through the window.

Elroy's eyes popped when he saw it. His stereotypical good ole boy disposition suddenly changed as he muscled his way past Mike and walked to his truck, took out his CB and radioed a friend. "Hell, Fred, I got me a bunch of Northerners out here, they got them one of the biggest durn rocks you ever seen. You git yourself down here with some boys and we'll see if we can't help these fellas out with it, heh, heh."

Mike pulled Jim inside as Elroy hung up the CB. Mike was starting the Bounder when Elroy raced to the side and hollered, "I think one good turn deserves another. I'd say this little tow job here ought to cost you a nice-size rock. Maybe something about the size of what you have sitting right there in the back of your rig."

"No thanks. We appreciate your help. But we have the Good Sam Emergency Road Service. They'll be glad to pay you." Michael took out his Good Sam card.

Elroy's eyes flared. "That's not what *I* had in mind."

"Well, uh, no? Then how about this?" And Michael stuck out two crisp twenty-dollar bills.

But Elroy violently shook his head and locked his mean eyes onto the Monks. "I don't think you heard me quite right. I said that rock would do fine, and if I have to bring in some boys to convince you otherwise, then that's just what we'll have to do."

Michael jammed on the accelerator.

"You try moving this rig one foot and I'll—"

The Bounder jumped forward, lunging past a startled Elroy, who leapt out of the way as the slow-moving RV picked up speed, turned a sharp right, swerved around the two truck, scraping the Monkmobile down its side, and charged for the road with Elroy cursing right behind.

"What the hell are you doing, Mike?"

"I don't know what I'm doing. What *am* I doing?"

"You're going to hit that tree—watch out!"

Mike swerved to the left narrowly missing the tree with the Monkmobile rocking on the road, grinding its gears, the accelerator pushed to the floor.

"We're picking up speed. Where is he?" Mike yelled.

"Oh, my God, he's on the back!" Jim hollered with his head leaning out the passenger window.

Elroy was hanging on the ladder, ascending toward the roof of the motor home.

"Get him off of there!" yelled Mike.

"What am I supposed to do?" Jim pulled himself inside.

"Throw something at him. He'll break our roof in."

Elroy was now up on the roof with his heavy boots, stomping madly on the thin frame, cursing his lungs out. The roof was bowing with each kick as the madman marched forward toward the front.

Jim ran to the cupboards and started to grab some dishes.

"No, not our new dishes, something heavy."

Jim grabbed a couple of books and arched out the window, tossing them up at Elroy, but they simply crashed down on the front windshield.

"No! You're throwing them the wrong way." Mike could see Elroy's foot above the air vent. Then Elroy popped open the vent with the heel of his boots exposing six inches of his mad-as-hell red face through the vent screen.

"You fuckers. Pull this thing off the road or I'm going to kill ya." His voice crackled with rage.

Jim started frantically pulling out the drawers throwing everything he could lay his hands on out the window, but not once hitting Elroy.

Mike opened his window and started heaving river rocks from the Monks' stash. He could hear them cracking on the roof bouncing along the edge and rolling off the side.

Boom!

Elroy's boot crashed through the other vent, leaving a gaping hole. He was putting his face down to the screen.

"Dadgumit! I'm goin' to git you little shits!"

Mike picked up speed on the country road driving like a maniac, swerving from side to side as he tried to dump the raging monster on top. Elroy rolled to the front. The low-hanging trees were brushing across the roof and Elroy stayed low to the Bounder.

Jim opened the fridge and started tossing long daikon radishes, lotus roots, giant Hokkaido pumpkins, beet juice, any food he could find.

"No, not the pie, that's for tonight!" The pie splattered on the top of the motor home.

Mike continued a constant spray of rocks. He threw a bottle of water and then resorted to throwing pennies.

Elroy was back at the vent. Jim grabbed the bug spray and dosed Elroy's face through the vent, but that didn't stop him. He was so mean, he was beginning to tear at the roof.

"Stop him, he's going to tear our roof open!"

Jim took a bottle of dishwashing soap and started squirting it up on the roof.

Elroy was pounding, sending shock waves through the speeding Monkmobile. Dolly was darting back and forth meowing frantically in the aisle.

"Quick. Give me something to heave!"

Elroy was back dangling over the front windshield.

"He's going to break the damn windshield. Give me that fucking brain machine!"

Mike heaved the brain machine in an arc around the side just missing red-faced, raging Elroy, who now stood up and marched back toward the vent ready to crash through in one final kick and kill.

"Do something!" Mike screamed.

"What! *What?*" Jim panicked.

The Monks scanned the Monkmobile and spotted the case of soy milk.

Jim ran for the box, ripped it open and started hurling cartons of soy milk through the screen. A solid barrage of soy milk flew through the air. Carton after carton, bouncing off the roof leaving a trail of soy down the road until suddenly Mike put on the brakes to slow for a low-hanging tree, hit a huge bump, and Elroy came sliding across the roof as Jim heaved four more cartons, which splattered on a falling Elroy, who gyrated wildly in the air, as he grabbed for a branch and crashed to the hard ground.

The Monks jammed down the road heading another three miles out to the highway, passing a red pickup filled with country boys coming in just before Mike turned west.

Mike went another fifty yards and then did a wide loop in the road, coming back east.

"What are you doing?" screamed Jim.

"If that red pickup was his friends, when they find Elroy, they'll tell him we headed west."

"Smart thinking, Mike!" Jim was proud.

The Monks were panting, afraid to move a muscle, as the Bounder sped down the highway. Jim was frozen in a squat position by the passenger window where he'd been heaving, with Mike arched over the wheel with his knuckles white as ice.

"Soy milk. We got him with the soy milk." Jim dared to laugh.

After five miles the Monks took another detour down a side road into Hot Springs and a mile later turned back onto 70 heading to Little Rock. Then we finally took a sigh of relief. Mike kept looking in the rearview mirror for a sign of Elroy, but knew that by the time Elroy and his friends figured out which way the Monks had gone, there would be no trace.

Jim was recounting the escape, blow by blow, when all of a sudden Michael screamed out, "Oh, my God, Mr. Burris!"

The Monks' hearts stopped with visions of Mr. Burris, a hostage back in the campground, tortured at the hands of Elroy and his henchmen.

"We've got to turn back!"

Mike was just about to turn back when a tall, thin man stumbled forward, rubbing his eyes out of a cortisone daze, waking from his blissed-out nap in the back.

"Gentlemen, what has happened?" He smiled a goofy, sleepy smile.

"Oh, just a little adventure on our way outta Dodge."

Riding on that midnight RV to Graceland. Destination: Memphis, Tennessee. Well, this train we call the Monkmobile, and it'll be gone five hundred miles before the day is done.

Ole Woody couldn't have been more prophetic. The Monks hightailed it to Memphis. The Monks and Mr. Burris had a meeting with the King, and we best not be late.

Rumor had it that Elvis was alive and well somewhere in the gaudy catacombs of Graceland. Another rumor had it the King wouldn't come out until he met the Monks. Seems Elvis had recently taken an interest in the finer aspects of Buddha dharma and wanted Jim Monk to help him brush up a bit on the meaning of the Heart Rock Sutra.

Never ones to leave an errant bodhisattva in distress, the Monks kicked ole Bounder into high gear and headed east with an ever-watchful eye in the rearview mirror. Maybe Elvis could give us a few tips on loosening up our pelvic lock. Seemed like a meeting made in rock 'n' roll heaven.

There was only one problem.

Elvis was dead.

But the Monks and Mr. Burris decided to visit Graceland anyway.

Mike reluctantly agreed. "But *God*, was he sleazy."

Mike had lived through the Elvis heyday, when his mom used to stand outside Graceland praying for an autograph. Mike felt Elvis was a stupid redneck, and he never forgave him for sucking up to Tricky Dick during the heat of the Vietnam War. Even still, Mike had enough of the tourist bug left in him to still be a little curious. And besides, maybe the Monks could unload the Rock for a solid piece of Elvis gold.

The Monkmobile shimmied up Elvis Presley Boulevard to Graceland at about ten A.M. We parked a mile down the road, rather than pay the parking fee for motor homes. We hiked back to Graceland where we found ourselves in the company of dozens of fawning tourists, most of whom seemed either to be British art students or American fundamentalist Christians, per-haps one of the few places on the planet where these two came together.

Mr. Cortisone Burris was in Elvis ecstasy, as he realized he'd finally reached his destination. But for the Monks there was a different reaction. Once inside, it immediately hit us. Graceland was just a poor cousin to the Hearst Castle, but far more popular because it's exactly what most Americans dream of when they think of opulence: a pink Cadillac, a dune buggy, a Hell's Angels—

style motorbike, and an extensive gun and badge collection. Elvis had pedestrian tastes to say the least, but because he was so faithful to them, the Graceland estate struck as true and pure campy Americana.

Jim was busily engaged in deciphering cryptic messages left by the King in the downstairs billiard room, while Mike approached the estate manager proposing they buy a three-hundred-pound piece of quartz to go with the Meditation Garden. The management declined.

Somewhat miffed, Michael carefully studied the Elvis wardrobe for clues in planning the Monks' next fashion statement.

"Lavender polyester bell-bottomed cuffed jumpsuit, cut to the belly button with silver lamé cape, orange Nehru collar and gold, glass-beaded trim. . . . Pink pigskin leather harem pants with green tassels and a wickedly cut green velvet cape on the bias with virgin white lace and chartreuse studs. . . . Did this queen have an eye for color or what?" muttered Mike.

Graceland was a shrine not so much to Elvis, but to what can be bought when millions of dollars filter through the hungry heart of a poor white Southern greaseball. And the Monks were taking copious notes, just in case they ever had a spare million to revamp the skunkmobile.

"Let's see . . . I'd put purple velvet drapes over the sacred windows." Mr. Burris was getting into the swing of things. "Gold-leaf the steering apparatus, hot pink brocade upholstery on *all* the chairs, six-inch lime green shag, glass beads over the doors, baby blue metallic on the wheels, a miniature Taj Mahal next to the yoga room, a row of Greek columns and a statue of Dollface with a most holy fountain in the bathroom."

Burris was on Elvis overload. And the Monks were pulling our silly cortisone-infested pundit out the door when we spotted the Elvis shrine. Jim was the first to feel an ominous throbbing presence as we stood next to the tomb of the King. Jim, the Channeling Overlord of Sedona, was beginning to have hot revelatory flashes that someone was near. Someone the Monks knew but not well.

"Hey, guys, I'm getting this funny feeling in the pit of my stomach," said Jim.

Mr. Burris stood at the foot of the shrine staring at the inscribed words on the stone. Michael could feel it too. We stood there sensing an approaching energy. Something bigger than the three of us together.

"What do you think it is?"

"Maybe it's a message from the other side. Maybe it's the spirit of Elvis. Maybe the King still—"

"Lives!" A low, grungy Southern voice boomed from behind them.

The Monks jerked around. And there stood . . .

"Elroy!" we screamed. "How the hell did you get here!"

"I have your fucking license. Every trucker in the country has their eyes out for you turkeys!" He chuckled his low, sadistic, mean-ass laugh.

Yep, there he was again, Elroy and his two ugly bubba men towering from behind.

"Ya'll's up shit crick without a paddle, aren't ya?"

Just then Elroy and his boys charged for the Monks and Mr. Burris as we took off sprinting for Elvis Presley Boulevard.

Fortunately for the Monks, Elroy and his gorillas were no match for the lightning speed of Mike, Jim and the cheetah-fast Burris.

"Dadgumit!"

The Monks charged across the lawn, weaved through traffic and caught a cab just as Elroy rushed out onto the street in front of a Memphis bus.

We could hear the rubber screeching and then a loud bang. But we didn't look back as the cab raced up the Boulevard to the waiting Bounder.

"Gentlemen, I think it would be a most appropriate moment to leave your fine company," stated a dazed and disheveled Mr. Burris. "It's been most enjoyable, but you can keep my piece of the Rock. I'm heading back to Santa Fe. Dollface, we shall meet again. . . ."

After pit stops to drop off Mr. Burris at the nearest bus terminal. . . "I leave you my dream, my dream I leave you" . . . and to see the waddling ducks at the Peabody Hotel, the Monks hightailed it east.

from CRAZY IN ALABAMA

Mark Childress

~

LUCILLE

Hollywood

Lucille spent a whole afternoon choosing just the right outfit, having her hair twisted up in an elegant chignon. The minute she walked into the General Services Studio they whisked her off to costume and makeup, took her apart, and started over from scratch. They washed out her hair and blew it up into a great shiny bouffant. They pasted fake lashes on her eyelids, painted her cheeks with rouge and her lips with red gloss. They put her in high spike heels and a tight dress with a frilly bosom. Of course she was playing Patsy Belle, the sexpot of Sibly, Arkansas; the hairdo and dress were part of the joke, but she felt silly—as if they'd seen through to her recent indecent behavior and dressed her as a whore on purpose.

Lucille had to remind herself that "The Beverly Hillbillies" was the number-one television comedy in America, thank you very much. She was lucky to be here.

She met most of the stars at the read-through rehearsal, Buddy Ebsen in a Hawaiian shirt and Bermuda shorts, Irene Ryan looking about half Granny's age, in a sweater and skirt, with lovely auburn hair . . . if these normal-looking actors weren't afraid to put on ridiculous costumes and act silly in front of America every Wednesday night, Lucille wouldn't be either.

Max Baer was just as cheerful and lunky as Jethro, but not the least dimwitted—in his tweedy clothes and horn-rimmed glasses, he seemed rather intellectual. Donna Douglas was sweet-natured like Elly May, with a twinkly smile and a sharp sense of humor. These people read through the lines with assurance, every one a real professional. Lucille was starstruck, she stumbled a time or two trying too hard, but Max Baer just smiled and said, "Let's do it again."

At the end Buddy Ebsen said, "Honey, you'll do fine. Just relax."

Now she towered in her heels over the little foreign woman who kept trying to put on more makeup. "They vant a heavy look, much rouge," she said.

Lucille said, "If you put any more rouge on me, I'll look like I've got the flu."

A boy stuck his head in. "Carolyn Clay? Wanted on the set."

"See there? Thank you. I've got to go."

The boy pointed her across the lot to a pastel-blue barn of a building. She wobbled along in spike heels past a knight in armor, three clowns, and some kind of rubber-faced monster that reminded her of Chester with a hangover. At the door to Stage Three she met Max Baer in his Jethro costume: checked shirt, tight blue jeans rolled up at the ankles, rope belt, and that gee-whiz grin on his face.

"Morning, Carolyn! God, look what they've done to you."

"I know. I feel just like a floozy."

"Well that's what you're supposed to be. Don't worry, I'm the big stupid idiot every week and it hasn't hurt me yet. What's in the hatbox?"

"My hat." She was taking no chances today.

Baer ushered her past familiar sets with banks of lights instead of ceilings—Mr. Drysdale's office, the Clampetts' driveway, the entry hall with the curving staircase, the "courtin' parlor," the kitchen, the cement pond. Workmen scurried everywhere polishing floors and furniture, climbing ladders to hang lights. It was strange to see these rooms lined up beside each other, the Clampett mansion disassembled and overrun by strangers. On TV it all meshed into a seamless make-believe world, but in real life you could step from the cement pond into Mr. Drysdale's office, and directly into Granny's kitchen.

Max Baer introduced Lucille to Nancy Kulp, the tall, plain-faced actress who played Miss Jane Hathaway. "This is Carolyn, from Alabama."

"At last, a real Southern girl," she trilled in her Miss Jane voice. "We haven't had many actual Southerners on the set."

"It's so good to meet you, I really love Miss Jane," said Lucille. "She's got that wild streak in her. You remember when she—"

"Nancy, Ray, places please," called Bob Weed, the director. Lucille found a quiet spot behind two lightstands to watch Nancy

Kulp shoot a scene with Raymond Bailey, who played Mr. Drysdale.

"And . . . action!"

"Miss Hathaway," Bailey sputtered, "if you think this golddigging blonde is gonna get her hands on one dime of the Clampett fortune, you don't know Milburn Drysdale."

"Don't be so sure, Chief." Nancy Kulp pressed her hands together like a schoolmarm. "I didn't know Jethro was capable of such tender sentiments. I wouldn't be surprised if we're hearing wedding bells in the Clampett home before long. And after that, who knows? Maybe the patter of little feet?"

"If those two get married," Bailey snarled, "the only patter you'll hear is your little feet on the way to the unemployment line."

"Chief!"

"Cut! That's great, people. Next setup."

Yesterday, reading through the script, the actors had time to laugh at some of the jokes, but on the set nobody laughed. They shot it in snippets. The director yelled "cut!" and a buzzer went off and they moved on to the next camera angle.

The story was complicated for a twenty-six-page script: the golddigger Patsy Belle arrives from Arkansas all a-tizzy over Jethro, flirting and scheming to get him to marry her. After some comical misunderstandings involving Granny's secret love potion—a jug marked XXXX—Patsy Belle wins the trust of the Clampetts, who undertake elaborate preparations for a wedding. Getting wind of all this, the ever-suspicious Drysdale sends the prettiest girl in his secretarial pool to make an even bigger play for Jethro. In the end, all the fussing and flirting frightens Jethro. He bolts from the altar. The last joke is when Granny tries to persuade Jed to go on and marry Patsy Belle, since he's already wearing his Sunday suit.

The girl playing the pretty secretary came to sit beside Lucille on the prop crate. She batted gorgeous blue eyes. "Hello, we didn't get to meet yesterday. I'm Sharon."

"Carolyn," Lucille said. "Isn't this exciting?"

"I guess so. If you don't mind sitting around all day."

"At least they gave you a nice dress to wear," said Lucille. "I look like something from the circus."

"But you've got a real part. My character doesn't even have a name, see? 'Pretty Girl.' That's me."

"I'll be glad to trade you," Lucille said. "Tell you the truth, I'm a little nervous. I've never done this before."

"Don't tell me that," said Sharon. "It's taken me three years of hard work to get a part this lousy."

A script girl appeared. "Sharon? Your scene's next."

"Good luck," said Lucille.

"You too." Sharon followed the script girl to the Drysdale office set. She was a real California beach girl with a lanky, carefree swing to her stride. Lucille watched her work through her scene in ten minutes, three takes, no problem. "Anything you say, Mr. Drysdale," she chirped, as Raymond Bailey mugged and leered.

"Miss Clay? Follow me, please."

Lucille carried the hatbox to the set representing the Clampetts' front door. She placed it on a fake-granite pedestal out of the way.

"Places, everybody!"

Lucille stepped under the hot lights, and here was that foreign woman again, reaching up on tiptoes with her powder puff. "A little shine on ze nose."

Bob Weed came hustling down from the other set. "Morning Max, hello Carolyn, ready to go to work?"

"Oh, yes sir."

"You know your lines?"

"I sure do." She'd stayed up til two a.m. learning them; she had the twists and turns of Patsy Belle engraved forever on her brain.

The stage manager pointed out the chalk mark where she was supposed to stand. The cameras were big hulking hooded machines with men riding their backs.

Max Baer sat in a director's chair marked MAX BAER, reading a book called *The Philosophical Indifference of Sin*. When all the lights were in place and adjusted, he put down the book and stepped to his mark. His face grew serious. "Okay, Bob, give me my motivation here."

"Let's see, you've had a big crush on her for years," said Bob Weed. "You're a little flustered by her aggressiveness, but you're happy about it too. Kid in a candy store."

Max Baer closed his eyes to fix this idea in his mind. He took a deep breath, flexed his arms in the air. When he opened his eyes he was Jethro with a big googly smile.

Bob called "Okay, roll 'em! Aaaaaand . . . action!"

"Golly, Miss Patsy Belle," said Jethro, "I can't believe you'd come all the way out here to California just to see me."

Lucille grinned her sexiest grin and slung her arms around his neck, just as she'd done at the audition. "Why Jethro, you big ol' hunk of man, of course I came to see you!" she cried. "I was so lonesome back home—I just *couldn't* stop thinking about you!"

"Aw, gee," he stammered, "did Granny see you yet? She'll be plumb tickled to see somebody from back home!"

"Oh, she saw me all right," Lucille said. "She tried to give me a dose of her medicine. She's such a sweet li'l ol' thing."

"Hoo-ee, you didn't drink that stuff, did you? Uncle Jed says one dose of Granny's tonic is enough to put hair on a bald-headed possum!"

"I don't care, Jethro," Lucille breathed. "Just as long as I can have a dose of those big old muscles of yours."

"Cut! Okay, that's good, but I want another take," said the director. "Carolyn, go ahead and touch him while you're flirting with him. And Max, she makes you a little more uncomfortable, I want all the awshucks you can give me. Load it on."

They did three takes in quick succession. Lucille forgot about the cameras and concentrated on playing Patsy Belle to Max Baer's Jethro. It was just like acting on the stage at Cornelia Baptist, except in place of Dooley Simpkins as Captain Von Trapp she was playing opposite a real TV star.

When that camera switched on, Max Baer had no shame at all. He became every bit as sweetly stupid as Jethro—besides which he was cute, in a low-rent Elvis kind of way. Lucille flirted and simpered and hammed it up, just as she saw him doing.

"Cut! Print it! That's really good, people. Let's keep that energy going. Next setup ..."

"You're doing great," said Max Baer. "Having fun?"

"I am having a ball," said Lucille.

From the corner of her eye she spotted a cameraman making off with the hatbox. "Excuse me ..." She ran after him. "Excuse me, that's mine."

"Okay, lady, but keep it out of my shot," the man said.

"Carolyn, we need you," said Bob Weed. "Remember, time's money, let's go."

"Sorry." She stuffed Chester under a light rack and hurried to her mark.

Making television was hard work. Before long Lucille was grateful for the little woman stepping in between takes to dab powder on her face. She flubbed several lines, but Max Baer flubbed his share, too. Mostly it seemed a matter of facing the right way for the camera and keeping your gaze focused in the scene instead of letting it drift over to some stagehand pushing a dolly in the semi-darkness.

They shot four scenes before lunch, and six scenes after. Bob Weed liked Lucille's performance so much he added a couple of lines to her scene with Granny.

They did five takes of the scene where Patsy Belle kissed Jethro. Max Baer showed her how to do a movie kiss with your lips closed, but on the last take he winked and slipped her the tongue.

Weed yelled cut.

Lucille bopped the actor's shoulder. "You better watch it, buster!"

He grinned. "Couldn't help myself."

Late in the day they put Lucille into a big fluffy wedding dress for her left-at-the-altar scene. The whole cast was dressed for the wedding, Irene Ryan in a lace bonnet, Buddy Ebsen in an old-fashioned parson's suit with his hair slicked back, Donna Douglas in a pink-organdie bridesmaid number. Max Baer looked silliest of all in a tuxedo cut three inches short, so his hands and feet stuck out and looked enormous.

"Okay people, if we can get this scene it's a wrap and everybody goes to the beach tomorrow," said Bob Weed.

The wedding took place in the Clampetts' entry hall. The script called for Patsy Belle to enter down the curving staircase, three beats behind Elly May in her bridesmaid dress.

To reach the top of those stairs Lucille had to go around behind the façade of the entry hall, onto a rickety scaffold and up a narrow spiral staircase. Somehow she made it to the little platform in that voluminous hoop-skirt.

"Careful," Donna Douglas said, "these steps are a bitch."

"Thanks." Lucille swept her train around with one hand, and took a deep breath.

"Roll 'em!" The strains of a recorded wedding march echoed through the soundstage. "Aaaaand . . . action!"

Donna Douglas put on a big gooey smile and moved into the blaze of lights, tossing rose petals from the basket in her hand.

Lucille tossed her veil and stepped out, intending to be the most beautiful bride anyone ever saw.

The first stair was steeper than she expected. Her heel caught the lining of her skirt, she lost her balance and went somersaulting down the stairs head over heels crash bang past Elly May, flat on her ass on the floor.

"Weeee doggie, Jethro, that gal shore is in a hurry to get down here and marry you," Buddy Ebsen cracked.

The set exploded in laughter.

Lucille pushed up on her elbows, dazed, her veil askew. "Cut!" Bob Weed rushed over. "You okay?"

"I think so." She'd snapped the spike heel off one shoe; nothing else seemed to be broken.

"Great fall!" Bob enthused. "I'm gonna keep it! Buddy, what a line! We're keeping the whole thing. Greg, did you get that?"

"Sure did, Mr. Weed, that was swell."

"You get the wide shot on Buddy's ad lib?"

The actors gathered around Lucille. Buddy Ebsen knelt to help her. "Little lady, you all right?"

She got to her feet, her ears ringing. The crew clapped and whistled.

"I tried to warn you about those steps," said Donna Douglas, patting her shoulder. "If I was you I'd sue somebody."

"Don't say that, I'll make sure she gets a bonus for stunt work," Bob said. "Carolyn, that was inspired."

He went off to huddle with the writers while two ladies from the costume department helped Lucille put herself back together. When the director returned he'd added a scene in which Patsy Belle samples some of Granny's XXXX tonic before the wedding, resulting in her tumble down the stairs. This meant she had to act the rest of the scene drunk. "Do you think you can do that?" said Weed. "It'll play much funnier."

"Yeah, I can act drunk." She would just picture Chester on one of his Friday nights, and the rest would come.

"Okay, Maureen, put her back like she was, total disarray. We'll start from when Buddy helps her up, and Carolyn, your line now is 'I'm not as think as you drunk I am.' You got that?"

Lucille's heart was still pounding, but she did her best to play the scene just the way he wanted, reeling and tottering on her broken shoe.

Everyone pronounced it hilarious. Bob said it was much stronger than the original finish. They did four takes before he got it just the way he wanted, and after that they had to shoot the new bit with the jug of moonshine.

By the time he called, "Cut! Thank you, folks, that's a wrap!" Lucille was so exhausted she was swaying on her feet for real. She had no idea acting was such hard work. Watching movies and

TV, she had imagined that a movie star's job was to stand up, say a few lines, and ride home to her mansion in her limousine.

Technicians began snapping out lights. Bob Weed took Lucille aside. "I know you didn't mean to fall, but you were a real trouper, you took it in stride. The show will be a lot better for it."

"Thanks a lot, Mr. Weed. Do you need me in the morning?"

"No, tomorrow we just clean up odds and ends. You'll get paid for the full three days. Hope we'll be working together again. Good luck."

Lucille looked around for someone to wash out her hair, but the makeup people had gone home. She found her street clothes in a locker with "C. Clay" masking-taped on the door. She changed quickly, and peeled off the tape as a souvenir.

She was almost out the door before she remembered Chester.

She hurried through Granny's parlor, around the edge of the cement pond—then she saw the hatbox under the lightstand where she'd left it, and allowed herself to breathe.

"Come on, Chester." She grabbed him up.

"Lou-see-yul," he whispered, "I love you, honey."

"You shut up."

It was dark outside. The only human being in sight was the guard in the booth at the gate.

Lucille rapped on the glass. "Can you call a taxi for me?"

"Sorry, no outside line. You can walk up to the corner and wave one down."

"Thanks." Her toes ached from those pointy-toed shoes, but she felt pretty damn good about the job she had done. Nobody would nominate her for an Emmy—but nobody had pointed her out as a rank amateur, either. They hadn't had to stop a scene on her account more than three or four times. Even her inelegant pratfall had turned into the comedic high point of the day.

Her tailbone was sore, and also her shoulder where she'd hit the stair-rail. She couldn't keep a big smile off her face. She had done exactly what she'd set out to do, that very first moment when the skull-and-bones winked at her from the can of D-Con, when the devil's voice whispered the idea in her ear. She threw over her whole life and came to Hollywood and made good. Chester never believed she could do it. She'd brought him along to witness the whole thing. Now his humiliation was complete. Lucille had won a monumental victory over him and everyone else who'd ever doubted her.

Anything that happened after this was pure gravy.

Traffic raced in both directions. The occasional taxi seemed to speed up when the driver saw Lucille out in the street, waving.

This neighborhood was nothing like Beverly Hills: blank-faced warehouses, vacant lots, arc-vapor streetlamps casting everything in a violet light. She should have arranged for a car from the hotel.

Where was Norman when she needed him?

A police car slowed down for a look. The cop's face swiveled to follow her as they drove past.

Lucille quickened her step down the block.

A pair of Yellow Cabs cruised by. She waved both arms over her head but neither driver slowed down.

The cop car swung into view at the next corner, coming back around for another look.

Lucille set off down Las Palmas toward the studio gate, keenly aware of the hatbox in her hand.

She felt the headlights on her back. *Don't run, Lucille. Do not run.* The gun was tucked in the tissue paper alongside the money and Chester, just where she could not get at it.

The black-and-white car slid up alongside. "Good evening."

The cop had a bland, chubby face, curly blond hair. Also he had a partner, so the gun wouldn't be any use even if she could get at it.

"What's the problem, Officer?"

"You got some identification?"

"No, sorry. I left it back at my hotel."

"Where would that be?"

"The Beverly Hills."

He looked her up and down. "You don't say."

Suddenly she saw her image reflected in the glass of the back window—Patsy Belle's big poufy hair and the layers of garish makeup. She'd been standing out in the street waving at cars. . . .

"Oh my God—oh, I see what you're thinking. You know, it's the strangest thing how many people have been making this mistake lately."

"Really?" he said. "How long's it been since the last time?"

"No, listen, Officer, you've got it all wrong. I'm an actress. I was in this studio here shooting 'The Beverly Hillbillies' today. This is stage makeup."

"What's in the hatbox?"

Lucille saw that her only hope of escape was a swift counter-assault. She would have to brazen her way out of this. "It's a hat. What's the matter, is that against the law?"

The partner spoke up: "I think this *is* a studio, Ed."

"You're damn right it is," said Lucille. "Haven't you got anything better to do than going around bothering innocent women?"

"That guy up there," said the first cop, indicating the guard in the booth. "Can he vouch for you?"

"Well he better, he just sent me to the corner to find a cab. I couldn't get one to stop." She marched toward the gate.

The cruiser edged along after her.

"Hey Mister," she called, "would you please come out and tell these men I've been working in there? They seem to think I'm working out here."

It was more than the makeup and hair. It must be something about the way Lucille carried herself, something that revealed her awakening to the power of sex in these last few weeks. Or maybe it was all in the eyes of men, maybe they saw whores everywhere they looked, maybe they thought all women were whores except their mothers and the Virgin Mary.

The guard stepped out with his hand up to block the headlights. "She was on Stage Three. I signed her out myself." Lucille stalked back to the cruiser. "I hope you're satisfied. You owe me an apology."

"Listen, lady," the cop said, "it was an honest mistake, in this neighborhood. We have to keep an eye on things."

"Not only do you owe me an apology," she said, "but I think you ought to give me a ride to my hotel."

Lately she could not resist flirting with danger every time it wiggled a finger at her. The best defense, as Chester used to say, is a good offense.

"Can't do that," the cop said. "We're on duty."

"Yeah, you're real busy, I can tell." You Can WIN! At Roulette.

"Aw, let's give her a ride, Ed. It was our mistake."

"It sure was," Lucille said, "and I can't wait to tell my lawyer about it."

"Get in the back," said the first cop.

That is how Lucille came to ride from the studio to the Beverly Hills Hotel under the protection of the Los Angeles Police Department, with Chester's head and a gun and eighteen thousand dollars in a box on her lap. It seemed like a pretty good joke. The cops were friendly. They wanted to know inside stuff about Jed and Granny and especially Elly May.

The doorman at the Beverly Hills did not bat an eye. He stepped to open the back of the black-and-white car as if it were a limousine. "Good evening, Miss Clay. Welcome back."

"Thank you," she said. "Thanks for the ride, boys."

The cops waved and rolled off down the drive.

"Wasn't that nice," Lucille said. "They gave me a ride home. Everybody is so friendly out here."

Harry Hall called for her in his white Rolls-Royce on a warm summer Saturday night. He looked splendid in his tuxedo at the wheel of that car. Lucille twirled to let him admire her latest fashion splurge, a black sparkly party gown with sequins and a filmy shawl to cover her bare shoulders. "You like it? It's new."

"It's marvelous," he said, "but haven't your ill-gotten gains begun to run out on you yet?"

"Not yet."

"And of course the hatbox, as always." The Rolls purred off into the soft summer night. "It's one of my great ambitions to have a look at that hat one day."

"It's not just a hat, Harry. I keep all my important things in here."

"Most girls I know get by with a purse," he said.

She smiled. "I'm not like most girls."

"You can say that again. Walter Weitzman called me, all excited. Apparently you had some kind of mishap, and they were able to use it?"

"I fell down the stairs." Lucille drew the shawl around her head to protect her fancy French twist from the wind. "They thought it was funny."

"They sure did. From what Walter says the film is hysterical. He's offered us a contract. They want to write Patsy Belle into four shows for the fall season."

"You're kidding! Oh Harry, that's terrific."

"Yes and no. It's terrific they liked you, but I'm not sure we want to lock you into anything just yet. It may turn out Alexander Powell has something bigger for us at Paramount. This is his party tonight. Be nice to him but don't promise anything."

They followed a narrow, winding road into the hills. The smell of eucalyptus washed through the car. City lights sparkled in the distance, twinkling like the string of Christmas lights inside Lucille. These days in Hollywood had been the very best of her life. Every day she tempted fate, and every day fate handed her another plump bundle of good fortune wrapped up in shiny paper. While the people back home were fighting and marching and dying and having their eyes put out, the old ways of life unraveling, Lucille was forging a wonderful new life for herself. She didn't know how long her luck could go on getting better and better, with no price to pay for what she had done.

For days now she had sensed a shadow trailing her, a dark silhouette running along underneath her happiness. She knew this was not her real life but only a wonderful vacation from life, a vacation now moving toward its inevitable end. She had stayed on in her bungalow because she had a feeling this part of her journey was almost over, and she wanted to savor every moment.

Lucille had some terrible qualities—she was vain, selfish, quick-tempered, with a certain late tendency toward violence and sex—but stupidity was not one of them. Along with the glow of her sudden success came the knowledge of the huge risk she was taking, living out her dream this way. She could not hide her face in the gray cloud now. The cloud was nowhere in sight. She knew what would probably happen Wednesday night when her face was broadcast onto twenty million television sets. She could not put herself out over the airwaves of America and hope to remain anonymous.

She clung to the vague hope that Patsy Belle's makeup and hair might have transformed her so completely no one would recognize her, but that was a very slender thread.

She had her bags all packed in the closet of Bungalow Six, ready to go at a moment's notice.

She didn't know when, or where. She knew only that she had to stay one step ahead. She could do it, she could keep going, if only she could find the right place to get rid of Chester. She simply had to stop dragging him around. The load was becoming intolerable. That hatbox must weigh fifty pounds by now.

"You're quiet tonight," Harry said.

"Just thinking. I'm so lucky, here, lately."

"You make your own lick, kiddo. Take me, for instance. I started out with nothing. I worked for everything I've got."

She lit a Salem. "Listen, Harry, if anything should happen, if I should decide to take off for a few days, don't make a big thing about it, okay?"

"What do you mean, take off. We're just getting started! Two days' work and you want a vacation?"

"I'm not sure." She breathed smoke. "I might have to go someplace for a while. I have some unfinished business."

"What's going on, Lucille?"

"Please, Harry, don't ask me questions. And remember it's Carolyn now."

"No, I want to talk to Lucille. Face-to-face, Harry to Lucille. What are you up to? Are you going to quit and go home just when I'm about to make things happen for you?"

"No, I'm not going home. I probably won't go anywhere. I just wanted you to know not to worry. If I did. And also how grateful I am."

He touched the brake. "You're serious, aren't you. What is this all about?"

"Nothing! I'm sorry I mentioned it."

"Because the truth is I've invested quite a bit of time in you already. I have a stake in this now. If you've got something up your sleeve, I want you to tell me. I don't like surprises." '

"Look Harry, no sleeves." She tried to turn it into a joke.

He drove uphill in silence, glancing from the road to her face.

"Don't do anything without talking to me," he said. "I don't say this to everyone, but I see a real future for you. You're not a leading lady, you're a year or two on the wrong side of thirty for that, but you have the makings of a really fine comic actress. Walter said you took that pratfall like Lucille Ball."

"I didn't mean to, believe me," she said. Hollywood! The only place on earth where you could become a fine comic actress by falling on your ass.

They pulled up to a stone gate which swung open as if by magic. The driveway led over the ridge to reveal a magnificent white stone palace spread in a natural bowl on the hilltop, a kingdom of gardens and pools glowing with people and music and lights in the trees.

From this ridge, Hollywood stretched out forever, a glittering carpet of lights and possibilities. The lights overwhelmed all the stars in the sky.

Lucille gaped. "This is his *house?*"

"One of them. Alexander has houses in Malibu, Paris, Cap d'Antibes. Also a flat in New York."

A snappy young man came to park the car. Lucille and Harry walked up a stone path. "You mean that nice-looking gray-headed man? The one who was so busy looking after his wife's little dogs?"

"That's the one."

"I should have paid more attention to him," she said.

"Don't pay too much attention," he said. "Joan bites. She never lets him out of her—whoa, hello, Alexander, good evening!"

"Harry, you scoundrel, welcome! I see you've brought your lovely Miss Clay."

"Well hey, Mr. Powell," she said. "Thanks for inviting me to your party. I just love your house."

"Well, thank you, we like it too. Make yourself at home—oh there you are, Bob! Dolores, don't you look lovely!"

Dear Lord, that was Bob Hope coming up the sidewalk with his wife, not five paces from Lucille. She had an urge to find a phone and call Mama. Mama always had a big thing for Bob Hope.

Harry clasped her arm. "Come along, dear, close your mouth, now, that's good. There will be a lot of film people here tonight, I don't want you to stare. They hate that."

"Okay. I'll try."

A waiter floated by with champagne in long flutes.

"Oh my God," Lucille said, "Cary Grant."

"And don't point. Hello, Cary."

"Harry Hall! How are you?" They shook hands. He was gorgeous, though a bit older than Lucille had imagined.

"I'm fine. This is Carolyn Clay, a client of mine."

"And a lovely one, too." Cary Grant took Lucille's hand in his, and kissed it just above the knuckles.

She melted. "Oh thank you, Mr. Grant. I've watched you in so many movies I feel like I ought to kiss *your* hand."

"By all means." He extended his hand.

She bowed to the kiss. She would always carry the moment: her lips against Cary Grant's hand.

"A charming custom," he said, "I must teach it to all my friends. Good to meet you, Miss Clay. See you, Harry." He smiled, headed off to the bar.

She wanted to tell him she had named her second son for him, but she'd been too shy. "I could die right now and be happy, Harry. Did I embarrass you?"

"Not at all. Kiss all the hands you like. But do me a favor and stash that hatbox somewhere. Just for ten minutes."

"All right . . ." The house unfolded as Lucille stepped down into it, ever larger rooms opening out to a wall of plate glass, a glowing turquoise pool, the shimmering city beyond. A pianist in white-tie-and-tails sat at a white grand piano playing "Rhapsody in Blue" for the glamorous people smoking and drinking and talking.

"Harry, I'll find someplace to put this."

"Don't get lost, now."

All the rooms were designed in a severe super-modern style, bare white walls with white furniture and white carpets, no decoration at all. Lucille carried Chester down a long empty corridor, checking in each door. If these people owned anything that wasn't white, they had hidden it well.

At last she found a room with a welcome clutter of fur stoles and evening wraps on a bed, handbags lined up along a wall. She tucked Chester under the bed and whispered for him to keep quiet.

She nodded at the uniformed maid coming down the hall with an armload of furs. This place seemed more like a sleek new hotel than somebody's home. Lucille could not begin to understand why you would have such a big house with nothing in it. She supposed it was elegant, in a cold, empty way—but can you imagine what a couple of kids would do to all these white rugs?

Of course the dazzling people at this party had no kids and never spilled their drinks. Lucille had finally gone above her raising: she was in a room full of movie stars and people who knew how to talk to movie stars without gushing and turning red. No one was making a move to have her thrown out.

She spotted Harry near the fireplace in a group that included Joan Blake, the tall blonde from poolside at the Beverly Hills. She looked very flashy in a gold-beaded dress and a huge platinum bouffant, not altogether unlike the hairdo that had nearly gotten Lucille arrested on Santa Monica Boulevard. Joan's chihuahuas were off their chains, snapping and yipping at everyone's ankles as if they were on diet pills.

Lucille gazed upon the spectacle of Richard Chamberlain, Donald O'Connor, and Mitzi Gaynor in the same end of one room. Richard and Donald shared a private joke. Mitzi held forth in a circle of admirers, telling a story that had everyone's eyes dancing. The pianist played "Taking a Chance on Love."

Lucille held up her shoulders and moved through with her glass poised in one hand, as she'd learned from the movies. Harry said, "Joan, you remember Carolyn, don't you?"

"Of course I do."

"Your house is just beautiful, thank you for having me." Lucille felt a tug, and looked down to find one of the chihuahuas yanking at the hem of her new dress. "No, doggie," she said, trying to shake it off. "Go on, now." The dog wouldn't be shaken lightly. It bared its teeth and tugged harder.

Lucille managed a smile. She bent over, tried to shoo it away. She heard the *zzt!* of cloth ripping.

Joan's voice turned squeaky. "What's the matter, Binkums, you smell something? Huh? Does he smell sumsin?"

The dog growled and ripped a three-inch strip of hem from Lucille's new dress.

"Get *away* from me!" She gave a backhand swat to its hind end. The dog shrieked and let go.

When she thought about it later, Lucille could have sworn that dog gave her a dirty look. There was something mean in its little black eyes.

The second and third chihuahuas entered the fray, yarping and jumping up on their hind legs.

Joan Blake said, "Well you didn't have to hit him!" She knelt down and let the dogs jump all over her. "Come here sweetie, did she hurt you, no, he's okay. He's okay."

"Joan, have you ever given any thought to having actual children?" said Harry.

"Shut up, Harry." She drew herself to full height. "Excuse me. I'll go put them away." She stalked off to the back of the house, trailed by the trio of yappers.

"Damn dog tore my new dress," said Lucille. "Sorry, Harry, I guess I shouldn't have hit it."

"Don't worry about it. She used to have four of the little bastards. One of them bit my ankle once. But only once."

Lucille laughed. "You killed it?"

"No, no. It died of natural causes, I think. Maybe one taste of my leg was fatal. Listen, darling, I see two or three people I must speak to, then I'll introduce you around. Will you be all right just to mingle?"

"I'm fine, Harry. I'm just wonderful."

She went to stand beside the piano man. He glanced up from his keyboard with a wink. She wished someone would take her picture right now, so she could remember forever how she looked in that gorgeous black gown reflected in the wall of glass, while the city lights trembled in the distance and the man played "Whatever Lola Wants" just for her.

Someone stepped up beside her, a hand on her elbow. She turned with a smile but it was not Harry.

"Hello, little baby."

A shock: It was him. The man of her dreams, in a tuxedo.

His smile was brilliant, his face more handsome than she had ever realized in the dark.

"Oh my Lord." She took a step back.

"I can't believe you're here," he said. "I thought my eyes were playing a trick on me."

She blushed. "Go away," she whispered.

"Did I startle you?"

"Someone might see us."

"Oh, I get it." He backed up a step, his hand upraised. "You're married. Sorry. Forget I was here."

"No, wait, that's not it." She wished the pianist would play louder; she felt as if the whole party had ground to a halt and everyone was looking at her and the man who had come to her bungalow, the man whose name she did not even know. "I just—I didn't expect to see you again."

"Me either, what a stroke, huh? I'm not staying at the hotel anymore, I've rented a place just above Sunset." He dropped his voice. "Are you still in your bungalow?"

"Well, yes, but I'm leaving any day now."

"Where?"

"I don't know, Japan. Argentina. Somewhere far."

He said, "I'm Toby Clark. I don't think we ever . . . I mean, we didn't introduce ourselves, did we."

"I'm Carolyn." She cleared her throat, forced a smile. "Listen, would you mind getting me some more champagne? All of a sudden I'm dry as a bone."

"Of course, give me your glass. I'll be right back." Even in his formal suit he looked like a soldier, built solid and close to the ground, with that pink scrubbed face and the boyish crewcut. And now she knew why. He was Toby Clark. Lucille had made love to Toby Clark. Oh, if the women of Cornelia ever heard that, they would drop dead from pure envy.

She'd known his face since he was a second banana in all those beach movies, but he'd only lately become famous as Private Dolan in *The Last Man Standing,* the World War II picture that won all the Oscars. She remembered his big dying scene, when his leg was blown off above the knee and he thought he was back home in Kansas. He cried out for his mother. Lucille had wept for him then.

Just think—Toby Clark, that poor wounded all-American boy, was in real life the kind of man who would call up a perfect stranger in her hotel room, talk his way into her bed, make wild love to her, and leave without saying his name.

But then, Lucille was the kind of woman who unlocked the door to let him in. Didn't that even things out, pretty much? What gave her the right to cast judgment on him?

Here he came with that grin and two glasses of champagne.

"You should have told me who you were the other night," she said. "Now I'm embarrassed. I loved you in *The Last Man Standing.*"

"It didn't seem important at the time, but thank you." He lifted his glass. "Cheers."

They clinked.

Lucille said, "If you'd told me your name on the phone, I would have invited you over for a proper introduction."

He grinned. "Oh, but I liked the way it happened. Didn't you?"

"Yes. I did." There, she'd said it. The truth was out of her mouth. "It was a different kind of evening for me."

"Me too. I'd love a return engagement sometime."

"Uhmmm . . . no, I don't think so," she said. "I'm not staying here long."

"That's right, Argentina. You told me." He clinked her glass again. "To Argentina."

"Listen, would you mind if I got an autograph? It's for my—my niece, she's a big fan of yours."

He smiled and said okay, but she could tell it pained him. Just that fast she had become just another fan searching for a pen and a cocktail napkin. The moment was ruined.

"Make it out to Lucille," she said. "Put something, you know, kind of mushy."

He wrote "For Lucille—yours from here to eternity—Love, Toby Clark." "Here you go."

"Oh, that will make her so happy." Lucille folded the napkin. "I'm sorry, I know you must get tired of that."

"Never," he said, with a professional smile. "Listen, Carolyn, I see my producer over there. I'll come back and see how you're doing in a bit, all right?"

"Sure. That's fine. It's—it's nice to see you again." She smiled and watched him walk away. What a fool! She'd had Toby Clark in the palm of her hand, in her very own bed—the same Toby Clark whose pretty face made thousands of women warm and squirmy in the darkness of the matinee—and she'd run him off, just that fast.

She wished he had stayed in her dreams instead of materializing out of nowhere, only to lose interest in her.

At that moment there came a scream from the back of the house—a wild harrowing scream that silenced the piano and froze conversation to the far side of the swimming pool.

Everyone turned.

Joan Blake appeared in the door at the top of the room, shrieking, flailing her arms as if hornets were stinging her to death. She stumbled and got up and ran blindly through the room, pursued by some demon no one could see.

People stepped back to get out of her way. Propelled by her desperate screams she ran clawing at the air, tripped and fell, got up again and ran full speed through the plate-glass wall at the end of the room.

The glass burst over her in a dazzling white downpour.

Joan Blake toppled, bleeding, into the pool.

When something like that happens, one person reacts by instinct and everyone follows. Lucille always liked to remember that it was Toby Clark who dashed through that shattered glass and leapt to Joan's rescue in the pool, leading everyone else to rush after him out of the room—everyone except Lucille, who went the other way.

She hurried down the hall toward the sound of dogs yapping.

She had an idea what she would find, and she braced herself—Yes.

Chester was out of his box.

He was out of his box and his Tupperware, he was on the floor by the bed, encircled by chihuahuas barking their little lungs out. One of them had Chester by the hair and was trying to drag him across the rug.

It startled Lucille: he still looked so much like himself. That was his face. His skin wasn't the right color, he was purplish-black, but those were his features, unmistakably. She did not linger on the sight of him. She kicked the dog loose, grasped Chester by his greasy hair, and stuffed him back in the Tupperware bowl with a squishing sound that made her stomach flop over.

She had to push down to wedge him back in there. She swallowed the acid taste in her mouth. A dark fluid had spilled from the lettuce keeper all over the immaculate carpet.

The dogs barked and barked.

Holding her breath, rummaging among the furs on the bed, Lucille found the plastic lid and snapped it back on. She ran her thumb around the press-and-lock seal, wedged the bowl back into the hatbox, and crammed on the box-lid just as Harry Hall rushed to the door.

He stared at the stain on the rug. He caught a whiff of Chester and paled. The Tupperware seal had worked wonders, it surely had, but Chester had been in there for weeks now and you could not deny that smell.

"Hello, Harry." She fumbled to tie the ribbons. "I guess Joan didn't care for my hat."

"Yeah, but—but—"

"She was poking around where it wasn't any of her business." She snatched up the hatbox, kissed Harry's cheek, and slipped past him down the hall, past the noisy confusion around the swimming pool and the tuxedoed men running through the house. She marched straight out the front door to the first limousine in line.

"I'll give you one hundred dollars to take me to the Beverly Hills Hotel," she said to the driver. "I mean right now."

His face lit up. "Get in!"

She jumped in beside him. The big engine roared to life. The car jumped ahead with a screech.

Lucille got the hell out of there.

from NUDE MEN

Amanda Filipacchi

I AM PLEASED TO ANNOUNCE THAT LAURA IS OFFICIALLY MY girlfriend and I'm her boyfriend. It's been the case since the first night, in fact, but I'm mentioning it now in case it wasn't clear. We are very good for each other. She makes me more normal, and I make her less normal. I've told her about sleeping with my elephant. She took it well.

She also took it well when I "quit" my job. Although she works only for the respectability, not for the money, working is not something she requires of others. She's extremely well balanced. People who are very well balanced don't need ambition to be happy. They don't need goals. They appreciate life. They live one day at a time and love each day. She evokes this same serenity in me.

Laura is tallish, but not extremely tall for a woman, which is good because I'm not very tall for a man. She is perfectly proportioned, and she's as beautiful as a magazine model, her body too. She has light-brown hair and warm brown eyes. She's a brown person: brown as in brown haireyes. Very sensible, but sensitive; down-to-earth, but warm; moderate, but able to be extravagant. In addition to being a brown person, she happens to be so gorgeous physically, mentally, and emotionally that any man would marry her instantly if he were lucky enough to be the object of her love, like I am.

Her face always glows with health, and her cheeks are pink. She has healthy-looking teeth that are not too white: they are very real-looking and blend well with the color of her skin. One eye wanders out sometimes, but ever so slightly and imaginatively— I mean "rarely"—that I always think it's my imagination. It gives her an air of reality, of being a human, alive, who will die, which humans do.

Her personality, as well, is brown. Brown as in earth, down to earth.

We spend most of our time together at her place, not at mine, because although I keep my apartment clean these days, hers is bigger, more comfortable, more luxurious, paid for by her parents. It's a big, pale apartment with lots of light and few cumbersome objects, except for a shiny black piano. She does not play it well but loves to play, anyway, and likes the look of the instrument. She says she has always felt happy in a room with a piano. We sometimes toy with the idea of living together but decide to wait until the perfect moment, a time when it will happen naturally, almost without our thinking.

I go to practically every one of Laura's shows, to be nice and because I love her. I privately feel sorry for her and wish I could help her. It makes me suffer to see someone make such a fool of herself. Especially someone I know. Especially someone I like.

I finally decide I cannot let her go on with her pathetic show without at least trying to shake her up a bit. So one Sunday afternoon, at her apartment, I introduce the subject by making a casual comment.

"You know, I was thinking, it might not be a bad idea to show the empty boot first, before you take the flower out of it."

"My foot's in it. Isn't that enough proof the boot is empty?"she asks.

"Of course not," I say gently. "You know, I was wondering: You never told me if you know how to do any traditional magic tricks."

"You don't like my show," she states flatly.

"Yes I do! I just thought it might perk it up a little to do some traditional magic, like when things seem to really disappear and stuff."

"I don't do that sort of thing. I do modern magic."

"It seems more like baby magic to me," I say. "Any kid can do it. No offense."

"That's what ignorant people say of abstract art. This is abstract magic, modern magic, postmodern magic, naïve magic, experimental magic, avant-garde magic, an acquired taste. The dancing makes my work slightly more accessible and commercial. I could add singing, but that might overwhelm them."

"To do modern stuff, you have to know the traditional stuff," I tell her. "You can't resort to modern stuff just because it's easier. Good modern stuff is done out of choice, not out of inability to do anything else. Picasso was able to do extremely realistic portraits of people. He simply chose not to concentrate on that style."

"I just don't *do* realistic magic. It's not my thing."

"I know, but do you know *how* to do it?"

"Of course."

"Could I see some of your tricks?" I feel like a policeman. Could I see your driver's license?

She stares at me for a few long seconds and then goes into her bedroom to get her equipment.

She comes back and stands in front of me, holding a top hat and a wand. She proceeds to do the well-known, traditional magic trick, which one has seen a dozen times in the subways and on TV, of pulling a toy rabbit out of a top hat, after having shown me the empty hat first. She does it stiffly and clumsily. She truly has no talent for it. Not very coordinated.

"Pretty good, pretty good," I tell her. "I wouldn't compare you to Picasso, but pretty good. Can't you do anything better than that, though?"

She makes an ugly face at me and does the well-known trick with the silver loops, of attaching them and detaching them, when they seem unattachable and undetachable. The tip of her tongue is stuck out in concentration. Truly nothing impressive. It's almost worse than the baby magic she does onstage. You need a minimum of grace and assurance.

"Isn't there *any* trick you can do well?" I ask, in a joking tone. I don't want to seem too harsh, but I don't want to be too soft either, or it won't help her.

"You are ruffling my feathers, Mr. Acidophilus." She really is offended. It's nice she can joke about it and put on a light air. Perhaps I poked at a sensitive spot of hers. Perhaps she has a terrible complex about being incompetent at magic.

But she calmly proceeds to do the trick of making a card disappear under a handkerchief. She moves like a robot. She does it so badly that I can almost guess where she hid the card: in the lining of the handkerchief, or in her sleeve, or wherever cards are hid.

"Don't you do *anything* well?" I ask.

She angrily slaps a coin into her palm, and it disappears before my very eyes, while her hand remains open.

"There, that's more my territory," she mumbles.

I look up at her face. She quickly looks away and repeats the traditional trick with the silver loops. I stop her.

"Laura, that thing you just did. What was it?"

She blushes, pouts, looks distressed, and quickly blurts out, "You just pushed me too far. You humiliated me. I wasn't thinking. Let's erase the slate. I want to lose consciousness."

"I'm sure you do," I say, stunned. "I'm sure you do," I repeat involuntarily. "That seemed mighty much like real magic to me."

"Of course not. That's the only trick I'm good at. I just happen to do it well because it requires no sleight of hand."

"*It requires no sleight of hand?* Then it sounds even more like real magic to me."

"Well, it's not."

"Then show me how you did it."

"It's too complicated to explain."

"Try."

"No. Magicians are absolutely never supposed to reveal their tricks, no matter what. But you can go to any magic store and buy the kit with the instruction book."

I do exactly that. Early the next day, I go to a magic store and ask for a trick that enables you to make a coin disappear while your hand is open. They do not sell such a thing, of course, because such a trick can be performed only by fairies or witches or TVs. When I get home, I tell her I didn't find her trick for sale.

"Yeah, well, I didn't think you'd go check," she says. "I just wanted to get you off my back. It was actually my grandfather who taught it to me."

"I don't believe you for one second, just for the record."

"The only reason you're obsessed with it is because it involves a coin, like when you were little," she says. "If it had been a button in my hand, or a thimble, or a ring, or a pebble, you wouldn't have given it another thought."

"Not true."

"Yes true."

"Not not not."

"Yeah yeah yeah."

"No, I tell you."

"Yes, absolutely."

"Not on your life."

"Yes on my life."

"Forget it," I say, waving my hand. But I then turn toward her eagerly and exclaim, "Do it again!"

"Never. Drop your fixation."

"Never."

We stare at each other, almost panting. I suddenly plop down on the couch, exhausted. "I understand your dilemma," I drawl. "You're obviously not good at traditional magic, and it would be too risky for you to do your *real* magic, because even if you tried to make it look like fake magic, there's always the chance you could get discovered. So all you can do is your postmodern baby magic. I understand your problem, and I now respect your decision." I close my eyes. My case is closed: There is nothing you can say that will make my words untrue.

"Oh, *please!* Give me a break," she says. "My *real* magic? Yeah, right, Jeremy."

Nothing you can say.

I observe Laura carefully whenever I'm with her, to try and catch her doing some of her real magic. I often wonder if I might have been wrong about that coin trick. Perhaps she can't do real magic. Perhaps the quarter did not truly disappear from her palm as I thought it did. Maybe I hallucinated, though I'm convinced I didn't.

How strong is her magic, I wonder. What other tricks can she do? Can she make a chair disappear, or only small things? Can she make things appear, or only disappear? Can she make people love her?

Can she make people love her? Am I under her spell?

I sometimes ask her to show me more of her real magic, and she tries to ridicule me, to make me stop pestering her. She'll say things like: "I can't believe you, Jeremy. You're such a baby! You still believe in magic. How many times do I have to tell you I'm not a fairy?"

You would think that since she's so eager for me to drop my fixation, she'd simply reveal to me how she performed her coin trick. But she doesn't, which I'm convinced means that there's nothing to reveal, no solution, no secret; it's just pure, undiluted magic.

*   *   *

I keep going to her shows, and I sometimes fall asleep halfway through. One evening I wake up suddenly from my doze because I hear clapping. What? What? What are they clapping at? The show's not over yet. So what are they clapping at? I sit forward in my seat and squint at the bright lights stinging my sleepy eyes. I don't notice anything strange or different. Did she do her real magic? Could that be it? No, I doubt it, because if she had made things really disappear onstage, in front of their very eyes, using no sleight of hand, they wouldn't be clapping; they'd be fainting, or getting the police, or running out, or screaming madly, or kissing her feet and worshiping her like a god. Perhaps I'm getting carried away. But at the very least, they'd be staring at her with complete astonishment, like me when she made the coin disappear. They would be too stunned to clap.

I did not notice what she did to deserve the clapping. I missed it. Oh well, I'll have to ask her about it later. But suddenly there is clapping again, and my eyes are not closed, and I can tell you that she did *nothing* to deserve it. It's her same old marble-out-of-mouth trick. For the rest of the show, there are two tables of people who clap at every lousy rotten trick she does, and I stare at them with disbelief and then look at Laura to see if she is troubled, or pleased. She does look a little stunned. She has trouble concentrating, I can tell, takes longer than usual to accomplish every trick and every interlude of dance. Sometimes she glances at the clapping tables and then quickly looks away. But she does not look displeased. Her eyes are brighter than usual, and her lips are blushing and smiling in a lovely soft manner.

The clappers look like students. Some are older, and wiser-looking, as if they might be graduate students. They have beards.

After her show, I tell her I don't understand. She says, "Maybe it's you, Jeremy. Maybe you bring me good luck."

At her next show, three nights later, there are five clapping tables.

The waiters have to bring in more tables, and they eliminate the open dancing area. Her show goes from ten minutes to twenty to half an hour, but not more. She doesn't want to overdo it. She wants to leave them unsatisfied, dying for more. And then we realize that she is an overnight sensation.

But don't think it's her same old dumb tricks that are attracting so much attention. No. It's her new tricks, which are even more moronic. Laura has great instinct and intuition about people. After her first successful evening, she was able to sense which tricks people were clapping at particularly loudly, and she went in that direction. Her most admired tricks are the ones that are barely perceptible as tricks, the most subtle ones, like when she takes off her brown jacket and reveals that the inside is red.

Her tricks get progressively more idiotic, and the clapping and the number of clappers increase. Laura unwraps a candy and smells it, and people clap. Such tricks cannot even be called magic anymore, yet people call them that with delight, and calling them that contains a message about modern life and society, which goes something like this: In our times, routine, habit, drudgery, and repetition are so ingrained, so inescapable, that it seems as though nothing short of magic can break the pattern of eating the candy. Breaking that pattern, by doing the unexpected, even ever so slightly, like smelling the candy, is so unusual and extraordinary that it is certainly worth being called magic and certainly worth clapping for.

When Laura takes a Kleenex out of her pocket and wipes her forehead with it, everyone roars with clapter because the primary function of a Kleenex is to receive a nose's wind. By wiping her forehead (a less common, secondary function), Laura is fighting drudgery and expectation.

The most refined people are those who can detect the subtlest tricks, and they clap. If someone claps wrongly, at one of Laura's "trick tricks," like when she looks at the time on her watch, well, she'll shake her head ever so slightly, and the person is horribly humiliated, given crushingly subtle looks of disdain and contemptuous clucks of the tongue by the other members of the audience. If, on the other hand, someone claps alone in the right place, Laura's lips twitch into a slight smile, and everyone joins in on the clapping and bestows on the first lucky clapper looks of endless respect and admiration.

A typical evening consists of the following repertoire of basic tricks:

Laura winds her watch. One courageous clapper dares a few claps. She smiles slightly. They all roar, with clapter, and reward the fortunate first clapper with smiles and "Ah!"'s of awe. The primary function of a watch is to indicate the time, which is worth no respect because it only contributes to the monotony of modern life. To be wound is a watch's secondary, less common, function and is worth great respect.

Laura takes a comb and brush out of her box of objects and starts combing the hair out of the brush. One clapper claps, she twitches her lips, the entire room claps.

She takes off her pearl necklace and puts it on the table on the stage. Someone claps, she turns her head one inch to the side, which everyone knows is a negative response, and people cluck, snort, and snicker to the now ruined first clapper. People have become bold. Sometimes they even allow their disdain to be expressed verbally. You'll hear "God," "Really!" and "He's out of it."

One of the reasons her show is so beloved is that there's a lot at stake for the audience. People can build or destroy their reputation with a single clap. It's the quick way to success. Or failure.

After her show, people talk to one another enthusiastically, saying things like: "She's a genius; her choice of tricks is superb, exquisite. The vocabulary is rich, and the language, my goodness, the language is sublime. When she revealed the red inside of her jacket, I thought I would die!" The ultimately chic thing to say is: "How did she do that?" and to ask her directly, "Is there any chance you might ever reveal how you did that jacket trick?" And she wisely answers, "I'm sorry, I never reveal my magic tricks. I'd be out on the street without a job. You understand."

"Of course; how thoughtless of me." And the person walks away, saying, "Ah! The deceptive simplicity of it! I *love* the way she magics."

How real is her magic, I wonder. How big are her powers? Can she make people love her? Are they under her spell?

Tables are reserved weeks in advance. People order a meal, but many of them barely touch their food, they are so moved and affected by the show.

People send their kids to her for lessons. She has so many students that she has to divide her class into three levels of difficulty. The lowest is for traditional magic, where ordinary tricks are taught, such as pulling rabbits out of seemingly empty hats. These basic tricks provide a good foundation and background. In the second and slightly more difficult class, students learn how to take flowers and wands out of their boots, and marbles out of their mouths. The last and most difficult class focuses on tricks like taking off jackets whose insides are of a different color than their outsides.

It feeds into the system, the fact that the beginning classes are more difficult than the advanced classes, the fact that students progress from learning sleight of hand to smelling candies to winding watches to wiping their foreheads with Kleenexes. They love it that way, the parents and the public, but the children have trouble understanding this system and are told they are too young to understand; it's experimental, abstract, avant-garde, intellectual, an acquired taste.

One day, in the subway, a man is doing magic tricks. We watch him pull a rabbit out of a hat, and Laura laughs.

"Why are you laughing?" I ask.

"I'm thinking of what my audience would think of that. They would find that so vulgar, so base."

Laura has eliminated the dancing from her show, as you might have noticed by now. ("The more cultured the person, the more stark they like it," she explains to me.)

Articles come out on her magic.

There are imitators, but they are not accepted by the most cultured people. She is considered the best, because the first.

Two ballet companies have been fighting to get her.

"But it's not ballet," I tell her. "You don't even dance anymore."

"That's the whole point. Just as it's not magic."

Nevertheless, people still call her "The Dancing Magician."

Laura has raised magic to equal the most important art forms.

How big are her powers? Can she make people love her? Are we under her spell?

*   *   *

I often catch myself not wondering if I can have a happy life with a woman who may have cast a love spell on me. I really should wonder about such a thing, logic tells me. So I wonder about it.

from ALL ABOUT MAN

Frank Gannon

~

OF ALL THINGS OF GREAT IMPORTANCE, THE SUBJECT OF MAN is the least understood. For a long time, everything except MAN was being studied. We studied animals, but we seemed to ignore MAN, perhaps because of what we were afraid to find out about him.

We seemed hesitant to investigate MAN. Even now, we are really careful not to get MAN upset because we know that he would cause trouble. If we found out anything "sensitive," we were very reluctant to reveal it.

Some MEN say, "Hey, leave me alone. It's not your job to investigate me. Back off." I, for one, cannot accept this as a valid response. It is only by careful, scientific scrutiny of MAN that we may perhaps discover why MAN is here and what MAN should do. Perhaps we need to point out the direction that MAN should take in the future. Perhaps we may need to tell MAN to leave.

The present volume is principally an overview of my findings and suggestions based on my study of MAN. I know MAN isn't going to like some of what I say here. Some of it is painful reading, but then reading about MAN has got to be painful. It's got to be dogmatic and it's got to be tedious. It's got to be vague, and it's got to be indefensible.

It's got to be fair, yet it also has to be triple-checked against an inevitable slant towards frothiness and a celebratory air because the writer has found, after so many years of researching MAN, he's become prejudiced. With one or two exceptions, he just likes the hell out of MAN.

That's what I've tried to do.

MAN: HIS ORIGINS

Many, many years ago, before there was George Jessell, the earth was a simmering cauldron, an amalgam of the elements, the very stuff of existence itself, slowly cooling, much as today's jello molds do in the refrigerator.

There was a lot of hydrogen and oxygen and silicone (which would become important in the creation of breasts, as we will see later). There was latex and bondo and naugahyde, but one thing was conspicuous by its absence.

MAN.

There weren't even any animals. There was just a big, bubbly, slowly-cooling thing. And while it cooled, you could listen to Stravinsky's "The Rite of Spring." MAN didn't appear until much later—at least a half-hour after Mickey Mouse and the water that got out of control.

When MAN did finally arrive on the scene, he was naked, short, and a chain smoker. It took him a very long time before he learned to talk. At first he just made Brando-like mumbles. But then, just as suddenly as he had appeared, he started talking. He talked about all kinds of things, but his speech was dominated by one theme: I WANT SOMETHING TO EAT AND SOME PANTS.

In time, he found both.

MAN first appeared in northern Africa. There he assembled with other MEN into "tribes." These early tribe MEN were very busy attempting to establish "culture." Their effort involved a lot of discussion and, ultimately, fist fights. Soon, ashtrays were invented, and civilization as we now know it started to fester and coagulate.

The first MEN were little, short aggressive guys. Today their progeny live in north Jersey, but back then they were the emperors of the species. They pushed other primates, such as monkeys and gibbons, all over the place. They insisted that the "lesser apes" pay them protection money, and the lesser apes went along with it. They had no choice. By now, MAN controlled everything. A few gibbons got beat up in the weight room, and the rest of the apes caved in.

MAN was now in an extremely powerful position. At this time, MAN ran all of the continents and the water in between. If you even wanted to fly over MAN's "turf" you had to arrange some form of payment. Many birds resisted this. Finally the leader of the birds met with MAN in an attempt to form some sort of compromise. Some sort of compromise *was* met. MAN came out of the bathroom after dinner and shot the leader of the birds six times in the head.

MAN owned everything. The land. The seas. The air. The police.

The era of MAN had begun.

There is, of course, a big question. How did MAN, himself obviously a monkey, learn how to do all this stuff that obviously beat the living crap out of the other monkeys? Why didn't a well-prepared gibbon, for instance, discover electricity? Why didn't a baboon, who had crammed really hard and pulled all-nighters, figure out how to make a driver's-side air bag?

This is a big question. That's why we say that it's a big question. Some even call it THE big question.

But like most puzzling conundrums, this one seems to have an easy answer. I don't know.

MAN was certainly no smarter than, say, a spider monkey. He was outweighed by the orangutan, and a gorilla would have probably beat him up really bad and just left him in a parking lot.

Yet MAN triumphed. He triumphed because I, for one, was behind him. I hated those other monkeys. I hated the way those baboons would just sit around with that smirk on their faces like they owned the place. And the lemurs, don't get me started on those assholes. They'd just hang there with those stupid eyes.

At least I respected the gorillas. If you had a problem, they would help you out. Sure, they were surly. That's just the way they are. But they'll help your ass out. That I will tell you.

I know—MAN can be sneaky, but he's a *lot* better than mandrills. You can keep those mandrills. Make a weekend guest out of a mandrill and then tell me about mandrills.

MAN is a shaper of his landscape. MAN can build his own landscape, or paint it. MAN can paint his landscape, take it downtown, lean it up against a building, sit next to it, and try to sell it. Fat chance.

Every landscape in the world contains animals that have adapted to that landscape. (We're not talking about painted landscapes anymore. That was last paragraph. Pay attention.) In the eighteenth century, for instance, Indians used to talk about "dancing fish" that came out at high tide on the California coast. This is an extreme example of animal adaptation. These fish would dance to almost any kind of music, but that classic "big band" sound was what really turned them on. Late in the day, as the sun slowly disappeared into the Pacific, the Indians would gather and watch the dancing fish twirl and gyrate to the sounds of Benny Goodman and Kay Kaiser.

Every place in the world is filled with examples of animals that have adapted to their environment. MAN, however, as the "boss hawg" of animals, doesn't have to adapt. If he doesn't like his particular environment, he can change it. A hedgehog will just crawl under a bush, fall asleep, and wait for spring. If MAN wants spring, he can get spring. He can crank up the outside heaters and head for WalMart to buy any variety of plastic flower. Then he can watch video tapes of baseball games while he washes his car. MAN doesn't have to adapt. Adapting is for losers. Like hedgehogs. If, however, MAN happens to, for whatever reason, admire the hedgehog, MAN can adapt too. He too can crawl under a bush and wait for spring. But MAN doesn't *have* to. The hedgehog does. That's the key difference.

I once had a cousin who would, every year, come December 21, the first day of winter, crawl under a bush (making sure that there weren't any hedgehogs already there). MAN is free. If he wants to go the hedgehog route, that's an option that he has.

Biological evolution has, then, not shaped MAN into any specific form to fit into any specific environment. Compared to the sturdy hedgehog, for instance, MAN has hardly the equipment to survive on this planet. I, for instance, don't even have a good winter coat. Yet MAN not only survives, he prospers. This is because MAN, using his great intelligence and subtlety, doesn't really need any equipment. Indeed, MAN has turned his deficiencies into assets. For example, I have used my lack of a winter coat as an excuse to get out of shoveling snow. I have used the fact that I don't have shoes on as an inventive way of avoiding taking out the garbage. The history of MAN is filled with examples of MAN using his deficiencies to his advantage. This ingenuity is, along with his nice ears, one of the greatest of MAN's qualities.

MAN has changed a great deal over time. Today's MAN hardly looks like earlier MAN. MAN's thumbs are longer today. His head is larger. He's taller, and he has a better tan, although he's beginning to lose a little bit of his hair. That's why he's combing it funny, but one of the great ironies of MAN is just this: he's not fooling anybody.

We have found skulls that are two million years old. By studying these skulls, we have come to two striking generalizations. Ancient MAN was called *Australopithecus,* and ancient MAN, primitive as he was, knew how to spell his name.

It is very odd to think that today's MAN came from these ancient origins, but he did. We know this because of exhaustive research and the fact that we saw it on PBS.

There are many animals that are sort of genetic cousins of MAN. The lemur is one of these. Just last week I remember feeling very guilty because I hadn't called my cousin Bill, a lemur, since last Christmas. I walked right over to the phone and started to look up his number when I remembered that the last time he was over, he ate part of my sofa. So I said screw it.

The biggest difference between MAN and the primates who preceded him was the size of his brain, which made complex behavior possible. While the size of the brain is not a true indicator of an organism's intelligence, it's a lot surer than going by the number of nostril hairs, a measure which early anthropologists, in a sad display of backwardness, used to employ.

Even a really big gorilla doesn't have that big a brain. Even King Kong was a relative "pea brain" when compared to the awesome grey matter that MAN packs. MAN's brain has been known to be as large as 2,000 cubic centimeters, which is really big, but I couldn't tell you exactly how big because I'm pretty confused about the whole metric thing, to tell you the truth. Suffice it to say that MAN's brain is plenty big enough to do the job. Nuff said.

MAN's brain was not only larger than everybody else's, it was very, very, very complex. MAN was capable of taking twenty semester hours and pulling a three-five. However, there are no fossil remains to show us what the insides of his brain looked like. Modern MAN's brain is composed of grey, squishy-looking stuff, so we might surmise that primitive MAN's brain looked the same, but maybe with less squishy stuff.

With this brain, MAN did a lot. He made tools and weapons. He went on hunts. Large groups of primitive MEN dressed in camouflage clothes and went out in the woods and killed animals and, occasionally, each other. The women usually stayed home tending to the fire and secretly ridiculing the MEN for their stupid macho posturing. But MAN didn't care. He would hunt antelopes and gazelles, and afterward, as the ancient sun disappeared into the ancient horizon it was what these ancient MEN called "Miller Time."

One of early MAN's first breakthroughs was the discovery of fire. MAN soon discovered that all of the other animals were afraid of fire, and this made MAN very smug. When the first MAN came out in his lab coat and told the other MEN about fire, there was much excitement. Unfortunately, we don't know who it was that came up with fire, so we can't thank him.

Soon after fire, of course, came cooking. No longer would MAN have to eat tartar after tartar, which must have been tedious and very hard on the teeth.

With cooking, however, came another problem. Tipping. But we will get into that matter later, after some coffee.

Where is MAN today? At what stage of development? Has he gotten better? Or has he gotten worse? When we look at MAN today, are we proud of him? Do we want to run up and give him a big hug and tell him that he's just the nicest, tallest thing?

I don't think so.

MAN today obviously needs work. Some need a kinder, more caring outlook. Some need a heightened appreciation of WOMAN, HIS FELLOW CREATURE ON THE PLANET WHOM HE HAS BEEN NEGLECTING LATELY. Some MEN you just want to run up to and slap. Others have bad posture and poor eating habits. MAN needs major work, and I'm afraid it's going to be expensive.

When I began life as a MAN, it was the fifties. Although I was very young and short I noticed the way that the older, taller MEN were. It was enough to make you sick.

In the fifties, MEN never cried. They were taught to suppress their emotions. This restraint was their only good quality. They were otherwise completely loathsome. They lacked compassion. When they saw a flatbed truck go by packed full of little screaming children, a fifties MAN would just start scratching himself and talk about football. Also, MAN in the fifties was dangerously unbalanced and actually thought of himself as male.

In the sixties, things got a little better—mainly because I was taller now and could influence MEN to be better. But still, try as I might, MAN kept acting poorly. In 1969 I told MAN that if he didn't stop acting like an asshole I was going to have to slap him. This aggressive posture worked for a while, but the improvement wasn't permanent.

Of course, then came the part of the sixties that most people are talking about when they say, "the sixties." As in, "I'm an accountant now, and you actually trust me with your money, but back in the sixties I used to like to eat a heck of a lot of LSD. And my hair was very long and looked stupid."

The sixties changed everything, and MAN was no exception.

MEN questioned old values, rejected old truths, drove old cars. MAN was clearly becoming something new. And vibrant. And exciting. The Age of Aquarius was upon MAN, and MAN started to "do his own thing." MAN broke through old barriers and grew really ugly, thick sideburns.

This was a time of great transition. I, for instance, was barely three feet tall in 1960, but by 1969, I was big, mean, and bad, and was, for a time, the last white heavyweight champion. I had only recently gotten laid. Vast vistas stretched before me. It was really almost slightly better than average.

MAN in the sixties. Think of the names. Kennedy. King. Picasso. Ed.

In the sixties MAN was really one of the most "together" things that were happening. MAN could look forward and back. He could also turn sideways. Some could stand on their heads, and many could juggle.

I remember seeing a whole bunch of MEN. They were stardust. They were golden. They wore ridiculous clothes.

They were MAN in the sixties.

A long time ago, anthropologists thought that MAN was a relatively simple subject. Many anthropologists of that era considered MAN a "crip course."

"What are you taking this quarter, Bo?"

"Organic. Psych."

"What else?"

"I'm taking MAN. I gotta get my grades up or Dad's taking back the Mazda."

"Bummer."

Today, of course, we know that this is far from true. Today MAN is a real gut-buster, and only serious dweebs even think of signing up for it. Walk into today's MAN classroom. You won't see any Budmen in there.

In those ancient days, though, anthropologists thought MAN was a relatively simple matter. They called him HOMO ERECTUS ROBUSTUS. Since they were all MEN, it is not surprising that they gave themselves such a cool name. Today, though, we realize that they were way off. MAN is much more complicated than they thought, although he is, I grant you, quite robust.

It seems that there were really many more types of MAN than had been originally thought. There were dozens of them. They kept finding old skulls with different characteristics. They had to invent names for these MEN and somehow assimilate them into the big picture.

Roget Man

Between 1935 and 1936, in Biliton, a small island off the coast of Sumatra, in the Java Sea, a skull was found in a quarry. Robert Pikestaff of the University of London found the skull on July 13, 1935. Paul Wrensnest, a colleague of Pikestaff, confirmed that they had found the skull, but not in a quarry. Wrensnest insisted that they had found it in a pit. Pikestaff said that they had found it in a quarry, not a pit, but he would find the term "open cut" acceptable. Wrensnest replied that he could never call it an open cut or a quarry, but he would find any of the following terms more than suitable: "vein," "load," "dike," "shoot," "lodestuff," "speed metal," or "esophagus." Pikestaff, at that point, turned to Wrensnest and told him to "fuck" himself.

Robo Man

In 1992, in Pennsauken, New Jersey, a partially decomposed MAN was found. He was far smaller than any previous species of MAN. Robo Man was less than half a meter in standing height. Yet he possessed an outstanding musculature. Also, astoundingly, Robo Man apparently had no dick.

Chevalier Man

In 1950, in Cotes-Du-Nord, France, near the village of Dinan, in a deposit of the Second Interglacial period, a skull was discovered which sent an earthquake through the world of MAN studies. The portion of the skull that still retains its original structure shows clearly that this early MAN was completely incapable of pronouncing the letter "H." For instance, scientists theorize that he probably said things like "Tank eaven for lit tell girlz. Dey grow up in day most ay light full way."

In Chevalier MAN we see strong evidence that even very ancient MAN was capable of making you sick to your stomach.

Raging Man

He was found on the streets. Brooklyn. 1949. Once, before they got him to the lab for the autopsy, he asked the scientists to do him a little favor. The scientists said sure. So he asked them to hit him, as hard as they could, right in the mouth. Then he told the scientists that they punched like girls.

MAN AND HIS MYTHOLOGY

From his very early days, man has always had myths. The word *myth* is a part of MAN's everyday language. Every schoolchild is familiar with that mythical figure, Santa Claus. Our myths are all around us: that "Mercury" guy outside of the florist; the giant rabbit who delivers eggs, the symbol of fertility, to our children; that doctor who doesn't care about money and is actually working because he wants to alleviate suffering; the MAN riding a zebra who throws women's panties on your lawn every February. All of these, though not real, are quite familiar to us, so familiar that they seem, in a way, more "real" than the world we actually see around us.

So MAN needs myths. Originally, they probably explained things to man. Ancient MAN saw a big flaming thing go across the sky every day, and his pathetic ancient mind was probably comforted in thinking, "That thing in the sky? That big yellow thing? That's Apollo in his chariot. Every day he drives it across the sky. When he leaves, it's night time. That's what I believe. It gives me comfort. You don't like it? You got a problem with that?"

Even today, when we know that that's not some guy in a chariot up there (give me a break, what do I look like?), even today, modern MAN, for all of his staggering accomplishments, still needs myths. Today, modern MAN may look at the ancient myths from a different perspective, but the myths themselves still speak to MAN's deepest fears and desires.

Why can't MAN live forever? If he trains and eats sensibly, why can't he continue to exist until the end of time? This bothers MAN. It bothers the crap out of him. I'm having a good time, MAN thinks, why can't I continue to have a good time? Just when it gets good, some idiot has to pull the plug. Why? Why?

The answer to this question has evaded MAN since MAN started looking for it. Cagey bastard that he is, however, MAN has actually found the answer and written it in code.

One of the oldest myths on this subject comes from ancient Corsican fragments. It explains MAN's peculiar fate.

Our first ancestors were named Edna and Jerome. Jerome was a barbarian, but Edna came from the sky. When Edna's father found out that Edna wanted to marry Jerome, he stole Jerome's magic calf and took it with him back to the sky. Jerome went to the sky to prove himself worthy and get his magic calf back. He did this by completing a series of difficult tasks, like touching his nose with his tongue and brushing his teeth in the mirror. Jerome was given back his magic calf and allowed to marry Edna. They returned to earth, but as soon as they got there Jerome walked out back and died. This is how "death" started. Now go away.

The simple eloquence of this ancient tale still speaks to the deepest part of me, and probably to you.

Today we think of science as "real." We think of science as "verifiable" or "true," yet science is just as mythological as mythology itself is. That's why conversations like the following, though commonplace, are so regrettable:

"Well, Bob, this looks like a rough quarter. I'm taking Calculus II, Organic Chemistry, and Advanced Genetics. What are you taking?"

"I"m taking Mythology."

"Get away, you scab."

Take "the black hole" thing, or "the big bang" idea. Scientists call things like these "theories," but those in the know dismiss them as the mumbo-jumbo they are. If you happen to be one of those who "buy" science, good luck. You're going to need it. Give my regards to the tooth fairy when you run into him.

Because, Mister Smart Guy, science doesn't really tell you anything. It just offers theories and you buy them or you don't. Sure science is useful. Science helps us make dinner and watch television and relieve our indigestion, but it's not going to tell you what you're doing here. When science tries to tell you what you're doing here, it turns into mythology. Thus the famous explanation of Einstein's, "The most beautiful thing we can experience is the mysterious," and later, "Something deeply hidden had to be behind things," and later still, "Sock it to me."

And later still, "Who do you have to have sex with to get a drink around here?"

Perhaps by doing a little comparative mythology, we might discover certain strange parallels between these ancient stories, parallels all the more alarming because of the absolute separation of the cultures that produced the myths. Why, we might ask, does one culture, say Australian, have a creation myth that exactly mirrors the creation myth of a culture, say New Jersey, that is so remote from its own? Why are there these odd parallels between the mythologies of people who had absolutely no chance of ever seeing each other? What is going on here? Is mythology the language of God talking to MAN? Is there some sort of collective unconscious that we all share, much the way birds and other animals share certain instinctual knowledge? Is mythology telling us something almost unfathomable about our truest nature?

Personally, I doubt it.

Consider the myth of the deluge or flood. Almost every culture has its version of this ancient "occurrence," but did it really occur? It is impossible at the moment for science to tell us with any degree of certainty whether or not there really was a flood. Nevertheless, mythology seekers have compiled sixty-three versions of the flood story. These versions differ in details (in some, no water is mentioned, for example, and in another the deluge turns out to be a trick pulled by some kids). But the basic story is the same: it rained.

Perhaps the deluge story is metaphorical. Perhaps these ancient stories are merely symbolic. The deluge story, for instance, might stand for the state of human beings on the planet: it is always raining and they are always bitching and moaning about it. Yet they endure. Sorry, I didn't mean to say that. They don't just endure. They conquer. They prevail. Even though it rains, these ancient stories might be telling us, there's no reason to get all mopey. Look at Kathie Lee Gifford. Surely she is what our ancient ancestors had in mind when they told their deluge stories. It rains and many die. But not all die. And those that do not die are perky.

How, then, is myth to be defined? In general, a community's myths are the stories that are traditional to its people; the stories that the older people tell the younger people. These are stories that have developed over long periods of time and through many retellings. It may be said that they convey the collective wisdom of many generations.

Here are a few myths peculiar to contemporary American culture. No doubt you're familiar with them.

- If you wash your car, it will rain.
- A watched pot never boils.
- If you are tall and wearing a suit, if you tell someone to do something, no matter how stupid, that person will do it. Provided you pay him what he usually gets.
- Take lessons, you'll do better.

from THE ROAD TO WELLVILLE

T. Coraghessan Boyle

~

THE CIVILIZED BOWEL

Will Lightbody fell into the wheelchair as if he'd been dropped from a great height—say, from a spot just to the left of the chandelier. His knees had suddenly lost their elasticity, his calves gone slack, and there he was, in the wheelchair, staring up at the ceiling like an octogenarian with egg in his lap. The Doctor—Dr. Kellogg, the Chief, the great and famous healer in the white spats and matching goatee—had disappeared, hustling off down the hallway till he receded in the distance like a scrap of paper blown by the wind. He'd been cordial enough—Will couldn't fault him there—but he'd seemed distracted, frazzled, not at all the solid and immovable rock he'd expected.

Not that it mattered. Not anymore. Not in the face of that cursory but terrifying examination. The great man had stuck his fingers in Will's mouth, though he was so short—another surprise—that he had to go up on tiptoe to insert them, and Will had seen the look of alarm in his eyes. It was a look that penetrated to the core of Will's being, a look that prefigured the coffin and the funeral wreath, and suddenly Will had felt as sick and weak as he'd ever felt in his life. He felt rotten. Light-headed. Doomed. And his stomach—there it was, as palpable as the hands before his face—his stomach clenched as if he'd caught a whiff of the grave.

"As severe a case of autointoxication as I've ever seen," the Doctor pronounced.

The words hit home like a storm of bullets. Will tottered, actually tottered, and then the wheelchair was there and he lost all conscious control of his muscles just as surely as if he'd drunk down a pint of Old Crow in a single gulp. He was frightened. His heart beat like a hammer in his chest. The ceiling seemed to fall in on him and then recede again.

"Eleanor!" a voice cried out, and the sound of it, hearty and bold, smooth as a surge of water over the buffed blue stones of a stream, brought him out of himself. The muscles of his neck tightened, the cords and sinews did their work, and all at once the ceiling was a memory and he was staring into the boyish eyes, cleft chin and brilliant naked teeth of Dr. Frank Linniman. "But you've lost weight," Dr. Linniman chided, clutching Eleanor's gloved hand and practically twirling her like a ballerina.

Eleanor called him "Frank." Not "Doctor," not even "Dr. Linniman." Just "Frank." "Yes, Frank, I know it, I know it, but it's just about impossible to eat scientifically in Peterskill, New York"— the way she pronounced the name of their hometown, she might just as well have been describing some huddle of huts in the Congo—"and Cook, though she's a dear, just can't seem to get the hang of Dr. and Mrs. Kellogg's recipes." Eleanor was glowing, her color high, her eyes struck with the light of the chandelier. She made a little moue, shrugged one shoulder, dipped her head ever so slightly to set the artificial bird atop her hat in motion. "I tell you, Frank," she breathed, "it's just heaven to be back here again."

In that moment, Will's fear of his own mortality was replaced by another emotion, one more often associated with the youthful and vigorous: jealousy. This was his wife, after all, the woman he loved, the woman who had borne his baby girl in tragedy, the woman whose breasts he'd held in his hands and whose curves and intimate places he knew like no other, or used to know . . . yes, and here she was fawning all over this, this *doctor* with his starched white suit and sunny grin. Good God, he looked more like a baseball player than a medical man, more like a brawling ham-fisted catcher or lumbering first baseman. Will cleared his throat. "Will Lightbody," he said, or tried to say, but unfortunately all that came out was an incoherent croak.

"Oh," Eleanor gasped, a hand to her bosom, and in that moment the little group that was gathered round Will—his wife, the bell-hop, the attendant at his back and Dr. Linniman—seemed to converge, the whole world and universe radiating out from that little gasp. "Forgive me," Eleanor went on, "but Frank, Dr. Linniman, I'd like you to meet my husband." And then, in a rush of breath: "He's a very sick man."

Suddenly, Frank Linniman's earnest face was hanging over Will's and his big friendly mitt of a healing hand was pumping Will's limp scrap of wrinkle and bone as if he were trying to draw water from a well. "Never fear," the physician was saying, conversant with the usual platitudes, "you've come to the right place. We'll have you scaling mountains in no time."

And then the hand was withdrawn, orders were given, the luggage vanished (and with it, Eleanor) and Will was being propelled across the lobby by an attendant as brawny, fit and eudaemonically sound as Frank Linniman himself. The wheels moved noiselessly, effortlessly, and the faces of his fellow patients—as jolly and robust a group as he'd ever seen—floated past him, barely curious. To them, Will was just one more sick man in a wheelchair.

But what they didn't know, what Will wanted to cry out to them, was that he'd never in his life been in a wheelchair before. Wheelchairs were for Civil War veterans, amputees, invalids, the superannuated, the infirm, they were for withered crones and doddering old pensioners with one foot in the grave. He thought of Philo Strang, the oldest living human in Peterskill, a blasted relic of a man who'd lost both his legs at Sharpsville when he was forty-two and had sunned himself outside his son's tobacco emporium in his rusting homemade wheelchair ever since, his eyes gone, hearing shot, clumps of yellow hair sprouting from his ears and nostrils and a dangle of phlegm caught in his beard. Well, now they had something in common, old Philo Strang and he, though Will was barely thirty-two and had been as spry as the next man a year ago.

Spry. He'd been spry, that's what he wanted to tell them.

Yet what did it matter? Now he was in a wheelchair. Now he

was helpless. Old before his time. Used up, cast aside, hung out to dry. Gliding across the lobby through the hum of conversation and muted laughter that bubbled up round him as if the whole thing were some social affair, some cotillion or ball, Will felt a yawning cavern of self-pity open up inside him: surely he was the sickest man alive.

The silver wheels eased to a stop at the mouth of the elevator and Will felt himself swung gently round as the attendant expertly rotated the chair and drew it backward. The sensation was oddly familiar, a feeling of airiness and effortless suspension that wasn't altogether unpleasant, and Will realized that he'd gone from an old man to an infant in that moment, from Old Philo Strang with the snot in his beard to a babe in a perambulator. "Good evening, sir," the elevator man said, beaming at him out of a missionary face, "you look all tuckered," and he clucked his tongue. "Floor, Ralph?" he inquired of the attendant.

The attendant's voice spoke behind Will as if in some trick of ventriloquism: "Five."

"Oh," murmured the elevator man, winking an eye, "very nice, you're going to enjoy it, sir. Best air in the place, and a lovely view, too." He paused, sighed, reached for the grate. "Rail travel," he said, shaking his head. "Poor man looks all tuckered, Ralph."

At that moment, just as he was about to pull the grate across, a nurse slipped in to join them. Will was in a funk and delirium, and he didn't take any notice of her at first, but as they ascended, defying gravity, she turned to him with a smile of evangelic intensity. For all his exhaustion and despair, for all his pain and ruination, Will couldn't help feeling the force of that smile. He looked up. "Mr. Lightbody?" she inquired.

Will nodded.

"I'm Nurse Graves," she said, and her voice was a tiny puff of breath, as if she were unused to speaking above a whisper. "Welcome to the University of Health. I'll be your personal attendant throughout your stay here, and I'm going to do everything in my power to make the time both pleasant and physiologically sound for you." The smile held, perfect, confident, soothing. This was the smile the first cave woman had used on the first cave man, a wonder of a smile, a novelty and an invention. Who'd ever thought of smiling before this nurse came into the world? "But you must be tired," she said, and the smile faded ever so slightly to underscore the concern and sympathy of her words.

Will wanted to answer in the affirmative. He wanted to be undressed and put to bed like the antediluvian infant he'd become, wanted the surcease of the liquor and narcotic cures, wanted to drop dead on the spot and get it over with. *Yes,* he was going to say, *yes, tired to the marrow of my bones,* but the elevator man beat him to it: "Rail travel, Irene," he said, heaving another sigh. "It's as like to torture as anything they did in the Inquisition, let me tell you."

"Well," she said in her hushed, breathy tones, "I don't doubt it for a minute, though I've never been farther than Detroit myself," and she cocked her head alertly as the fourth floor rolled by beyond the grate. She stood there like a monument, like an advertisement for biologic living, breathing cleanly and deeply, chin held high, her spine so erect you could drop a plumb bob from it. And her uniform: it was an unbroken field of white, from the hem of her skirt to the cap perched atop the pinned-up mass of her hair, and it was perfectly—and naturally—contoured to the shape of her body, which was free of the corsets and stays the Chief railed against. Even in his fog, Will couldn't help admiring the fit of that uniform. And from his vantage point in the wheelchair, just behind and below her, he could make out the blades of her squared shoulders, the swept-up hairs at the back of her neck and the delicate little shells of her ears. He fixated on those ears. In that moment they seemed the most precious things he'd ever known. Little jewels. Little monkey ears. He wanted to kiss them.

"But Mr. Lightbody is at the very end of his journey now," she added, turning from the waist to beam that smile at him, "and we're here to receive him and comfort him and make him well again."

Will didn't mean to stare, but he couldn't seem to help himself. Something had come over him, a quickening in this groin, a heat he hadn't felt in months. Sick man that he was, bundle of bones and extruded nerves, he looked up into that smile, studied those ears and more, much more—that rump, those ankles, the bosom presented in profile—and all of a sudden he saw Nurse Graves spread out on his bed in all the glory of her naked and pliant flesh, and he, Will Lightbody, mounting her like a hairy-hocked satyr. Breasts, he thought. Vagina. What was happening to him?

"I haven't slept in twenty-two days," he croaked.

Nurse Graves held his eyes. She was young, very young, no

more than a girl, really. "You'll sleep tonight," she said. "That's what I'm here for."

The elevator man announced the fifth floor, the grate drew back, and in the next moment Will found himself passing down a brightly lit hallway, Nurse Graves at his side, Ralph providing locomotion. There seemed to be quite a crowd in the corridor, seeing that it was nearly ten-thirty on a Monday night in November—nurses, attendants and bellhops hustling to and fro, men and women in evening clothes sauntering along as if they'd just come back from the theater, patients in robes lingering at the doors of their rooms and chatting in low tones. *Grand,* one robed and turbaned woman said to another, *simply grand.* But for the white flash of the attendants' uniforms, Will would have thought he was at the Plaza or the Waldorf.

And then an odd thing happened. Just as Nurse Graves pushed open the door to his room and Ralph swiveled the chair round to enter, Will had the strange feeling that he was being watched. Nearly devoid of volition at this point, he let his head loll against the leather padding of the chair and gazed up to see a young female peering at him curiously from an open door across the hallway. She was tall, striking, well formed, and the salacious thoughts began to flood his head again...but then the flood ceased as suddenly as it had begun: there was something wrong with her. Desperately wrong. Her skin—it had the color of bread mold. And her lips...they were dead, blackened, two little eggplants fastened beneath her nose as a morbid joke. Sick. She was sick. This was no hotel. He tried a sort of wry grin, commiserative and sad, but she only gave him a blank look and shut the door.

"There, now," Nurse Graves said as they entered the room, "isn't this cheery?"

Will took it in at a glance: Oriental carpet, drapes, a sturdy mahogany bed, matching armoire, private bath. He tried to respond, tried to seem interested, but he was sick to the very core. "Breasts," he said. "Vagina."

Nurse Graves's smile fluttered briefly, a hundred-watt bulb flickering between connection and extinction. "Beg pardon?"

Ralph's voice, blissful with enthusiasm: "He says it's very nice. But don't try to talk, Mr. Lightbody, not in your condition, please."

Nurse Graves—Irene, hadn't the elevator man called her Irene?—instructed Ralph to lift Will from the chair and lay him out on the bed. Will didn't protest. Ralph thrust one arm under Will's knees, wrapped his shoulders up in the other, hoisted him from the chair without so much as a grunt of effort and lowered him to the bed. There, Will found himself supported in a sitting position as two pairs of hands removed his jacket, tie, shirt and collar, and then his shoes, socks and trousers, until he sat before them in his underwear, too far gone to worry about modesty. No woman, save for his mother and Eleanor, had ever seen him in his flannels—and no man, for that matter. And here were Ralph (he didn't even know his last name) and Nurse Graves standing over him in his underwear as if it were the most natural thing in the world. Perversely, his groin began to stir again. He sank into the bed and closed his eyes.

He heard the rattle of a tray, the whisper of the chair's wheels. Nurse Graves—Irene—was going to put him to sleep. He wished her luck. He did. He hadn't slept in twenty-two days—had barely eaten or moved his bowels or even drawn breath, for that matter. It was Eleanor, of course. As soon as she'd announced that they were going to the San, both of them, for an indefinite stay, he began to lie awake through the eternal nights, his stomach churning with fear. Fear of what? He didn't know. But the Sanitarium was a club from which he'd been excluded, a club that had taken his wife, his baby girl and his stomach, and it loomed nightmarishly through the dark hours of the night. He longed for the oblivion of the Sears' White Star Liquor Cure, opium dreams edged in red and pink and opening on nothingness. *Then* he would sleep, oh yes indeed. But he fought the urge, fought it like a man on the brink of extinction—which is exactly what he was. And so he hadn't slept. Not at all. Not a wink. Every time he closed his eyes he was immediately swept down his own esophagus and into his stomach, where he lodged like an undigested lump of food— chops, fried potatoes, tumblers of whiskey and oysters with human faces gamboling and cavorting round him as he churned in his own juices. He wished her well, Nurse Graves, but how could she hope to accomplish what Sears and Eleanor and the Old Crow could barely manage?

There was the sound of water being drawn in the bath, and then Ralph's hands were on him again, unbuttoning his long johns. "There, now," Ralph murmured, "just lift your arm up." Will flashed open his eyes. Nurse Graves, her back turned, seemed preoccupied with a tray of instruments. "Right leg, that's a boy, now your left," Ralph coached, peeling the garment from Will's ankles and feet, and suddenly Will was naked, fully naked, in the presence of strangers. The stirring in his groin died stillborn. He was mortified. And what if she should turn around? What then?

Ralph, white-smocked, sure-handed, square-jawed Ralph, produced a swath of linen, a flap of white cloth the size of a dinner napkin and supported by a thin band at the waist. Nothing more than a diaper, really. Will took the garment from Ralph's outstretched hand, slipped his feet through the leg holes and hurriedly pulled the thing up over his loins.

"All set?" Nurse Graves chirped, swinging round on them in that instant as if she were clairvoyant. Will gazed up at her in helplessness and surrender. "Good," she puffed, rubbing her hands together. "We'll have you fast asleep in no time at all. Ralph, would you help Mr. Lightbody into the bathroom?"

Will gave her a startled look.

"Neutral bath and colon wash," she said, her voice as light as the air itself.

"Colon wash?" Will could only gasp out the words as he staggered to his feet and Ralph took hold of him and assisted his plodding steps across the floor.

"An enema," Nurse Graves said. "Hot paraffin, soap and tepid water. You haven't been thoroughly examined yet—we'll put you through a series of tests tomorrow—but the Chief and Dr. Linniman have both diagnosed you as suffering from autointoxication, among other things. In effect, Mr. Lightbody, you've been poisoning your own system. We find it's very common among meat eaters."

They were in the bathroom now, and Will was perched on the edge of the toilet in his pristine diaper. Ralph nodded his head and ducked out the door. "But I don't eat meat—or not anymore," Will protested. "My wife won't let me. It's been nothing but Graham gems, parsnips and tomato toast for the last six months."

Nurse Graves was watching him closely. The apparatus—a sort of syringe, with a big distended ball of India rubber at its base—lay cradled in her arms like a sacred object. "That's very admirable, Mr. Lightbody; it's a very good start. But you must realize that all those years of abuse have severely taxed your system. I'm not a doctor, and I know you haven't been thoroughly examined yet, but if you're like the thousands of patients who come here from all over the world, I'd say your intestines are absolutely putrid with disease and germs—*un*friendly germs."

It was seventy-two degrees in that bathroom, a temperature Dr. Kellogg maintained throughout the San, winter and summer, seventy-two degrees, and yet Will felt a chill go through him. "Unfriendly?"

Her hand was on his back, hot as a little nugget against his bare skin. "Bend forward now, Mr. Lightbody, yes, just a touch, that's right." He felt her probing at the diaper, felt it slip down round his hips. "Yes," she breathed cheerfully, "there are so many types of bacteria—people don't realize that—and so many of them are a natural and necessary part of the human organism—particularly in the alimentary canal." She paused, probing, probing. "We need to rout the bad ones so that the beneficial can . . . flourish. . . ."

Her hands. The warm bulb of the apparatus. What was he doing? What was going on? "Eleanor," he blurted. "My wife. Where's Eleanor?"

"Hush," Irene whispered. "She's fine. She's on the second floor, room two-twelve, no doubt undergoing this very same proce-dure . . . to flush her system, relax her."

Will was stunned. "Then she, she won't be staying here, with me?"

The nurse's voice caressed his ear, soothing, soft, as much a part of him as the secret voice that spoke inside his head. "Oh, no. The Chief keeps couples separate here. For therapeutic rea-sons, of course. Our patients need quiet, rest—any sort of sexual stimulation could be fatal."

Sexual stimulation. Why did those two words suddenly sound so momentous?

"Relax," she whispered, and all at once Will felt the hot fluid surprise of it, his insides flooding as if a dam had burst, as if all the tropical rivers of the world were suddenly flowing through him, irrigating him, flushing, cleansing, churning away at his deep-est nooks and recesses in a tumultuous cathartic rush. It was the most mortifying and exquisite moment of his life.

That night he slept like a baby.

In the morning, after his wake-up enema, a sitz bath and a dry-friction massage administered by a mannish-looking nurse who was as mechanical as Irene Graves had been tender, Will, under his own power, hobbled down the corridor and took the elevator to the dining room for breakfast. When this second nurse—Nurse Bloethal—had produced the colonic apparatus, Will had protested. It had been disturbing enough to have the lovely and delicate Nurse Graves administer the treatment, but this woman— well, he felt it would be impossible. "But I just had one last night," he said, a hint of nasality creeping into his voice as he took a defensive posture on the bed and self-consciously adjusted his cotton robe. Nurse Bloethal, fortyish, arms like hams, hams like sacks of grain, with a squarish face and a smile full of crooked teeth, burst out with a laugh. "You'll forgive my saying so, Mr. Lightbody, but you've got a lot to learn."

She was referring, as Will would discover, to the Chief's obsession with interior as well as exterior cleanliness. Dr. Kellogg, tidy son of a broom maker, not only believed in a diet rich in bulk and roughage to encourage the bowels to exonerate themselves, but he was a strict adherent to the five-enema-a-day regimen as well. The inspiration for this mode of treatment had struck him some years earlier during a visit to Africa. He'd had the leisure there to study a troop of apes living in a tumble of blanched rock and sere trees at an oasis outside of Oran. The doctor studied them for a week, sometimes up to sixteen hours a day, hoping to gain some insight into the hominoid diet from these gregarious and frugivorous primates. What he discovered, so obvious, really, and yet till this point so easily overlooked, was that the apes moved their bowels almost continuously. Practically every mouthful they took was accompanied by a complementary evacuation.

Simple. Natural. The way it was meant to be. None of that tribe suffered from constipation, autointoxication, obesity, neurosis, hypohydrochloria or hysteria. But man did. Because man had civilized his bowel, house-trained it, as it were. Man could not, in the course of daily life, go about eliminating his wastes at will— society simply wouldn't be able to function, and the mess . . . well, the Doctor felt, better not to think about the mess. At any rate, through this observation of the Oran apes, Dr. Kellogg hit upon one of his greatest discoveries: the need, the necessity, the imperative of assisting the bowel mechanically to undo the damage wrought upon it by civilization. Hence, five enemas a day, minimum. Hence, Will on the toilet and Nurse Bloethal with the already familiar apparatus.

Will was met at the dining-room door by a motherly little

woman with an enormous bosom and tiny recessed eyes so blue they looked artificial. She wore a prim white cap perched atop an explosion of hair the color of cornstarch. "Mr . . . ?" she inquired, the Battle Creek Sanitarium smile frozen into her features.

Tall, self-conscious, smarting from his recent encounter in the bathroom and broiling in the depths of his gut, Will gave her a curt glance. "Lightbody," he said in his hollow booming tones. A few of the diners in the vast room before him looked up from their plates.

"Yes, of course," the woman returned, "I've got you right here on my list. 'Lightbody, William Fitzroy.' " She paused to squint up at him for reinforcement. Will nodded. "It says here that until your examination is completed, you're to be put on a low-protein, laxative, nontoxic diet. But, oh, do forgive me"—and here she held out her hand—"I'm Mrs. Stover, the head dietician. I'll be overseeing your diet during your stay with us, under the direction of your physician, of course. Now, if you'll look out into the dining room a moment, you'll see a number of girls in white caps like mine. Do you see them? There, there's a girl, Marcella Johnson, she's one of mine. If you need any help or advice in choosing your dishes scientifically, please just flag one of us down, won't you?"

Will took her hand, released it, and promised that he would. He made as if to move on, but Mrs. Stover lingered there in the entranceway, blocking Will's path to the comestibles as other patients sauntered casually by her and were seated in that grand and quietly seething room. Will didn't care much about eating— he couldn't remember the last time he'd experienced hunger or when he'd last eaten anything that didn't set his digestive tract aflame—but he wasn't particularly keen on standing there all morning like an idiot while several hundred cud-chewing diners studied him surreptitiously. "Yes?" he asked. "Is there anything more?"

"One thing only." Mrs. Stover stoked up her smile a degree. So much cheer, Will thought bitterly. And for what? They were all of them hurtling toward their graves, scientific living or no. "Where would you care to sit? We do try to accommodate our guests as to seating arrangements, though not everyone gets an opportunity to sit next to a Horace Fletcher or an Admiral Nieblock, of course."

Will shrugged. "With my wife, I guess."

Mrs. Stover's smile contracted till it was just the template of a smile pressed into her dry and faintly reproachful lips. She looked hurt, offended. "Oh, no," she crooned, "you wouldn't want to do that, would you? Don't you think you might prefer to mingle, to meet some of your fellow guests?"

Will thought not.

Mrs. Stover looked crestfallen. She began to speak in a rush, barely pausing for breath. "I'll try my very best, for dinner, that is, but I'm afraid—well, I'm afraid I've already seated Eleanor, Mrs. Lightbody—such a charming woman, you're a very lucky man— and her table, number sixty, is full at the moment. You're quite certain you wouldn't prefer to sit with someone else?"

"Do I have a choice?"

Mrs. Stover studied the floor a moment before answering, and when she answered, her smile fluttered and her voice couldn't seem to hold its note. "No," she said, "I'm afraid not."

The waitress, a robust young thing who suggested Nurse Graves in the color of her hair and the set of her ears, led him into the huge palmy room with its skylights and twin colonnades. Will tried to hold himself erect, conscious of his fellow patients' scrutiny, but he felt unstable and weak and his shoulders seemed unnaturally affected by the tug of gravity. He saw a mass of bent heads, a hundred bald spots, mustaches, beards, the rats and fluffs of the women's monumental coiffures, the flash of silverware and the serene but constant movement of the host of waitresses in their dark dresses and white aprons. A murmur of conversation bubbled up round him: laughter, repartee, a smatter of economics and politics—he distinctly heard Teddy Roosevelt's name as he passed a table of six mustachioed gentlemen, none of whom seemed in imminent danger of starvation. He saw, in fact, that all the tables were set for six—no doubt the Chief had determined this to be the optimal number for conviviality and physiologic dining, not to mention superior digestion. A phrase popped into Will's head—"The Peristaltic Optimum"—and he had to smile despite himself.

He craned his neck to look for Eleanor, but she was nowhere to be seen in that sea of scientifically feeding heads, and when the waitress stopped abruptly at a table in the far corner, he wasn't quite as alert as he might have been. For a moment he lost control of his feet, which were narrow but overlong, and he suddenly found himself pitching forward in a spastic sprawl just as the waitress pulled back a chair for him. *The embarrassment,* he was thinking, *oh, the embarrassment,* when at the last moment he shot out an arm to clutch at the rigid spine of the chair and managed to rake himself around, swivel his hips and collapse heavily across the seat—but not before barking both shins and cracking his kneecap with a sudden sharp sound that echoed through the room like a gunshot.

"Are you all right, sir?" The waitress looked stricken.

All right? Was he all right? The immediate and shooting pain of shin and patella was nothing, kindling to the inferno raging in his gut. He wanted to bay at the moon, claw at himself, get down on all fours and tear out his innards like a poisoned dog. All right? He'd never be all right.

Tears of anguish in his eyes, he looked up into the startled faces ranged round the table before him and found himself staring into the chartreuse eyes and high green cheekbones of the girl he'd noticed in the hallway the previous night. Seeing her there flustered him, and he glanced down at his hands, into which the waitress, with a thousand apologies, inserted a menu.

"A bit eager today, aren't we?" a voice spoke in his ear. The voice belonged to an Englishman, sixty or so, with a white tonsure and teeth like a mule's. He was sitting to Will's immediate right. "Champing at the bit, eh? I know the feeling. All of this simple living builds an appetite, and there's no arguing that."

Will agreed with him, wholeheartedly, his eyes affixed to the menu.

"Endymion Hart-Jones," the Englishman's voice announced after a pause, and Will at first thought he was recommending a dish—but no, he was introducing himself.

Will had grown up in a proper household and gone to proper schools. He knew how to behave in society. In fact, he was normally gregarious, barely containable—but to say he was out of sorts would be an understatement. He locked eyes with the Englishman. "Will Lightbody," he said in his rain-barrel tones.

The Englishman introduced the others, Will nodding at each in turn. The heavyset woman to Will's immediate left was Mrs. Tindermarsh, of Indianapolis; beside her, a dwarfish man with a tiny pointed beard and bulbous head, a Professor Stepanovich of the Academy of Astronomical Sciences, in Saint Petersburg, Russia; at the far end of the table, Miss Muntz, the greenish girl, from

Poughkeepsie, New York; and beside her, Homer Praetz, the industrialist, from Cleveland.

"The Nut Lisbon Steak with Creamed Gluten Gravy is absolutely divine," Mrs. Tindermarsh offered without a trace of irony.

Will could only blink at her. He could feel the presence of the waitress—or was it one of Mrs. Stover's dieticians?—hovering at his elbow as he tried to make sense of the menu:

BREAKFAST

Tuesday, November 12, 1907

		Prot.	Fats	Carb.	Oz.	Portion
SOUPS	Bean Tapioca	2.17	0.4	8.9	4½	½
	Brown	0.54	0.2	5.24	4½	¼
	Peas Consommé	7.1	5.2	8.6	4½	1
ENTRÉES	Nut Lisbon					
	Steak	22.89	34.47	16.8	2	1¼
	Protose Patties	18.6	21.85	9.15	2	1
	Nuttolene &					
	Jelly	12.0	22.0	26.0	2½	1½
VEGETABLES	Corn Pulp	3.7	2.9	23.2	2½	¾
	Stewed					
	Tomatoes	1.4	0.5	4.7	2½	¼
	Creamed Celery	1.9	11.9	4.6	4½	¼
BREADS	Bran Biscuit (2)	21.0	31.0	73.0	1	1¼
	Graham Bread					
	(1)	10.0	4.0	61.0	1	¾
	Granose Biscuit					
	(2)	7.0	1.0	42.0	1	¾
	Rice Biscuit (2)	8.5	0.9	96.6	1	1
FRUITS	Stewed Pears	0.7	1.1	23.3	4	1
	Sliced Banana					
	w/ Beaten					
	Meltose	2.6	2.0	106.3	4	1½
	Prune Fritters	3.4	10.5	24.0	3	1¼
CEREALS	Gluten Mush	3.2	0.3	14.68	5½	1
	Graham Grits	2.1	0.3	14.9	5½	1
	Granuto	19.1	5.0	91.8	1¼	2
	Corn Flakes	10.8	1.4	91.3	¾	¾
	Granose Flakes	13.4	1.0	83.8	¾	¾

	Prot.		**Fats**	**Carb.**	**Oz.**	**Portion**
BEVERAGES	Kaffir Tea	1.0	1.0	8.0	4	¹⁄₁₀
	Sanitas Koko	13.0	89.0	23.0	5	2¼
	Kumyss	3.3	5.6	6.3	5	¾
	Hot Malted Nuts	36.0	96.0	68.0	1¼	2
	Milk	23.0	67.0	35.0	6	1¼
DESSERTS	Squash Pie	4.27	22.7	36.5	5½	3½
	Indian Trifle	3.64	9.4	23.3	3	1

"Do you feel up to an entrée today, Mr. Lightbody?"

Will gazed up into the broad honest faces of the table waitress and dietician, buxom girls and young, radiating health, wisdom and the secret knowledge of diet and health to which their Chief and idol had made them privy.

"My name is Evangeline," said the taller of the two, "and I'll be your dietary advisor during your stay with us. And this"—indicating the second girl—"is Hortense. She'll be your waitress. Now, if I might explain the menu to you, sir." She cleared her throat. "I hope you'll notice the numbers printed beside each food item. . . ."

Will clutched the menu as if it were a rope suspended over a pit of crocodiles. His fellow diners had fallen silent, absorbed in his deliberations: this wasn't merely eating, this was science.

"Well," she went on, "these numbers, when summed up, will give you the total calories consumed—simply add the figures in the first, second and third columns and put down the sums at the foot of the respective columns. Mark each item eaten, sign the bill of fare, and hand it to your physician—for each meal, each day. It's really quite simple."

"Yes," Will agreed, his eyes jumping from the dietician's to those of Miss Muntz and the others, "yes, I suppose it is."

"Well, then," Evangeline said brightly, "may I repeat my original question: Do you feel up to an entrée this morning? Either the Nuttolene and jelly or the Protose patties would be very therapeutic for a man in your condition."

Will ran a hand through his hair. His stomach began to announce itself, an old adversary backed into a corner but not about to give up without a fight. "Uh, well," Will fumbled, "uh, I think I'll just have the toast. And water. A glass of water."

"Toast?" the girls harmonized, a look of shock and incredulity on their faces. "But surely—" began the taller one, and then she trailed off. "We can get you your toast, of course, if that's what you like, sir, but I'd recommend a serving of the corn pulp, the brown soup and prune fritters to go with it. At the very least. I can appreciate that you're not yet up to digesting a large meal, but I do advise you to eat generously and flush your system of its poisons."

At this point, the Englishman got into it: "That's right, old boy, flush the system. You'll be getting your flora changed, too, I'll wager"—and here, inexplicably, the whole table burst into laughter—"and it's never too early to give the little blighters a hand."

Will's face reddened. Flora? What on earth was he talking about? And the menu. That was nonsense, too. Nuttolene, Protose patties, Meltose and gluten and all the rest of it—Eleanor's concoctions, as unlike food as anything he'd ever had in his mouth. His jaw hardened. He fastened on the eyes of the waitress. "Toast," Will repeated in a firm tone. "Dry. And that will be all, thank you."

Suddenly meek, the girls melted away from him. When he turned back to the table, he found himself staring into Miss Muntz's startled yellow eyes, until she turned abruptly to the bulbous Russian and began talking of the weather—terribly cold for this time of year, wasn't it? The Englishman had suddenly become absorbed in studying his shirt cuffs, and Mrs. Tindermarsh gazed out the windows into intermediate space. Homer Praetz, he noticed, was carefully chewing a bit of something that looked vaguely organic. It was then, in that moment of relative calm, that Will again thought of Eleanor. Where was she? Why hadn't she come to the table to wish him a good morning? Was this the Kellogg method—to drive a wedge between husband and wife? To segregate them? Well, he'd be damned if he'd sit here and eat his toast without her.

He was just rising from the table when the waitress reappeared with his toast and a glass of kumyss for Mrs. Tindermarsh. Reluctantly, Will sank back into his chair, all the while looking over his shoulder for a glimpse of Eleanor. She was nowhere to be seen. Other women were, though—hundreds of them, ranging in age from fifteen to eighty, every last one of them dressed in the latest styles (as modified by their Chief, of course) and enjoying a healthy, bubbly, convivial meal. Their chatter was electric, all-pervasive, the buzz of a field of insects droning toward the intersection of afternoon and evening. Will bowed his head and morosely lifted the toast to his mouth.

No sooner had he taken a bite than his stomach began to rumble—or not just rumble, but growl and spit like a caged animal poked with a stick. "Down, boy!" the Englishman exclaimed, playing to the table with a show of his horsey teeth. Miss Muntz put a pretty green hand to her mouth and tittered. Will gave them a sick grin and munched his toast.

Just as he was transporting a second spear of scorched bread to his mouth, his stomach rumbling like Vesuvius and his coated tongue swelling in his throat, he felt a pressure on his shoulder and turned to find himself gazing up into a great shrewd globe of a face that hung over him like a Chinese lantern. The face belonged to a rubicund, snowy-haired man built on the Chief's mold—that is, stocky, foreshortened and expansive round the middle. The man had his hand on Will's shoulder. His look of sagacity almost immediately turned to one of consternation, and he began emitting a moist clucking sound. "No, no, no, no, no," he said, wagging a finger for emphasis, "you've got it all wrong."

Will was baffled. Did he know this man? He studied the blistering blue eyes, the firm jowls, the hair leached of all color dancing round the great pumpkin of his head . . . come to think of it, he did look vaguely familiar. . . .

"Chew," the man said, and he made a command of it. "Chew!" he cried, his voice corkscrewing upward. "Masticate! Fletcherize!" And he removed his hand from Will's shoulder to point to the ten-foot banner draped across the wall just under the entranceway at the far end of the room. The banner, in bold black letters three feet high, echoed the stocky little man's exhortation:

FLETCHERIZE!

Understanding began to dawn on Will. This was none other than Horace B. Fletcher himself, standing there before him in all his mandibular glory. Will knew him—of course he did. Was there a man, woman or child in America who didn't? Fletcher was the naturopathic genius who'd revealed to the world the single most fundamental principle of good health, diet and digestion: mastication. Thorough mastication. Fletcher maintained (and Dr. Kellogg concurred with all his heart) that the nearest thing to a panacea for gastric ills and nutritional disorders was the total digestion of food in the mouth. And he wasn't content merely to chew each morsel of food once for each of the thirty-two teeth in the human mouth, though he'd admit that it was a good start; rather, you were to chew a given bit of food fifty, sixty or seventy times even, until it dissolved in the mouth, the "food gate" opened and the mouthful was gone. With a shout of acclamation, the entire alimentary community had heralded this simple but momentous discovery. And now here was this celebrated figure, this hero of the oral cavity, standing before Will in the midst of this dining room crowded with luminaries, this great man coaching him in the intricacies of masticating a scrap of toast. Despite himself, Will was impressed.

He chewed slowly and thoughtfully, chewed as he'd never chewed before, the fluid mentorial tones of Horace B. Fletcher counting off the strokes in this ear: ". . . ten, eleven, twelve—that's it—thirteen, fourteen, yes, yes." And even in the depths of his concentration, Will felt the touch of the Great Masticator's strong square fingers as they gently wrapped themselves round the nape of his neck and forced his head down in the proper Fletcherizing position. Will chewed. And chewed. At the count of twenty, he felt a sharp pain in one of his lower rear molars; at twenty-five, his tongue went numb; at thirty, the toast was paste; at thirty-five, it was water; at forty, his jaw began to ache, and the toast was saliva. And then, miraculously, it was gone.

The whole table watched this operation in silence. When it was completed, and Will cautiously lifted his head, the Great Masticator gave him a congratulatory slap on the back, winked one sharp blue eye and sauntered off with an air of satisfaction. Will saw that Mrs. Tindermarsh was beaming at him—they all were, the whole table. For a moment, he thought they were going to burst into applause. He couldn't imagine how the simple act of grinding up a bit of toast could give them such a thrill, but it pleased him nonetheless, and he smiled shyly as he bent forward to repeat the performance.

It was not to be. For at that moment the thread of a single voice disengaged itself for just an instant from the general hubbub—a voice he knew as well as his own—and he jerked round in his chair as if electrified. *Eleanor.* And then he was on his feet, the chair thrust back from him as he scanned the crowd for a glimpse of her. Her voice came to him again, this time as it rose to cap off a witticism and trail away in the musical little laugh he'd already begun to miss. *Eleanor.* The feeding heads dipped and rose, waitresses waited, dietary advisors dispensed dietary advice. Will felt frightened suddenly, frightened and sick. "Eleanor!" he cried like a stricken calf. "Eleanor!"

He saw her in that moment, rising startled from a table not thirty feet away, the dark silk of her hair piled atop her head, her quick green eyes fixing him with a look of shock and admonition. *Not here,* that look warned him, *not now.* He saw the faces of her breakfast companions gaping up at him, a distinguished company, a brilliant company, no doubt. And who was that beside her, the napkin folded surgically in his lap? Who was that with the flaxen hair and the adamantine jaw? Who with the perfect teeth and the subtle, healing hands?

Not here, not now.

Will didn't care. He was already lurching toward her, the fist in his stomach beating at him as if to force a way out—he didn't want to be here, didn't want to be in Battle Creek, didn't want to be in a place where his wife was lost to him and people had to tell him how to chew his toast. He didn't know what he was doing—it had been ten hours since he'd seen her last, ten hours, that was all, and here he was awash in loss and self-pity. "Eleanor!" he cried.

They were all watching him, every anointed, spoon-fed, Fletcherizing one of them, and suddenly he didn't care. He blundered into a chair occupied by an immovable fat man, ricocheted off him and felt the strength fall away from his legs. Still, he staggered on, thinking nothing, thinking to embrace her, claim her, right there in the middle of the room.

Eleanor stood poised at the table, and she didn't look startled or even angry anymore. No: she looked embarrassed, only that.

from A PLAGUE OF DREAMERS

Steve Stern

~

HYMAN THE MAGNIFICENT

I. The Straitjacket Challenge

I was in the audience at the Idle Hour Cinema with my mother and father for my friend Hymie Weiss's Amateur Night debut. This was on North Main Street in the spring of 1927. Of the several acts preceding Hymie, the first was Mr. Dreyfus the jeweler, who'd aspired to be a comedian ever since Mogulesco's touring company had played the Workman's Circle lodge hall. The problem was that Mr. Dreyfus knew only a couple of jokes, which he repeated at each performance, so that everyone already had them by heart. As a consequence the earnest jeweler found himself in the role of straight man to his own shtik of riddles and gags.

His favorite was the one that went, "What hangs on a wall, is green, and whistles?" to which the audience would answer in a chorus so loud that plaster fell from the ceiling, "A herring."

Says Mr. Dreyfus, flapping his baggy pants in case you hadn't noticed: "Since when does a herring hang on the wall?"

Audience: "Who stops you from hanging it?"

Mr. Dreyfus, adjusting a rubber nose scarcely larger than his bulbous original: "Is a herring green?"

Audience: "You could paint it."

Mr. Dreyfus: "But who ever heard a herring whistle?"

Audience: "Nu, so it doesn't whistle!"

Mr. Dreyfus does a modest hornpipe to Mrs. Elster's organ, exiting to raucous applause.

Next the little Elster girl, done up in blackface like Topsy, commenced a bubble-eyed tapdance, making window-washing gestures with the flat of her hands. Her mama, the resident organist, accompanied her in a medley of Stephen Foster tunes. Wearing a false beard that covered his goiter, Ike Taubenblatt, the shoe repairman, did the "Blow wind, crack your cheeks!" speech from Shakespeare. Mrs. Padauer juggled three rolling pins and Mannie Blinkman swallowed a light bulb, only to belch it back up again. Cantor Abrams sang his three-handkerchief rendition of "The Czarist Recruit's Farewell" through a megaphone. Then it was Hymie's turn to perform what he'd talked Mr. Forbitz, the theater manager, into announcing as the evening's pièce de résistance.

He came on dressed like the Phantom of the Opera in a getup borrowed from Nussbaum's Drygoods Emporium. With a flourish he doffed the top hat and removed his silk cloak, revealing a sleeveless undershirt that showed off his stringy physique. When he handed the hat and cloak to his assistant, my sister Miriam, there was polite applause, though whether it was for Hymie or Miriam (who was an uncommonly dishy girl) was hard to say. In either case Hymie had the attention of the house.

Having placed the accessories over a chair, Miriam took up the stiff sailcloth straitjacket trimmed in leather. This while Hymie, running a hand through his upstanding auburn hair, announced gravely, "Ladies and gentlemen, for your express delectation I will attempt Houdini's famous punishment suit release." Then, as Miriam held the straitjacket in front of him, Hymie thrust his hands into the sleeves, which overlapped the ends of his outstretched arms. He gave her the nod and Miriam turned to the tittering crowd.

"Hymagnimummm . . . ," she mumbled to her sandal-shod toes, nervously flouncing the handkerchief points of her skirt. But when some of the onlookers demanded she speak up, she repeated almost defiantly, "Hyman [pronounced High Man] the Magnificent requests volunteers from the audience."

Practically all the young men in the theater, eager to assist Hymie's assistant, rose and stampeded the stage. Miriam glanced sheepishly at Hymie, who maintained his rigid pose but rolled his eyes, as the small stage was overrun by the sons of North Main Street. Conspicuous among them was Bernie Saperstein, the most aggressive of my sister's suitors, looking spruce in his canary blazer and waxed mustache. Shouldering his way to the forefront of the would-be volunteers, he left Miriam no recourse but to choose him to help fasten Hymie's restraints. She also chose, probably to compensate for Bernie's vigor, the consumptive Milton Pinkas.

Exercising somewhat more zeal than was called for, Bernie went to work on the buckles and straps, slapping down Milton's hands whenever he tried to pitch in. With his torso constricted until he'd turned the blue of moldy cheese, Hymie spoke in a voice trapped somewhere in his diaphragm. "The committee will confirm," he managed hoarsely, "that the punishment suit is secure." Bernie tugged at the jacket and smugly grinned his assent. "And now," croaked Hymie, "as I say the mystical word 'Anthropropolygos!' [which I mouthed along with him], Miss Rosen, if you please—"

Miriam rolled out a gauze hospital modesty curtain from stage left and folded its panels around Hymie. Then she said what she'd been coached to say, the phrase uttered by Bess Houdini before shutting up her husband in his various cabinets: "Je tire le rideau comme ça!" "It means 'I draw the curtain thus!' " I told my mama next to me, who grunted that I shouldn't be such a wisenheim. Stepping to one side, Miriam made an artistic gesture and smiled unconvincingly, embarrassed as always by her own drop-dead beauty.

Mrs. Elster played an appropriately suspenseful signature on her organ, while I pictured Hymie behind the curtain, drinking in the moment he'd waited for. Mentally I prompted him, reciting under my breath the pertinent passage from *Magical Rope Ties and Escapes:* "The first step necessary in freeing oneself from the jacket is to place an elbow on some solid foundation and by sheer strength . . ."

The ordinarily boisterous Amateur Night audience were subdued as they listened to the sounds of the struggle behind the curtain. They remained almost reverent, even as the curtain toppled over on its clattering frame, revealing Hymie wrestling furiously with himself. He thrashed around like a cat in a bag, flinging his hampered body here and there, assuming contortions certain to cause him an injury. Against the painted asbestos backdrop Miriam had begun to chew her braid, her pale cheeks gone intensely crimson. The jaws of the volunteers hung collectively open. Then Bernie Saperstein, always the joker, called out, "Somebody get the rabbi, there's a demon in Hymie Weiss!" and the whole theater split their sides. This was Mrs. Elster's cue to strike up a rollicking tune.

The general hilarity seemed only to encourage Hymie's violent behavior. Puffed with concern, Mr. Forbitz marched out of the wings, shooing everyone from the boards. "All right, Weiss," he blustered, dewlaps swaying, "that's enough already, shoyn genug!" "Stop it, Hymie!" cried Miriam, stomping her foot, but her agitation on his behalf if anything only fueled his abandon.

At length Mr. Forbitz returned to the wings and lowered the movie screen with a dust-raising thud, thus separating the spectators from Hymie's ordeal. He stepped back out again to signal the projectionist, upon which the lights went out, a beam shot over our heads, and the picture began. It was a John Barrymore melodrama entitled *The Beloved Rogue* ("Even torture could not quell the spirit of the vagabond poet," the posters read), for whose credits Mrs. Elster modulated her rollicking organ. The rooftops of medieval Paris, brooded over by Notre Dame, appeared to be caught in a blizzard of blackbirds, so poor was the quality of the film. What's more, as the dauntless vagabond swaggered into the frame, the screen, patched and seamed as an old topsail, began to flutter from the goings-on behind it. The crooked streets rippled as if in an earthquake and the audience howled over the distortions. Then, in the side of a house from whose window a bosomy lady was waving, a fissure opened and Hymie hurtled through. Still in the throes of his desperate struggle, he lurched headlong into the orchestra pit, breaking an arm.

*   *   *

"Hymie." Miriam softened her tone, unknitting her brow so that you kind of missed the imperfection. Like everyone else I was a helpless observer of the seasons of my sister's face. "Don't you think this is a little farfetched even for you?"

For a brief moment he did appear to reconsider. "Maybe you're right," he conceded, gnawing the inside of a freckled cheek. "You know, Houdini himself was afraid of going mad. He wondered how, when he lost his mind, they would ever find a cell that could hold him." Hymie was full of obvious admiration.

Miriam clucked her tongue, shook her head. "You're impossible," she sighed, placing the back of her hand to his forehead as if to check for a fever. There was a beat during which Hymie might have enjoyed the coolness of her hand before pushing it away.

"*You're* impossible," he countered, which seemed to surprise my sister, but I thought I knew what he meant. He meant it was impossible that the likes of her should care for the likes of him, though what he said was, "Sometimes I think you don't take me serious."

"Take you serious?" gasped Miriam. "I don't even take serious you should ask why I don't take you serious! Whoever takes Hymie Weiss serious, that person is meshuggah as Hymie Weiss." While you could see she'd hurt his feelings, she still wouldn't leave it alone. "Is that what this is all about? You want to impress me by becoming Houdini? Give me a break, will ya. You're as bad as Sy Plesofsky."

It was the worst thing she could have said. Hymie expanded his chest to show off what Eugene Sandow referred to as "Marine-tough pectorals," mostly imaginary in his case. "Not everything that goes on around here is for the amusement of the famous shainkeit Miriam Rosen," he assured her. "Some of us got ambitions of our own."

Miriam tried her best to stay nettled. He shouldn't have mentioned her beauty, which she regarded as a nuisance, the source of the hostility she suffered from all the guys she would never belong to. This was hitting below the belt. But you could see that she saw the justice, and even as she turned back to her phosphate she'd cocked a brow, as if it wasn't lost on her that for once Hymie had noticed.

"I mean it, Miriam," he persisted, "this is real. Next Thursday night North Main Street will witness the debut of the new Houdini, reborn in the person of Hyman the Magnificent."

Sucking on her straw, Miriam choked slightly, then swiveled toward Hymie with an expression of tolerance under pressure.

"I thought of 'The Hebrew Mahatma,' " he went on, idly flicking a fly from his sleeve, "but decided that 'Magnificent' says it all. Kind of no-nonsense, don't you think?"

She swept her heavy braid over the shoulder of her apple green pinafore, the better to search his face. It was the gesture that stopped them cold in the delicatessen and you could tell it was having its effect on Hymie. Craning, I saw how his eyes dodged here and there but kept returning to an uncovered blue vein in her neck, blinking with every pulse. Whether consciously or not, he'd reached for a soda spigot, holding on as if to steady his resolve.

"Hymie," Miriam said finally, "you want to do amazing feats? Try growing up, why don't you. Join the living." She swiveled her stool back toward the fountain, propping her elbows on the marble counter, her chin in her hands. "Find a girl, get married, have little Hymies, raise them up to be . . . magicians for all I care."

As this last was said dreamily, like sentiments having more to do with herself than with him, Hymie relaxed: the danger was past. Off the hook, he brazenly took up again the matter at hand. "And Miriam," wiping the sweat from his upper lip, "I'll need an assistant."

"Oh no." She shook her head fervently. "You want to make a horse's caboose of yourself in front of the whole neighborhood, that's your business. Leave me out of it. Ask your shadow there with the pisk full of tutti-frutti."

For a second I was scared he might actually take her advice. But when he only winked at me over his shoulder, I felt a little let down, though I wanted no more part than my sister of what I saw coming.

"You still don't understand, do you Miriam?" said Hymie, like it was him doing her the favor. "I'm—"

"You're cracked is what you are!" snapped Miriam, with perhaps more irritation than she'd intended. "You don't need an assistant, you need a keeper."

Above it all now, Hymie raised his eyes to the bossed tin ceiling, a move borrowed from his Aunt Frieda, who frequently called on God to give her strength. "Okay, I tried. Nobody can say I didn't try, even though I knew she'd only be in the way."

"Hymie."

"Even though she'd just hog the spotlight, being such a notorious glamor puss and all."

"Hymie." She'd given his cheek the gentlest slap to turn his head, forcing him to look her full in the face. I saw his nostrils flare from the chopped liver and pickle brine scent of her fingers, which on Miriam smelled somehow exotic. Satisfied that she'd brought him back to earth, my sister asked Hymie, "What is it you want me to do?"

II. The Procrustean Bed Mystery

When I saw him just after the Amateur Night fiasco, I could have sworn he'd learned his lesson. He was relieved to have gotten Houdini out of his system, and I expected that in a couple of days he would be riding another hobbyhorse. But by the time my sister had calmed down enough to go around to Nussbaum's, he'd relapsed. Sporting the plaster over his swollen eye at a jaunty angle, he grinned piratically with a pair of shears in his teeth. He was waiting on Mrs. Altfeder, the seamstress, unrolling a bolt of cloth with his good hand, stabilizing it with the elbow of his right arm in its sling.

Reading disapproval in Miriam's rueful countenance, Hymie took the shears from his mouth and cautioned, "Don't say it. I heard it already from my aunt and uncle." With a glance over his shoulder to make sure they weren't watching, he went into his Frieda and Shaky routine. " 'It don't look good for the Jews.' " This was Aunt Frieda, whom he had down even to her spitting against the evil eye. "So I tell them it looked good enough when Houdini did it, and my uncle says, 'Houdini don't fall off the stage, which it makes the whole theayter to pish in the pents. . . .' " He aped Uncle Shaky's wheezing laughter.

Mrs. Altfeder, waiting beside him for her yard of chenille, tapped her foot and hemmed impatiently. Right-handed, Hymie began trimming the cloth at a reckless zigzag with his left, declaring as he worked that next time he'd be better prepared. Almost to himself he mused, "If I can wow them so much by bungling, just think what they'll do when I succeed." He presented the ragged-edged fabric to Mrs. Altfeder, who huffed and turned smartly away.

"Did I hear you correct?" said Miriam, cupping an ear. "What next time? Am I wrong or wasn't that you they had to scrape out of the orchestra pit and carry the pieces to Doctor Seligman?"

Hymie admitted he still had some kinks to work out. "But by the time the doc takes my cast off, I'll be ready. I got a brand-new act in mind, what I call the Procrustean Bed Mystery."

"Come again?"

"It's my version of Houdini's Spanish Maiden Escape, only I plan to use a Murphy bed. There'll be these iron spikes in the mattress, see, and I'm standing inside the closet. . . ."

"Hymie, this is too much."

". . . then the committee folds up the bed. . . ."

"Hymie!"

Eyes that weren't already on Miriam turned toward her now, customers setting down dress suspenders and ribbed union suits to listen. Since there were no other sounds in the store but the creak of the ceiling fans and the zing of a receipt sent along an overhead wire, my sister stepped closer to Hymie and lowered her voice.

"What happened to my friend who knows the difference between real and make-believe?" she asked.

He tried to explain that the new act wasn't dangerous; in fact, it involved so little risk he was almost ashamed. But Miriam wasn't having any of it.

"It's not the act that scares me so much as you. All of a sudden I don't know you anymore."

"That's because," began Hymie in a phony theatrical tone of voice that assumed a certain dignity as he spoke, "Hymie Weiss fell off the stage, but it's Hyman the Magnificent that gets back on." He took his arm from the sling to reveal his stage name splashed in scarlet tempera across his cast. If I hadn't known him better, I'd have thought he was trying to get her goat.

Miriam stared hard at Hymie as if she were making an effort to believe him. Then she blinked, after which her features lapsed into pity, the pity dissolving to exasperation in another bat of the eye. Hymie followed the changes like someone observing a total eclipse.

"You should just hear yourself," she scolded, and her pleated skirt whirled, her flying black braid brushed his cheek as she turned on her heel. Watching her leave, Hymie touched the cheek gingerly.

"Women," shaking his head, "who can figure 'em, eh Stuart?" Now he was philosophical, the faker, shoving a ruler down his cast to scratch, still refusing to admit the pain of his bruises, the torn muscles and broken bone.

"Come off it, Hymie," I told him, encouraged enough by my sister's example to take a potshot of my own. "Who do you think you're fooling?"

He looked over with an expression so injured it could have fooled me.

Several weeks later a Murphy bed, unfolded from its upright mahogany cabinet, its mattress bristling with spikes, stood before the box office of the Idle Hour Cinema. Tacked inside the cabinet was a homemade handbill announcing in eye-catching colors:

! ! !
Tonite
HYMAN THE MAGNIFICENT
will attempt to escape
The Tortures
of the
PROCRUSTEAN BED
! ! !

Purchased from Shafetz's Discount, the bed had cost Hymie the better part of three weeks' wages. Then there was the expense of hiring Lieberman Movers & Haulers to shlep it over from the Emporium. Add to that the railroad spikes from Blockman's Salvage, the bolts, brackets, and tools from Hekkie's Hardware in Commerce Street, and you had quite a sizeable investment. But Hymie never doubted that this laying out of capital would have instant dividends. Who knew but some scout from the Pantage's Circuit would be in the audience, prepared to offer him top billing to take his act on the road.

"Then it'll be good-bye North Main Street, Stuart my man, and hello Atlantic City, Rio-by-the-Sea-o, Zanzibar. . . ."

In displaying the bed prior to his performance, Hymie had taken a cue from the master, who'd been, among other things, a wizard at self-promotion. So certain was my friend of packing the house that he felt justified in approaching Mr. Forbitz about a percentage of the take.

"Gruber yung!" This was Hymie's impression of the manager's reply. "Where you been, you don't know what it means the word 'amateur'?"

Hymie was the first to concede that it was early in his career to think in terms of a turning point. But with the Procrustean Bed—the name implied stretching and compressing rather than being impaled, but he couldn't resist the mythical ring—he felt he was expanding his repertoire. He was introducing an entertainment involving illusion and split-second timing, instead of mere physical dexterity. A measure of showmanship was called for that the straitjacket release, for all its drama, had lacked. Besides, his right arm was still weak after its removal from the cast, its color unwholesomely sallow, the bone somewhat crooked from not having properly set. So it made sense that his follow-up act should rely not so much on athletic prowess as technical expertise.

You couldn't have accused Hymie of being handy. In fact, he'd always congratulated himself on his *un*handiness, this for the doubt it cast on his descent from his supposed father, the tinker. (Albeit the Nussbaums had informed him that the tinker wasn't so handy himself, scholarship having taken precedence over his trade.) But in outfitting the dummy wardrobe of the Murphy bed to create his mystery, Hymie'd begun to take some pride. Rather than the ill-fated character in the snuff brown photograph, he'd decided it was his spiritual father who guided his hand. It was Houdini himself, in his alternate capacities as carpenter, mechanic, and locksmith, whose skill Hymie had inherited, and as he worked he was inspired to a less woolgathering, more hands-on attitude toward escapalogy.

When I got over the feeling that he was building his own coffin, I began to take an interest in Hymie's handiwork. What he'd done was to rig a sliding panel in the back of the wardrobe. Attached to a post itself attached to no other board in the cabinet, the panel was fitted with abbreviated screws that looked to be securely fastened. So neat was its construction that the mechanism could stand the closest examination without being detected. Further, Hymie'd chalked an outline of himself on the mattress ticking, then perforated the down stuffing with railroad spikes sharpened to glistening points with a file. He lay down in a flurry of feathers, satisfied that when the bed was folded up, the strategically placed spikes would never so much as graze him.

Despite myself I'd begun to grow convinced. I couldn't stay away from the backroom at Nussbaum's where he worked on his free-standing wardrobe, and when he asked me to help with a run-through, I spat on both hands. But soft in the spine, I couldn't lift the iron-clad bedframe alone. No one else other than Miriam was in Hymie's confidence, but after all it had taken to talk her into playing his assistant again, he didn't want to press his luck. Instead, taking up his position in the cabinet, Hymie simply described what would happen, which he claimed was all the rehearsal he needed.

"I stand inside the dummy wardrobe like this, right? Then the committee raises the bed. They close the cabinet doors and lock them with padlocks, and Miriam draws screens around the whole contraption. She says, 'Behold, a miracle!' " At that the screens would be removed, the doors unlocked and opened, the bed unfolded to reveal an empty space where the magician had been. While the audience gasped (Hymie made sounds of universal astonishment), he, having slipped out the back of the wardrobe and into the wings, would shout from the rear of the theater, "Here am I!"

As Hymie'd predicted, the Idle Hour was filled to capacity. Rather than excited, however, the North Main Street families who typically comprised the Thursday night crowd looked nervous to me. For excited you had our Irish and Italian neighbors, not normally in attendance though tonight they were out in force. Stomping and clapping, they demanded that Hyman the Magnificent appear without further ado. It seemed that Hymie's previous debacle had indeed stirred the local interest, if not the kind ("Your friend Weiss is a scandal," grumbled my mama beside me) the Jews were comfortable with.

In keeping with tradition Mr. Dreyfus the jeweler was scheduled to open the show. He was to be followed by Eddie "Kid" Katz's punching bag exhibition, after which Miss Bialy from the Neighborhood House would perform her eurythmic dance. The program also promised another dramatic recitation from Ike Taubenblatt and his pantomime beard. But due to the ruckus Mr. Forbitz was forced to delay the other acts in favor of starting with the headliner, which Hymie considered himself to be. Though he was backstage, I would've bet I knew what he was thinking: he was thinking how the other performers had been similarly preempted during Houdini's engagement at the London Palladium.

True to her word, Miriam came out alongside him, in a dress of airy chiffon sashes that floated around her like smoke. Her hair was loose and luxuriant, her tortoiseshell combs like trellises overwhelmed by inky tendrils. She looked so farputzt, my sister, you might have wondered if she was a little stagestruck herself, since she generally tended to play down her own luster. But I figured it was her way of showing good faith.

Behind them on stage Hymie's nightmare furniture had already been erected, its jagged mattress lowered like a cruel underjaw. Again a committee was invited from the audience, and again Bernie Saperstein, dapper in his Oxford bags, was foremost among the gang of volunteers. Having removed an orange toweling bathrobe, Hymie stood in a one-piece bathing costume that highlighted his ribs and knobby knees. (This was in lieu of the formal accessories the Nussbaums, boycotting the performance, had refused him the loan of.) He made a brief but impassioned speech describing the danger in whose face he spat. Then with a studied swagger that won him cheers from the Zanones and Keoughs—while the Shapiros, Pinskys, and Plotts groaned audible *oys*—Hymie took up his stance in the hollow wardrobe of the Murphy bed.

Miriam stepped forward to announce above Mrs. Elster's ominous organ roll that "Hyman the Magnificent will now be confined—" But whether owing to her self-consciousness, her anxiety for Hymie, or the constant winking that Bernie subjected her to, my sister got tongue-tied over the word *Procrustean*. She had such trouble that Bernie and his minions, rather than wait until she could spit it out, took the liberty of jumping the gun.

They lifted the bedframe at its foot, slamming it shut with such zest that the whole wardrobe fell over backward. It hit the stage with a loud report that hushed the house. The hush endured until the dust began to settle, the cabinet to rattle, muffled sounds of distress emanating from within. Then, as energetically as they'd knocked it over, the volunteers righted the Murphy bed. They opened the wardrobe doors and pulled down the mattress, revealing a stupefied Hymie squirming from the spike that had entered his thigh. As he was lifted limp and bleeding from the cabinet, that part of the audience who'd already broken their silence let loose a thunder of hilarious applause.

*   *   *

VII. Buried Alive

Released from the hospital, Hymie went where he must have felt that in his state he belonged, back to Blockman's. It was his own decision, since his aunt and uncle had come to his bedside to beg him to return to the Emporium. Forgoing the satire, he told me their mistake: they'd promised him everything would be the same as before.

He looked more a part of the junkscape than ever, more dilapidated than either of the resident ragpickers. Leaning on a stick to walk now, he was no longer certain which of his injuries had left him lame. Oddly, however, his spirits were good, almost you might say blissful. The painkillers had surely worn off, and while he sometimes resorted to medicinal snorts of Itzik's rotgut, I didn't think this accounted entirely for his mood. His smile was serene and he spoke in pensive platitudes, such as "Faint heart ne'er won fair lady" and "Only the brave deserve the fair"—as if, having reached these conclusions, he was at peace. In the end I supposed he was just exhausted, because after a week or so he snapped out of it, announcing somewhat grimly that his priorities were straight again.

He had a theory that the failure of his escapes, notwithstanding the fame they'd earned him among the gentiles, was Miriam's fault. A headache for the whole neighborhood, she'd been his special burden to bear. "It puts me in mind, Stuart," he said in the tone I had come to resent, "of Houdini's obsession with flying. You'll remember how it kept him awake for the couple of hours he slept each night. It left him muddled and spoiled his timing." The point being that Miriam was Hymie's obsession with flying.

"So what, you might ask [though I'd had no intention of asking], was the maestro's solution? He took apart the Voisin biplane, which by the way he was the first aviator to fly over Australia in. He packed it up and never flew again. Then he devoted himself with a vengeance to greater and more dangerous stunts."

Meanwhile my bar mitzvah had come and gone; I'd become a man and hardly anyone noticed, the affair having been overshadowed by preparations for my sister's wedding. Invitations had to be sent out, a bridal gown fitted, arrangements made to secure the hall at the Workmen's Circle for a reception. All day my parents made noises, which were boasts thinly disguised as complaints, about the lavish extent of catering involved. The whole street was caught up in the anticipation, since despite disappointment and envy in certain quarters, the marriage of Miriam Rosen would be a load off of everyone's mind. To tell the truth, I was a little exhilarated by it all myself. I barely flinched when Bernie Saperstein, strutting around the deli like a pouter pigeon, rubbed my head and called me "brother-in-law."

For her part, my sister couldn't manage to keep her mind on her work, which everyone said was natural in a prospective bride. Still, instead of the fussing and fluttering you would have expected, Miriam seemed merely distraught. She kept gazing out windows, ignoring customers calling for their kneydlach and buffalo fish.

Some remarked that the direction she looked in was forward to the date of her nuptials, though I wondered if she might be waiting for something else. In the evenings, when the deli was closed, she begged off Bernie's solicitations with the excuse of fatigue— "too much excitement, y'know." Then she went up to sit on the roof of our building. When I followed, she forgot to accuse me of snooping, but instead said aloud what I wasn't sure I was supposed to hear.

"He used to be my lost cause," she brooded, seated on the parapet, a silhouette but for the corona the streetlamps made of her hair. "Now he's everybody else's."

If there'd been any question as to whom she was talking about, she spelled it out soon enough. Again and again she asked how it was possible that a legendary beauty like herself, with such an angel head on her shoulders, could stoop to care for a zhlub like Hymie Weiss. Anyway, it was too late for him. It had always been too late for him, and if it hadn't been strictly speaking too late for him before he'd become such a mutilated fragment ("Oy, such a fragment!"), then it was certainly too late now. Because once the machinery of a Jewish wedding was in motion, no power on earth could turn it around.

I wasn't exactly neglecting Hymie. Since the only thing that scared me more than watching him was letting him out of my sight, I kept an eye on him. But with so much going on it was easy to forget about Hymie for days at a time. It was convenient to think he was finally too crippled to perpetrate any more funny business; though on my next trip to the junkyard I found I had another think coming. He was considering a new escape. Not just any escape, mind, but the one that had nearly been the maestro's own undoing—namely, being buried alive. The miscalculation that had resulted in Houdini's almost suffocating made it a kind of ultimate stunt, and Hymie was determined to pull it off without a hitch. It would be his crowning achievement, and afterward . . .

"But who cares about after, eh Stuart?" The escape was the thing, its faultless execution all that concerned him. Rising with a groan to support himself on his stick, he resolutely declared, "This one I'm going to rehearse."

To buy a little time I reminded him that, according to one of his own pet theories, you couldn't call a stunt accomplished without an audience on hand to applaud—to say nothing of saving you from your own botched devices. Hymie thought this over and said he was wrong; he'd been wrong all along. A stunt ought first to be perfected in solitude. Driven to the usual frustration, I could only state the obvious, that he was in no shape to perform anything more strenuous than tying his shoes. Cupping his good ear to hear me out, he agreed to a compromise.

"All right, Stuart, you be the audience."

He said it might be appropriate to do a dry run on the anniversary of Houdini's death, which was coincidentally Halloween. This was tomorrow.

He'd decided to try it out under cover of darkness, thus reducing the chance of being disturbed. For what it was worth, I pointed out a flaw in his logic, since Halloween was one of the more populated nights of the year. The neighborhood was swarming with pint-sized ghosts and witches, which the local Hasidim (who kept indoors) complained were indistinguishable from actual dybbuks on the prowl. I myself had left the apartment on the excuse of trick-or-treating, stretching the seams of the skeleton outfit my mama had made me two seasons ago. "Who ever heard of a zaftig skeleton?" she'd remarked at the time, and I'd put on a few pounds since then. But if I was keeping company with Hymie Weiss, I would just as soon be in disguise.

Of course I needn't have worried. Even with the additional handicaps of the shovel, coal chute, and toolbox he carried (I held the lantern), Hymie was virtually invisible to the residents of North Main Street. It was as if he moved in everyone's perpetual blind spot. Besides, given the evening's traffic in goblins, he was just one more clanking spook.

For the site of his rehearsal he'd chosen Catfish Bayou, a fetid sink just north of the Pinch, its banks bordered by ramshackle shanties and an old slave burial ground. To get there we crossed Auction Street, where the shops petered out and a row of dogtrot houses began. Though the only lights were the odd jack-o'-lanterns in windows, the moon was bright enough to upstage my oil lamp. It shone in the mud of the bayou, rippling sluggishly with what may have been the spines of snakes, and on the tin roofs and smooth headstones and the ring of fallen leaves where we halted. The place being deserted, I made a joke, which was only half a joke, about how its occupants might be returning soon.

Since my chum didn't seem to know the meaning of fear, it was up to me to be jumpy enough for the both of us.

Indifferent to sinister surroundings, Hymie'd already shrugged off his load and set to work. He banged together some slats from his toolbox, making an upright trestle against which he propped the coal chute. At the mouth of the chute he placed a tumbled wooden grave marker and tamped it into the ground. (Seeing him so industrious, who would have believed he didn't necessarily know what he was doing?) When he'd completed his incline, he began to dig, heaving damp clumps of earth onto the coal chute and rambling between grunts about Houdini.

"One time he does one of his bridge leaps . . . unh . . . and there's a corpse stuck in the weeds which he unsettles . . . unh . . . at the bottom of the river . . . unh . . . so before the maestro can get free of his chains, the corpse floats to the surface . . . unh . . . and that's what the crowd sees first, this decomposed dead man . . . unh . . . then Houdini pops up right after."

I could see that the digging was taking its toll, so I offered to spell him a while, which surprised us both. If I'd forgotten I was no great shakes at physical labor, Hymie's laughter, as he leaned against a mossy headstone, reminded me soon enough. Moreover, here was this situation where a fat kid in a skeleton suit was helping his only friend dig his grave. Amazed at myself, I climbed out of the hole, turned in the shovel, and begged him once again to reconsider.

His answer was to slide back into the hole and carry on digging, reassuring me there was nothing to it. "I lie in the hole with my knees to my forehead, see, which makes a nice pocket of air. You can live like this ten, maybe fifteen minutes, long enough so the audience goes crazy with suspense. Then it's a simple matter to scramble up through the loose earth." By the time he'd finished explaining, the dirt was piled high in the coal chute, the excavation chest-deep, and he was ready to demonstrate.

He took wads of cotton from the pockets of his ragged cardigan and stuffed them in his nostrils, mouth, and ears. Throwing off the sweater, he unwound a long linen croker sack from his waist. He pulled the sack over his head, poking his arms through slits in the sides, the golem become a Halloween ghost. Then he curled up in the hole and mumbled something that the cotton in his mouth made unintelligible.

"What?" I knew better than to ask.

Possibly needing an orifice to breathe through as well as speak, he must have spat out the cotton, because this time the request came loud and clear: "Open the chute!"

"Guess again," I replied.

"Stuart, old pal," he entreated, making what was under the circumstances a tasteless crack, "this is a strictly kosher burial, no casket or nothing. All it wants is some Jerusalem mud to finish the job."

But I stood firm.

Undiscouraged, Hymie got to his feet and began to grope blindly in the toolbox at the side of the hole. From among the collars and shackles he eventually dredged a large three-pronged fishhook with line attached. This, after a couple of clumsy efforts, he snagged like a grappling hook on the soggy marker at the lip of the coal chute. Then he lay back down with the line in his hand, shouted, "Anthropropolygos!" (which I hadn't heard in a while), and pulled the cord. The marker toppled but the huge mound of dirt stayed put.

"For God's sake, Stuart," pleaded Hymie like his heart would break, "give it a shove! This is what I was born for!"

So I did it, if only to shut him up, to stop his accusing me of coming between him and the fulfillment of his destiny. All right, I thought, Hymie meet Destiny, Destiny, Hymie. Then I placed my hands against the hill of cold earth, which was taller than myself, and pushed, but it refused to budge. I pushed again and it began to inch glacially down the chute, spilling over the edge, dumping its weight in an enormous dull avalanche on top of Hymie.

In the moment before I panicked, I was angrier than I'd ever been—angry at myself for having let him sucker me into this, angrier at him for not being what he claimed. Never anybody magnificent, he was only the screwball Hymie Weiss, whom I could wait for till kingdom come without his ever crawling out of the ground.

Then I fell on my knees in the unpacked earth and began to claw my way toward him, burrowing from above the way Hymie was supposed to have tunneled from below. I dug until I was certain he wasn't going to meet me halfway, and was nearly done in before I remembered the shovel. Grabbing it, I managed finally to scoop out the hole to the depth where he lay. Then I tossed the shovel and went back to clearing away the dirt with my hands, unearthing him enough to lift his head by the filthy linen shroud. I pulled off the sack and unplugged the cotton, which the killing weight had yet to expel from his nose, but I knew all along it was too late.

He was stone cold, no hint of a pulse in his marmoreal neck, and his moonlight-flecked eyes, opaque as ball bearings, stared starkly from a hollow face. It was said that Houdini, using the techniques of oriental swamis, could breathe so shallowly it took a stethoscope to detect his heartbeat. But shaking Hymie, beating on his chest, I was unable to elicit even the faintest sigh; though a sound like a wind through venetian blinds came from his sphincter, and a foul gas enveloped us both. Plunked down next to him, I began to cry for help through my tears. When my voice broke, the fractured word subsiding in whimpers, I tried to close his gaping jaw; I lifted an arm that fell limply, like a marionette's.

After a while a couple of colored kids, come down I suppose from the shanties, did in fact peer over the rim of the hole. They saw the stiff, pearl gray corpse in the arms of a roly-poly skeleton and, their curiosity satisfied, turned tail and fled. Or did they flee because they'd seen Hymie blink? He'd blinked once or twice as his eyes adjusted to the sight of me, then leapt to his feet and started to holler. I was hollering too, sitting splay-legged and pointing with one hand, holding onto my heart with the other. Then I remembered I'd yet to remove the rubber skull mask, and promptly did so.

"It's me, Stuie," I was able at length to inform him.

Hysterics ebbing, he caught his breath and said distantly, "Stuart," like he might have made my acquaintance in another world. When he attempted a grin, I thought I knew what was coming: he would tell me he'd been fine all along; he'd only been waiting for the suspense to build—after which I would pick up the shovel and send him back to wherever he'd been.

But instead of his standard assurance, he scuttled the grin and touched his own haggard features. He touched them the way a blind man might touch someone else's, hoping to recognize. "Stuart, I was dead," he confided in a voice thick with awe. "I was dead, Stuart," he repeated with growing urgency, hunkering down beside me in the hole. "Crushed under the weight of the clay. I wasn't alone, but I was lonely and I wanted to come back. So I escaped."

VIII. Metamorphosis

At first he said he couldn't explain it, then began to explain it. Death, he told me, was like being in an audience, looking toward a milk can or a packing case that contained your life. It was *your* life though you weren't in it anymore, and you could only see it taking place vaguely, as on the screen at the Idle Hour before the curtain was raised.

He told me everybody who was recently dead was there: "You name 'em. The Birnbaum kid, who was knocked over by a meat wagon? He was there. Mr. Klotwog, who died of that thing nobody will mention, and Mrs. Pinsky, who passed away in shul? They were all there. So I thought, maybe Houdini—we could put our heads together and figure a way to get out. But when I asked, nobody knew who I was talking about."

Instead he had himself been found, to hear him tell it, by a gaunt, bearded man in a dented bowler, holding a book. " 'Pardon me,' he says, 'but I was your papa, Berl Weiss, that didn't live to meet you. And this was your mama, Chanah Sarah, rest her soul.' She's standing next to him, this pie-faced lady in a babushka. 'We been watching your monkeyshines,' he tells me, 'which it makes us to wonder is this our own sonny, eh Mama?' 'Gevalt,' says the lady in the babushka."

At that point I exclaimed, "Have a heart!" out of habit, though I didn't really want him to stop. He said he told them he was sorry if he'd disappointed them, but he was likewise disappointed, since they'd blown his theory of the magician's bastard child and all. Then he asked them if they knew the way out of there.

" 'Give a listen, Mama,' says my papa. 'He wants out, this pisher, that's been trying so hard to get in. Well it ain't to my knowledge in the Five Books, the Zohar, or the Shulchan Aruk, the secret how to get out of here.' Then my mama speaks up, apropos I don't know what; she talks like this with a frog in her throat; 'Was you afraid? We was all the time afraid.' Papa gives a nod like she's hit on the heart of the matter. 'That's right, we was afraid of the Russians and the diseases and the whole gantseh megillah. Good riddance, says I. We was glad to leave the world.' "

This had set Hymie thinking: Was there something he'd been scared of? Certainly not danger or pain or even death, which he was here to tell me was no big deal. When it occurred to him to look back on his life from the other side, he saw how everything was faded already to shadows—everything, that is, but my sister in her smoldering anticipation, who was still lit up as bright as his own dead family.

"All right," Hymie admitted, as if he'd been bullied into confessing, "I was frankly afraid of her. But now I was even more scared that, if I didn't act quick, Miriam would turn to shadows along with the rest. And that's when it came to me, Stuart, how to jimmy the lock so to speak—which you'll understand is a professional secret I must take to my grave."

As he scrambled out of the hole and started for North Main Street, I noticed a definite spring in Hymie's limp. I pulled down my skull mask and hurried to catch up, following him back across Auction, wondering if there was anyplace I wouldn't have followed him to.

On the evening of my sister's wedding the entire neighborhood was gathered in the Anshei Sphard Synagogue. Women in the gallery wept openly or sniped in whispers; young men grumbled into their prayer books, as Miriam began circling the groom seven times. Veiled and trailing petal points of organdy and lace, she was a spectacle you could go snow-blind from looking too long at. Even Bernie Saperstein, despite the finery of his leather spats and silk lapels, looked humbled as she marched resolutely around him. In fact, he looked downright apprehensive, like a prisoner tied to a stake surrounded by savages.

Then she'd come to a full stop, my sister, and the two of them stood under the chupeh, facing the squat Rabbi Fein in his homburg reciting psalms. A hymn was sung and the blessing over the wine spoken, which was my cue to excuse myself. I rose from the front-row seat next to my father, who growled, "What's a matter, you got ants in your pants?" and made for the altar. I turned, sniffing the flower in my buttonhole. There, before God and my family—not to mention the Nussbaums (Uncle Shaky wheezing, Aunt Frieda shushing him from the gallery), the Forbitzes and Seligmans, the shnorrers hoping to double as wedding jesters, all of them muttering in a commotion that swelled like a stirred hive of bees—I pronounced the French phrase and pulled the cord.

Muslin draperies fell about the bridal canopy. (The bolts of muslin had been easy to come by since Hymie had resumed his old job at the Emporium. As for the rest, the rigging of the chupeh and so forth, we'd managed it all quite handily after breaking into shul the night before.) The congregation held its breath as I counted down from ten, barking the numbers to drown out the noise of scuffling behind me. Then I declared "Behold, a miracle!" and parted the curtain.

Hyman the Magnificent, restored to the top hat and cloak of his original performance, was standing astonishingly erect in place of the groom. He was presenting his case to my sister, whose arms were folded, her toe tapping impatiently. The green fire in her eyes seemed to have melted the ice of her veil, thrown back to reveal her dark hair braided into a garland.

"You want kiddies, I'll give you kiddies," Hymie was promising. "We can use them in the act. They'll pop out of flowerpots and picture frames, and when they're older I'll teach them escapes . . ."

"You're impossible!" accused Miriam, unfolding her arms in a gesture that released her bosom like doves about to take flight.

There was the sound of thumping and clanking that was Bernie, struggling in his chains, safe in a place known only to the magician and me. Meanwhile Rabbi Fein had evidently gone into shock, his mouth hanging open, the goblet fallen from his hands to smash on the floor. This didn't prevent him, however, from delivering the benediction—once Hymie, slipping a ring over Miriam's finger, had turned toward the little man.

"Blessed art thou, O Lord," said the rabbi, though his lips were never seen to move, "who plucked the bride and groom out of a hat. . . ."